Police
Management

To
Elizabeth, Ruth
and Timothy

Police
Management

A. J. P. Butler

Gower

British Library Cataloguing in Publication Data
Butler, A. J. P.
  Police Management
  1. Police Administration—Great Britain
  I. Title
  354.410074   HV8195.A2

Library of Congress Cataloging in Publication Data
Butler, A. J. P., 1944–
  Police Management
  1. Police Administration.   2. Police administration—Great Britain.
  3. Management by objectives.   4. Police administration—evaluation.
  5. Police administration—Great Britain—evaluation.   I. Title.
HV7935.b87 1984   351.74   84–10343
ISBN 0–566–00646–4.

Published by

Gower Publishing Company Limited, Gower House, Croft Road, Aldershot, Hants GU11 3HR, England

Gower Publishing Company, Old Post Road, Brookfield, Vermont 05036, U.S.A.

Type set by Regent Typesetting, Odiham, Hants.
Printed and bound in Great Britain
by Billings & Sons Limited, Worcester.

Contents

Acknowledgements

Anyone who has put pen to paper to write an article or book to inform others about their ideas is likely to recognise how much they owe to the ideas of other people. This book is no exception. It is the combination of ideas and experience gained through work and contact with colleagues and friends. I am pleased to acknowledge their influence on this book but it is impossible to mention everyone. Therefore, I start with an acknowledgement to police officers with whom I have worked over the past years.

My interest in police management strategy has developed over a number of years and I have been fortunate that opportunities have been provided within the West Midlands Police to learn more about management problems and issues. This book strongly advocates the use of sound research techniques to identify the true nature of problems before solutions are proposed. I have been able to develop and use these techniques within my Force and gratefully acknowledge the support I have received from Sir Philip Knights, the Chief Constable.

My introduction to Policing By Objectives occurred some years ago when I met Val Lubans and later Jim Edgar. The Policing By Objectives process can be seen in specific chapters of the book, but the contact and friendship with Val Lubans has made a contribution to the whole book. The chapters relating to Goals, Objectives and Action Plans are drawn substantially from the definitions and principles in the "Policing By Objectives". I am grateful for Val Lubans' permission to reproduce the PBO Cycle and the Linking Pin Model.

In 1982, I had the opportunity to work on the staff of the Police Staff College. This was an extremely stimulating period and I record my thanks to Mike Plumridge, head of the Management

Studies Department, for his interesting ideas and particularly his views on the human dimensions of organisations. Discussions with other colleagues, Bernard Gent, John Hood and Brian Hilton stimulated thought and ideas. Although he was not a member of staff, Bernard Stewart, a consultant to the College, gave me some interesting techniques for looking at problems. The use of matrices in Chapter 8 springs from his concept of the Organisation Development Grid and I am pleased to acknowledge his contribution to my exploration of the planning process.

During my time at the Police Staff College I was able to provide some assistance to the Northamptonshire Police. The officers provided a useful audience on which to test some of the ideas contained in the book. In thanking Mr Maurice Buck, the Chief Constable, for allowing me to become involved in the introduction of Policing By Objectives in his Force, I am implicitly thanking his officers for their opinions of an earlier version of Chapters 9, 10 and 11.

A central theme of this book is the need to evaluate the results which are achieved by police actions. Measures of effectiveness and efficiency are the keys to objective evaluation. My first involvement with the measurement of police effectiveness started in 1980, and since then it has become an important part of my research. Throughout the research and the development of techniques to measure police effectiveness, I have been assisted by Karen Tharme who has made a valuable contribution to this relatively new area of police management strategy. The experience she gained in this work enabled her to review an earlier draft of this manuscript and I am grateful for her comments on the application of management concepts to practical policing situations.

Foreword

By Sir Kenneth Newman QPM
Commissioner of Police of the Metropolis

My pleasure in being asked to write a foreword to Dr Tony Butler's book stems from two sources. First, from my personal knowledge of his contribution to the work done during my term of office as Commandant of the Police Staff College in developing the theory and practice of police management. Secondly from my feeling that I can honestly support and endorse his book as a useful addition to the corpus of professional police literature.

The book comes at an opportune time. Against a background of rising public expectations those of us who are entrusted with responsibility for the husbandry of valuable resources have never before been so concentrated in our efforts to ensure efficiency and effectiveness. Within my own Force, we have instituted an interactive planning system committed to measurable objectives at each level. Many of the issues discussed in the book are germane to these efforts and the work reflects both the rationale and techniques of the systematic approach to planning. From the strategic and policy level, to implementation and evaluation it contains sound and practically relevant material for police managers. Practical issues are confronted and useful examples are included with the important focus upon problem identification and analysis as precursors to problem solution.

This may not, of course, be a book only for police managers. Those with an interest in policing from a variety of fields will find it of interest, as may managers in other organisations, especially those concerned with effectiveness and efficiency in the public sector. It is not an "off the shelf".system but a useful source book of ideas and techniques. I was impressed to see that the objectives of each section of the book are clearly defined enabling those who wish to use it as a text for learning to do so in a systematic way and to evaluate their progress.

1   Police Management

Management is the process of motivating, directing and controlling the endeavours of others to achieve a result which is consistent with the purpose of the organisation. Therefore, a police manager is responsible for motivating, directing and controlling the officers and civilians under his command to achieve results which are determined by the policy of the chief officer. There is a world of difference between the person who is a passive supervisor, responding as one crisis recedes and another takes its place, and the manager who attempts to bring some order and structure to his role. The person who operates as a supervisor will be condemned to be a victim of his world, whereas the manager will seek to plan ahead and anticipate problems, and thus have more control over his world. A manager should know four vital aspects of his command responsibilities:-

1   The current performance of his officers set against the policy of the force – the 'here and now' of his command.

2   The desired level of performance he should be achieving – the objectives of his command.

3   The means which are available to improve effectiveness and efficiency, recognising all the constraints which exist.

4   The measure he will use to evaluate the achievements of his command.

All these issues will be addressed. Methods will be described to help a manager develop objectives, measure his current performance, develop performance measures, implement solutions to policing problems to pursue objectives within a rational management structure and process, and evaluate the results he has achieved. There is a realistic assumption that a police force will not solve all its problems in the first year, therefore, there is a need to develop a system of management which allows the process to develop and improve over successive cycles. Police forces must have a system of management which allows them to 'learn' as an organisation and develop in the context of a rational response to policing problems rather than ad hoc responses to individual crises.

Police management strategy should seek two goals, first to provide a better, more challenging and fulfilling job for all members of the force, and second, to improve the effectiveness and efficiency of the force thereby improving the quality of the service given to the community. The order of the goals makes the point that improvements are unlikely to occur in the performance of the force without a commitment from its members. To ask people to change their working practices or to become more productive, without offering them the opportunity to have some benefits from the changes, is rather shortsighted. In the future, police management will have to consider moving decision making down the organisational structure. The suggestion is based on the premise that the people most likely to know the solution to the policing problem will be the officers who are closest to it. Therefore they should be given the greatest opportunity to make the decisions to solve the problem. This policy will bring advantages to the force by developing a more responsive and flexible organisation. It will also bring advantages to the individuals involved because it will give them more control over their world, bring more opportunities to achieve a sense of personal satisfaction from their work and give them opportunities to develop management skills to improve their prospects of advancement in the force. Thus the policy will achieve the two goals of improving the working environment of individuals and the effectiveness of the force.

Introducing The Book

The purpose of this book is to explore practical methods of improving the effectiveness and efficiency of the police. The contents and sequence of the chapters form a working guide to the stages and processes which will enable a police force to make better use of its resources and measure the results it achieves. Practical police problems are examined in case studies to show how management concepts can be applied to police work to achieve improvements in effectiveness. It is essential that each part of the process is understood and related to the actual experience of the reader. To highlight the essential management concepts and issues, they have been summarised as Learning Objectives at the beginning of each chapter.

Before significant improvements in effectiveness and efficiency can be achieved additional training will be required for many police officers. This could be done in formal training sessions, or through a process of action learning 'on-the-job'. The Learning Objectives can provide the basic framework for this training and will be useful to an officer with the task of designing training courses. The Learning Objectives also provide a valuable guide to a sub-divisional superintendent, who wishes to improve the performance of his sub-division, by defining the concepts and issues which must be understood by his officers. He can take the chapter and the Learning Objectives and design his own training package for an action learning approach.

Within an operational context, this book is concerned with officers who have management responsibilities. Attention will tend to be directed towards the sub-division as the primary operational unit. Therefore, the term 'police manager' will tend to be a reference to the sub-divisional superintendent. However, the police manager could be located at almost any point in the police force, because it is a generic term used to denote any officer who has the responsibility to control the activities of others towards some defined target or goal.

The principles and concepts will be described in the context of a typical British police force. Allowances will have to be made for local variations which will not affect the principles, but may require some modifications in the process of application. To establish the context, a simplified organisational diagram can be found in Appendix 'A'.

The learning objectives of this chapter are:-

1 To understand the need for a rational approach to police management to bring an ordered framework to the complexities of the work.

3

2   To understand the two goals of management development in the police, namely improving the working environment of staff and the effectiveness and efficiency of the force.

3   To understand the value of decentralised decision making.

4   To recognise the limitations of current police management practice.

5   To recognise the future management needs of the police in the light of the increasing demands to demonstrate measures of effectiveness and efficiency.

The Current Perspective

One of the most important matters facing the police manager is the definition of the role and responsibilities of the police in modern society. Police managers are being asked to take account of competing priorities to be addressed by their limited resources. They must decide, for example, how they will balance demands for more resources to control crime with the time needed for police involvement in community relations activities. Police forces have to set their boundaries. Management text books refer to this issue as the determination of the mission of an organisation. The term 'strategic policy' will be used to embrace this central management concept. For the purpose of analysis, three groups can be identified as having a role in the definition of police strategic policy. In very broad terms 'policy' will be established through the community stating its priorities, needs and wishes in terms of crime control and police services. Government, both local and national, also make demands on the police, but this group hold the powerful position of being able to allocate resources to the police which brings an added dimension to their role in comparison to the community. The third group who have an interest in defining the police role are the police themselves, the term used here includes all aspects of the police organisation from individual officers to the Police Federation and other staff groups through to chief officers. (Figure 1.1).

Public consultation is a matter that has risen to prominence since the publication of Lord Scarman's report in 1981.[1]

Figure 1.1 Defining the police role

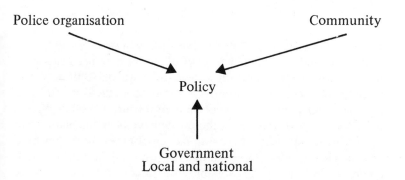

Police organisation   Community

Policy

Government
Local and national

Consultation by itself will not result in improved police services unless the consultation process is formally recognised as part of the policy making strategy of the force. Methods by which this can be achieved will be discussed later, but at this point it is important to recognise that the process must be sufficiently sophisticated to ensure all groups and levels in society have an opportunity to make a contribution. Consultation is not an end in itself but a means to provide an opportunity to improve police management. There may be many communities in this country who are entirely satisfied with the service they receive from the police and to force some formal consultation process upon these groups when it is unnecessary, is unlikely to improve the professional image of the police. In other areas however, there may be considerable local dissatisfaction with the service received from the police and it is here that consultation must demonstrate that the views expressed by the community are matters which are considered when police policy is formed.

In the formal sense, Government has the most power to influence the policy of the police, for example, by passing legislation which the police are obliged to enforce, or by withholding funds in the form of a reduced budget, which may for example restrict the amount of overtime worked by the police or the number of civilians recruited. The policy of the police can also be influenced indirectly by Central Government policy. Greater cost effectiveness is being demanded by Government, both national and local. The requirement to promote an efficient police force, which is contained within The Police Act 1964, allows Government to encourage a policy of cost effectiveness.

The police have a significant role to play in the formation of policy. The degree to which they can formally influence these matters will be directly related to the quality of their management. If they are unable to demonstrate by objective measurements their relative effectiveness and efficiency, they will have difficulty in resisting demands for an improved service from the community or demands from politicians for cuts in their resources. Following cuts in budgets over recent years, the police have been unable to state in unequivocal measures the consequences for the service they have provided to the public. Where crime has risen and the detection rate fallen, it has not been possible for forces to show a direct relationship between these measures and the reduction in resources provided by politicians. Police work is not an exact science, but if management is approached in a systematic manner, then the police will be in a better position to question unrealistic demands which may be made from the community and furthermore their request for resources from Government will be based upon a sounder appreciation of the relationship between resources and effectiveness.

In a review of Unit Beat Policing (UBP) in Chapter 2, it will be argued that it was shortcomings in police management that was the critical deficiency in the introduction of UBP, the policy, implicit in the concept, was determined almost exclusively by Central Government. The Home Office sponsored the Working Party which produced the report recommending the system. After the publication of the report, the Home Office enthusiastically encouraged chief officers to take advantage of new technology and provided the offer of financial assistance as incentives for the purchase of personal radios and cars. Local communities were not directly involved or consulted in the design or implementation of Unit Beat Policing but when public concern was expressed it did not, apparently, influence policy. At the time Unit Beat Policing was designed, the police and Government were facing the problem of continuing to provide a service with static or decreasing manpower. If the police had invoked a management response to the Government's recommendation to implement Unit Beat Policing, the analysis of available resources would have shown that in some forces, they did not have sufficient officers. Unfortunately, the police passively accepted the model and attempted to stretch

6

resources. As a result the first priority of the police, namely, responding to calls for service, inevitably took precedence over the second priority, maintaining contact with the community through area foot patrol constables.

The current perspective on policing can be summarised under two headings, first we appear to be no further forward than we were in 1966, in terms of objective measurements of police effectiveness and efficiency. Second, there is a diversity of opinion both within the service and outside as to the exact nature of the police role, its relationships with other social organisations and the methods to be employed in the pursuit of effectiveness.

Fundamental questions are being asked about the role of the police. Although the community are generally satisfied with the service they receive from their police, certain groups are looking for change and improvement and for an influence on the process of deciding policy. The police are open to change and appear to share some of these uncertainties which can be seen, for example, in the way in which they have extended the boundaries of their responsibilities into the realms of social/community work. It must be for the community to decide where the responsibilities of the police lie, but this should be based upon an objective assessment of what the police actually achieve through these social/community activities rather than a passive acceptance that any activities the police perform must have benefits for the community. A police officer cannot simultaneously enhance the public's feelings of safety by patrolling the streets and yet spend hours in youth clubs and community groups as a member of their management committee. Quite simply he cannot be in two places at once, and the community and the police will need to decide the priorities and subsequently how resources are allocated.

To speculate about the future of policing in Britain is dangerous, but on the evidence available we can be confident that the results achieved by any policing strategy, either existing or innovative, will be determined almost exclusively by the quality of police management applied to the efforts to solve policing problems. With hindsight it is relatively easy to establish the weakness of the management of Unit Beat Policing, but an examination of more recent innovations in policing suggests there is considerable danger of repeating the mistakes of the past. To talk naively about the introduction of community policing without having any clear managerial definition of the meaning of the concept and without considering the organisational, training and evaluation issues, is to set off down a road from an unknown point to an unknown destination. If you have no idea where you want to go, any road will take you there, but unfortunately there will be no way of determining when you have arrived.

The Future Perspective

Before police forces can improve their effectiveness and efficiency they must be able to measure their existing performance. Therefore, future management practice should emphasise the analysis of current performance using information from within the force and taking note of the needs and desires of the community expressed through the consultation process and public opinion surveys. The strategic policy which is formed through this analysis, will be significantly different to present policy formulation, insofar as it will identify the indicators or measures to be used to judge police effectiveness and efficiency. When policy and performance measures have been established, the police manager will be expected to critically review the present organisational arrangements by which policing strategy is pursued. During this review he will identify circumstances where there needs to be changes in the way work is organised, together with other preparatory measures, such as the training of officers. The introduction of change will be accompanied by a preparatory period in which unforeseen difficulties will hopefully be resolved. After the full implementation of the change, tactical evaluation in the form of day to day monitoring and controlling will occur and this will form the basis of the long term review, namely the strategic evaluation, which will complete the management cycle by providing information for the next planning phase. These management principles must be sustained within a rational management system. If a system does not exist there will be no formal means for co-ordinating the development of management strategy within the force. The management system, Policing by Objectives (PBO), is suggested as one means of providing co-ordination to the management strategy of the force.

There is no suggestion that Policing by Objectives is the only management strategy appropriate for the police, but it does contain all the critical elements to be recommended within this book. The PBO model was developed in the United States following a review of the use by some American police forces of Management By Objectives. After completing a nationwide survey of forces that had used Management By Objectives, it was concluded there were a number of significant differences between the police and traditional industrial organisations where MBO had been introduced with some success. Unless these differences were recognised by police management, the adoption of MBO was less than successful in most cases.[2]

This book will fall broadly into three parts, first this introduction and the police management context which it has described will be followed by suggestions to adopt a more systematic approach to problem solving and management strategy. Methods of measuring police effectiveness and efficiency will be described (Chapters 3 and 4). Having established measures, the first section will continue to describe methods whereby policy can be constructed (Chapter 5). This will include references to the present organisational structures (Chapter 6), and the role of individuals within the force (Chapter 7). The second part will be concerned with preparing the organisation for change (Chapter 8). The third, and final part of the book will be concerned with the adoption of a management strategy to combine the four essential phases in the management cycle. This part will recommend the adoption of Policing by Objectives as a coherent management process to provide a systematic framework on which police management can be improved.

It should not be assumed that this book is recommending change for the sake of change. If a police officer with command responsibilities can claim, in terms of objective performance measures, that his community is satisfied with the current effectiveness of his force and there are no means whereby that same level of performance could be achieved with the use of less resources, then he probably does not need any changes in his present policing methods. If this cannot be stated with confidence at present, then it may be considered worthwhile for the police commander to undertake a process of analysis and review, but if on completion it is established there is no requirement to change his present operational strategy, then once again he need read no further than the first part of the book. However, if after conducting this review he believes there are matters which could be changed to improve the overall effectiveness and efficiency of his command then it is recommended he continues to read the remaining chapters. This book has been written for practical police managers who are less concerned with theory and more concerned with improving the day to day operations of the officers under their command.

References

1 Scarman, L. J., *The Brixton Disorders 10 – 12 April 1981*, London: H.M.S.O., Cmnd 8427 (1981).

2 Lubans, V. A. and Edgar, J. M., *Policing By Objectives*, Hartford, Conn: Social Development Corporation (1979).

2   Problem Definition in the Management Context

Before improvements can be achieved to police effectiveness or efficiency a rational systematic management process must be adopted. The management cycle forms a framework which enables ideas to be developed and implemented. The evaluation process measures the results which have been achieved and also enables the lessons which have been learned to be included in the plans for the next cycle. The management cycle is only a means to an end, namely the identification and achievement of objectives. When improvements in police effectiveness and efficiency are being pursued it is usually as a result of some problem being identified, for example, an increase in the number of burglaries reported to the police demands improved effectiveness, or a reduction in the budget demands improved efficiency.

The learning objectives of this chapter are:-

1   To understand that management practice in the police is basically a system of problem solving.

2   To recognise the constituent elements of the process of problem identification.

3   To understand the elements of the management cycle.

4   To be able to apply the concepts of rational management to policing methods.

Problem Definition As A Management Responsibility

If the world was orderly, predictable and friendly then the need for managers could be challenged because employees would only need to be supervised within existing policy. Unfortunately the world of police work is far from orderly, it tends to be unpredictable and can be very unfriendly. Thus the manager's role is to take the world as he finds it and try to bring some order and predictability to his responsibilities. As he surveys his responsibilities he can identify those matters which are operating smoothly and do not demand his immediate attention. He will also identify matters where he must take steps to improve effectiveness and/or efficiency. These matters will be considered as management '*problems*'. The key to the problem solving process is to establish the exact nature of the problem. Before any attempt is made to solve the problem it should be stated in terms which indicates a complete understanding of the issues which it raises.

The process of analysis starts with a written description of what is known about the problem including the reasons which make it a problem. Using the description the analysis will consider a series of issues:-

1   Having described the problem the first step is to establish who is experiencing the problem. Officers in the force may be experiencing problems through increasing workload, lack of resources, such as vehicles or equipment, or deficiencies in training. Alternatively the community may be experiencing the problem. Unless the manager can identify the people involved in the problem he will not clearly understand the nature of it.

2   A manager must always have the concept of priorities at the forefront of his mind. He will not have sufficient resources to address every problem which may arise and therefore he will have to make decisions concerning those problems to which he will commit resources. Before he makes the decision he will have to establish the consequences of doing nothing in response to a problem. Where he believes he can live with the implications of doing nothing, he can use his valuable resources elsewhere.

3   The manager must establish if he has a responsibility for solving the problem. There has been a tendency in recent years to assume that the police have a responsibility to solve all kinds of social problems. The Home Office have cautioned chief constables about extending their boundaries and assuming the

12

responsibility for matters outside their traditional role (Home Office Circular 114/1983, paragraph 11). Thus before proceeding the manager must be confident that he has a responsibility to commit resources to solve the problem. The issues raised by this point concern what is sometimes called the mission of the organisation. In simple terms all organisations, including the police, have a mission or purpose. The founders of modern policing, Rowan and Mayne laid down the police mission in 1829, with their instructions to the Metropolitan Police. Over the years the purpose of the police has become extended to include being a friend to those in need (Royal Commission on the Police 1962). However, a manager should ensure that he does not stray beyond the purpose of the force which is set out within existing policy.

4   Returning to the description of the problem, there will be indications as to the cause of the problem. It is necessary to identify the extent and symptoms of the matter which is calling for attention. In this part of the exercise the indicators which identify the problem can be examined to determine if they can be developed as measures of success or failure when plans are implemented to solve the problem.

5   There is little point setting out to solve a problem if there are no means of establishing the results which have been achieved. The development of performance measures was raised in the previous paragraph, a manager should establish at an early stage the means he will use to satisfy himself that the situation has improved as a result of the actions he may take.

6   The final step is to rewrite the definition of the problem on the basis of the information obtained in the analysis and to give greater understanding of its nature, extent and causes.

These fundamental problem identification steps will be used as the foundation of the managerial process. However, the process will only tell the manager about the problem, he must have a system which will enable him to proceed to implement strategies or methods to solve the problem and thus improve the effectiveness and efficiency of his command.

The Management Cycle

To proceed from the definition of a problem to its solution requires a system of management to transform ideas into actions. There are four distinct stages in this process:-

1   The problem to be solved will be identified within the context of the defined purpose of the police force and thus will establish performance targets to be achieved. The planning process will explore alternative methods of achieving the desired results and choose the most appropriate.

2   The human resources will be organised on the basis of the plan.

3   When the preparations have been completed the plan will be implemented.

4   After implementation the work of the officers will be monitored and controlled to ensure they understand their role and instructions. At predetermined points the results will be evaluated on the basis of the performance measures developed in the planning stage.

The management process moves through four stages from the identification of the problem to the evaluation of the results achieved by a specific policing method implemented to solve the problem. The results of the evaluation are available to be used in the planning stage of the next management cycle. Thus the process continues as a cycle where the lessons of the past are used to improve future performance. The elements of the cycle are shown in Figure 2.1.

Planning

The planning stage starts with an examination of the 'here and now' in the context of the established purpose of the force, and follows the problem identification exercise to the point where the issue to be addressed is defined in a form from which performance targets can be identified. When the existing effectiveness and efficiency of the force has been established, alternative policing methods can be explored to seek improvements in existing performance. All the alternatives should be examined to identify

Figure 2.1   Management cycle

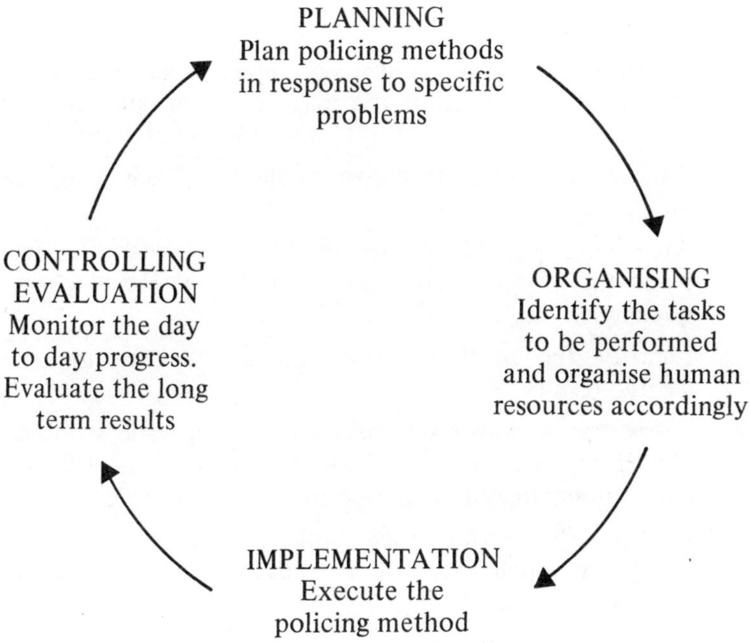

PLANNING
Plan policing methods
in response to specific
problems

ORGANISING
Identify the tasks
to be performed
and organise human
resources accordingly

CONTROLLING
EVALUATION
Monitor the day
to day progress.
Evaluate the long
term results

IMPLEMENTATION
Execute the
policing method

their positive and negative aspects and then the most suitable method can be chosen. It is not sufficient to simply choose the most preferred method, it has to be described in detail identifying the components, the sequencing of these parts and the resources which will be required. Finally, the monitoring and evaluation system, and performance measures have to be established.

The basic elements of the planning stage are shown in Figure 2.2. It is worth remembering that it takes far less resources to plan a policing method than it does to execute it. Therefore, time spent in planning is well invested because it should reduce the chances of operational officers wasting their time on poorly designed policing methods.

Organising

To organise appropriate manpower, it is necessary to examine

Figure 2.2   Planning

1   Establish and define the purpose of the force.

2   Identify the desired levels of effectiveness and efficiency.

3   Obtain information and assess the present performance of the force in respect of the defined policy and thereby establish existing levels of effectiveness and efficiency.

4   Produce possible alternative methods of achieving the desired results.

5   Assess each possible method in terms of its cost effectiveness, the resources required and any negative consequences.

6   Identify the most preferred means of achieving the desired results.

7   Transform the abstract means into a specific strategy, identifying the major elements, their sequence and costs in human and other resources.

8   Identify the performance indicators to be used, the means by which they will be measured, and the timing of these measures.

9   Determine the mechanisms for monitoring the progress of the policing method, anticipate variations and deviation from the strategy, establish methods for modifying the method when necessary.

the policing method in more detail to identify the various tasks and their constituent elements. Performance measures will be established to monitor the work of individual officers. Task analysis will be used to determine the relationship between tasks to construct job descriptions for individual posts. Task analysis will also facilitate the location of posts within an organisational structure, thereby establishing formal relationships between individual posts with specific responsibilities, accountability and authority. Task analysis is also a critical ingredient in determining the knowledge, skills and attitudes necessary for postholders to perform their work. These three matters follow in sequences, but the vital role of the task analysis is to link directly the policing method to the human resources who will execute the plan.

Before leaving the organising phase, consideration must be given to the allocation of resources. It is unlikely all resources will be made available for every project to be undertaken by the force and therefore some compromise has to be established on how limited resources will be shared amongst the force.

The key points in the organising process are summarised in Figure 2.3.

Figure 2.3   Organising

1   Identify from the method the various tasks to be performed, analyse their constituent elements and establish performance criteria for individual posts.
2   Determine the relationship between tasks and construct job description for individual posts in the organisation.
3   Locate posts within an organisational structure, establish formal relations between posts including responsibilities, accountability and authorities.
4   Identify the knowledge, skills and attitudes necessary to perform the tasks to the pre-determined criteria.
5   Establish the basis on which resources will be allocated.

Implementing

The implementation phase can be seen in two distinct parts, first, there is the completion of preparatory stages which involves all the personnel who will be responsible for executing the strategy. Second, there is the actual execution of the method accompanied by monitoring and co-ordination of the tasks being performed.

The first step will be to appoint officers to fill the posts identified during the organising phase. By using the information gained during the task analysis, the training needs of individual postholders will be identified, and a training and development programme will be conducted to prepare the officers for their new roles. During this preparation phase a wise manager will ensure his staff are fully aware of what is expected of them as individuals, and in collaboration with them, he will identify mutually agreed performance objectives for individual posts. Immediately before the execution of the method, responsibilities, accountabilities and authorities will be formally assigned to postholders. When the preparation has been completed the strategy will be initiated.

A major weakness of police management in the past has been a failure to co-ordinate and monitor policing methods. An integral part of the implementation and execution strategy is to ensure the tasks are monitored and co-ordinated.

The constituent elements of the implementation process are summarised in Figure 2.4.

Figure 2.4   Implementing

1   Appoint persons to fill posts.
2   Identify postholders' training needs and implement a training/development programme to prepare postholders.
3   Establish and agree in co-operation with individuals their own performance objectives.
4   Formally assign responsibilities, accountabilities and authorities to postholders.
5   Initiate tasks to be performed.
6   Monitor and co-ordinate the tasks to be performed.

Controlling And Evaluation

The monitoring and co-ordinating which is an integral part of the process of implementation can be seen as the basis of the tactical or day-to-day evaluation. The controlling which is an important part of the manager's responsibilities involves measuring the achievements of his officers against the targets which had been set. Changes may need to be made to tune the method to keep it on course. In the longer term the overall results will be measured in the strategic evaluation. The process of evaluation should be seen as an exercise which provides opportunities for the force and individuals to learn from their experiences. The force must know what has been achieved in the pursuit of the targets and its contribution to improving effectiveness and efficiency. Individuals must also have the opportunity to know what they have achieved during the process. In appropriate cases the achievements of individuals should be formally recognised.

The final step in this phase is the submission of a formal progress report. It will be processed through an established review procedure to enable the lessons learnt in the first cycle to be included in the deliberations that will take place before the next management cycle is initiated. The constituent elements of the controlling and evaluation stage are summarised in Figure 2.5.

Figure 2.5   Controlling – evaluation

1   Measure overall achievements in relation to desired results.

2   Identify reasons for results achieved and/or lack of achievement.

3   Assess the achievement of individuals against the pre-determined performance criteria.

4   Make modifications to the strategy in the light of the evaluation measures.

5   Recognise the contributions made by individuals and give appropriate rewards.

6   Submit progress reports into the established review process for consideration in the next management cycle.

A Management Case Study: Unit Beat Policing

The Working Party on Operational Efficiency and Management[1] which reported in 1967, established three aims for its review of police operational organisation. These aims were "to find ways of providing a better service to the public, to increase the interest and responsibility of the man on the beat and to achieve more economic utilisation of manpower."(paragraph 6) They conducted a review of existing police operations throughout England and Wales. It was concluded there was a general

19

inflexibility in the methods of deploying uniformed police officers and this worked against improvements in effectiveness and efficiency. They also identified a trend of increasing workload and either static or decreasing manpower. The Working Party believed chief constables should examine the ways in which they used their officers in an effort to improve the service the public were receiving from the police. Having identified the problem and established performance goals, they went on to consider alternative methods of policing and in an appendix to their Report they described a number of variations of uniformed police deployment. The most radical innovation in police deployment was found in the Unit Beat Policing concept implemented in Accrington, Lancashire. The Working Party urged chief constables to examine this method of policing to determine if it was relevant for adoption in other parts of England and Wales. The Report was at pains to point out that it was not recommending the universal and immediate abandonment of the traditional beat policing systems but was asking chief officers to review their own situation and performance in the context of a changing world.

The Working Party whilst striking this cautionary note, examined the Unit Beat Policing concept in a manner which would do justice to the planning steps set out in Figure 2.2.

The goals of Unit Beat Policing were identified as, improving the service to the public by a faster response to their calls, improved public relations by closer contact with the community, a systematic collation and rapid retrieval of information to enhance crime detection, improved morale for constables by a process of job enrichment and increasing police productivity by satisfying increased workload demands with no increase in manpower. A strategy to implement Unit Beat Policing was contained within the Working Party Report and included a job description for the area constable and a proposed organisational structure based upon a basic beat unit.

In hindsight, a critical deficiency in the Working Party Report was its failure to identify key performance indicators. The Report established with some care the problems the Unit Beat Policing System was designed to resolve, but it did not identify the means by which the achievement of those results could be objectively established. The absence of performance indicators was further

further exacerbated by the Working Party's failure to place the Unit Beat Policing concept within a management strategy which contained a controlling and evaluating mechanism for long term assessment.

The Working Party recognised the implications that would occur for officers when Unit Beat Policing was adopted. They were very specific concerning the duties and responsibilities of the area constable to the extent that they published a job description for this post. They also recognised the introduction of this policing system would radically alter the role and tasks performed by the patrol sergeant. The Working Party believed the sergeant would become a *leader and organiser* under Unit Beat Policing rather than merely a *supervisor* as he had been in the past. Unfortunately, they did not expand their ideas on this issue and furthermore, there was no recognition of the radical change that would occur in practice in relation to the sergeant's role owing to the introduction of the personal radio. When Unit Beat Policing was introduced the patrol sergeant remained responsible for the activities of constables on the street, but with the simultaneous introduction of personal radios it was the person operating the radio control, the controller, who had the most immediate knowledge of the activities of the constable. He was the officer who directly supervised and deployed those officers to incidents and furthermore, it was the controller to whom questions for advice and guidance on operational matters were directed in the first instance. This tended to undermine the position of the patrol sergeant and make his role somewhat ambiguous in the new structure. This ambiguity was exacerbated when the post of controller was held by a constable. With the passage of time, a new role has tended to develop for the patrol sergeant, a role which involves a significant proportion of office work as he is required to check and submit paperwork generated by the ever increasing workload of constables on the street. If a thorough task analysis had been conducted before Unit Beat Policing was adopted, then these problems may have been identified and resolved through the normal organisational process.

There are many other issues that arise in relation to the organising and staffing of Unit Beat Policing, not least of these was the role of the CID. Detective constables were given specific responsibilities under the Unit Beat Policing Model but, in a review report published some years after the introduction of Unit Beat

Policing, it was stated that the role of the CID could not be assessed as it had not been possible to find an example where the detective constable had become involved in Unit Beat Policing to the extent envisaged in the original design.

Despite the warnings of the Working Party that Unit Beat Policing should be seen as only one possible alternative for improving police effectiveness and efficiency, the concept was universally embraced by chief constables in the late 1960s. Some experimentation took place on a small scale in a number of forces, but generally Unit Beat Policing was imposed with the minimum of preparation for the majority of officers, almost no consultation and explanation and with no clearly specified objectives or performance measures.

The failure to identify performance measures made the final phase in the management cycle impossible. It was not possible to control and evaluate the performance of individual officers or the force as a whole if there were no benchmarks by which to judge performance. Thus formal evaluation formed no part of the management process of Unit Beat Policing. It is true, the original model has been modified significantly in many forces, but the exact reasons for these modifications and the consequences are not readily identifiable. In the absence of appropriate evaluative mechanisms, it is reasonable to say that the present form of uniformed patrol deployment in operation in England and Wales, has evolved through some form of random selection based upon a rather vague notion of the management process. The changes have not generally occurred through an objective assessment of problems, performance measures and systematic evaluation.

Have we learned from history or will we repeat the mistakes of the past? In recent years new systems of policing have been adopted in many parts of England and Wales. These innovations have generally been known as community policing and it is not the purpose of this book to review in depth the management of these new methods of policing.[2] This book does not promote one form of policing against another, but is primarily concerned with improving the effectiveness and efficiency of police forces through the systematic application of managerial concepts to all policing problems no matter where they arise or for what reason. The central issue in police management is not to examine the activities performed by police officers but to ask what results are being achieved and whether these results constitute a better police service to the community.

References

1 Home Office, *Police Manpower, Equipment and Efficiency* , Reports of Three Working Parties, H.M.S.O. (1967).

2 Weatheritt, M., Community Policing: Does It Work and How Do We Know? A review of research in Bennett, T., (Ed), *The Future of Policing* Cambridge: Cropwood Conference Series No. 15 (1983).

3   Measuring Police Effectiveness

After the purpose and the policy of the force have been defined, and performance levels established, then the present effectiveness and efficiency must be reviewed. These are the first three parts of the planning stage (Figure 2.2). The methods which can be used in performance reviews will be described in Chapter 8. Before the review can be performed there is a need to establish a means of determining police effectiveness. Police effectiveness can be measured by comparing the actual achievements of a force with the results it was seeking to achieve. In very simple terms, police effectiveness is a comparison between the results that the chief constable hoped to achieve during the year and the results that were actually achieved by his officers. Therefore effectiveness can be defined as:-

the progress which has been achieved towards a given objective.

Effectiveness and measurement are fundamental parts of the management cycle. It is impossible to use the term effectiveness without implying some form of measurement, therefore, the term 'performance measure' will be used to imply a measure of effectiveness. After the performance review has been completed, performance measures are used again in the planning stage to identify the means which will be used to evaluate the results actually achieved in the evaluation stage of the management cycle.

The learning objectives of this chapter are:

1   To understand how the concept of effectiveness fits into the planning stage of the management cycle.

2   To understand why measures are needed to review and determine the present effectiveness and efficency of the force.

3   To appreciate that a manager must have some means of measuring the results that his officers achieve.

4   To understand measures are essential to identify when improvements have been made in the performance of the force.

5   To know a working definition of effectiveness.

6   To understand that the definition of effectiveness is a comparison of measures.

7   To understand and be able to distinguish between a quantitative and qualitative performance measure.

8   To understand the concepts of reliability and validity when applied to performance measures.

9   To be able to apply the concept of effectiveness and define performance measures for police activities.

10 To understand the concept of preventable or suppressible crime when applied to performance measures.

Performance Measures

Performance measures are used within the management cycle to bring some degree of order to the sometimes confusing relationship between the activities of the police and the results that occur. It is obvious that a police manager cannot assume a simple relationship between the implementation of some policing method and, for example, a reduction in reported burglaries. It is possible that changes in the weather, levels of unemployment, improved amenities for young people or any of a number of other social and environmental changes could have had an influence on the crime rate. However, it is also possible that the introduction of the policing method also had some impact on the problem of burglary. It is the manager's task to establish the means by which he can measure the contribution the police have made to the improvements. If performance measures are not defined and used then the force will remain at the mercy of changes in the environment. When performance measures are defined then the force will be able to take the initiative and exert more control over the consequences of changes in the environment. Instead of being obliged to continually respond to the world, police operations will be able to be more proactive and less reactive.

Performance measures can be applied at all levels throughout the force. The definition of the performance measure may be identical throughout the force but the means by which it is measured may differ between the various levels. Taking the example of the reported rate of burglaries, the sub-divisional superintendent may use the direct measure of the number reported on his sub-division. However, when the chief officer is assessing the effectiveness of the entire force he will have to combine the achievements of all sub-divisions to produce an overall picture. On the sub-division it may also be necessary to apply the performance measure individually to uniformed patrol officers, detectives or area constables to be able to assess the relative effectiveness of these groups of officers. Performance measures can be seen as building blocks which are applied on a small scale and then joined together to produce a wider assessment of the performance of the force. The performance criteria of the force will be implicit in the policy established by the chief officer, for example a reduction in the number of reported burglaries. However, as a general rule, the actual definition of the performance measures which will be applied to specific police tactics should be done at the lowest operational level in the force, which will be closest to the point where they will be used as direct measures. There is a danger that a measure defined at headquarters may not always be capable of being applied in practice on a sub-division. Providing all the officers apply the same rules when they define performance measures, then the measures will be compatible and comparable throughout the force.

Performance measures are used in all four stages of the management cycle. In the planning stage performance measures are used to identify the strengths and weaknesses of the force and to establish the means by which future improvements will be measured. During the organising stage, performance measures which are attached to the various tasks are then communicated to officers during the implementation stage. Finally, performance measures are a crucial part of the monitoring and evaluation stage of the cycle. By using a rational management cycle with appropriate performance measures, it is possible to have an assessment of the overall achievements of the force and the effectiveness of individual members.

Basic Requirements Of A Performance Measure

The fundamental requirement of any performance measure is simply that it must be a measure. To achieve this criterion it must have a universal application and objective standards. If these elements are missing then it would be impossible to make reliable comparisons between, for example, the achievements of a police force before and after a change in policing methods. If a criterion of success for a new patrol method is a reduction in the crime rate, then the measure must include both crimes reported to the police and those which are committed but not reported.

Quantitative Performance Measures

Quantitative forms of performance measure are measures such as the numbers of persons arrested for crime, the number of crimes detected and the number of fatal road accidents. There are some problems with these data which will be explored later, but if the conditions of data collection are held constant between one time and another, then direct numerical measures of the number of crimes detected in one year compared with the number of crimes detected in another year can be a useful performance measure.

Qualitative Performance Measures

Qualitative forms of performance measures are primarily concerned with the public's opinion of the police. Research has shown that the public's satisfaction with, and confidence in the police, appeared to be more affected by the *quality* of police performance rather than the direct quantitative measures of such things as detection rates. In the past, police forces have tended to ignore, or at least treat qualitative measures in a very simple way without exploiting their full potential as performance measures. One of the main reasons for their lack of use is probably related to the difficulty in collecting qualitative data on which to base performance measures. Public opinion surveys of satisfaction with the police, are a powerful means by which the police can monitor their own performance and furthermore, by which they can identify areas for improving resource deployment, management and training.

Reliability

Performance measures involve comparisons either between one force and another, one sub-division and another, or between one time and another. The reliability of a performance measure refers to its consistency and accuracy. A measure of crime or vandalism taken in one location should measure with the same consistency and accuracy, crime or vandalism in another location. Some evaluations of policing projects have used as a performance indicator the number of cases of vandalism reported to the police during a given period. When the number of reported cases declines, the police may claim a success in deterring or preventing these types of offence. However, when public surveys are used as measures of vandalism in a community, evidence can show that less than half of the cases occurring are reported to the police. Therefore, it would be possible for the number of cases of vandalism reported to the police to double during a given period. However this could indicate either a real increase in the number of offences, if the proportion reported remained stable, or no increase at all, if the public simply reported a higher proportion. In these circumstances police records of reported cases of vandalism would not be reliable performance measures because they do not accurately and consistently measure the *actual* occurrence of these offences.

Validity

In this context validity is used to indicate the need for performance measures to actually measure what they purport to measure. For example, a traffic department might be trying to improve road safety on a particular stretch of road by increasing the number of offences of speeding reported by traffic patrol officers. A count could be made of the number of detected speeding offences on the stretch of road for a 28 day period. This figure could then be compared with the number of detected speeding offences in a subsequent period of 28 days. However, such a measure is not necessarily directly linked to road safety, as it is merely recording levels of police activity. Therefore the number of persons reported for speeding offences is not a valid measure of road safety.

To use the number of persons reported for speeding offences as a valid performance measure it would be necessary to demonstrate the following relationships.

1   There was a direct link between the average speed of vehicles on the road and the number of road accidents. Thus as the average speed increased the number of road accidents increased and as the average speed decreased the number of road accidents decreased.

2   As the number of persons reported for speeding offences increased the average speed of vehicles decreased and vice versa.

Consider another example, a force may record the number of visits made to schools by police officers and use this as an evaluation of the effectiveness of the schools liaison scheme. Obviously, there is not a simple relationship between the number of school visits and changes in pupils' attitudes towards the police. Therefore, if the objective of the scheme was to improve police/public relations then it is not a valid measure, it is simply a measure of the time spent on a particular police activity. A valid measure related to the objective would be a questionnaire survey of the attitudes of young people towards the police before the introduction of the scheme and an identical survey after implementation.

The issue of validity in performance measures raises the important issue of the difference between a measurement of *results* in pursuit of a specific goal, and the counting of police *activities* which may or may not produce the desired results. In the past the police have tended to emphasise the counting of activities to the detriment of measuring the achievement of results.

Police management practice in the past has tended to make assumptions about the link between activities and the results that they will achieve. The approach which is being recommended in this chapter makes the consideration of policing methods a secondary issue, which should only be considered when the policing problem has been identified in a form which defines a clear statement of the desired results. All police activities should have a clearly defined purpose which can be used to establish policing goals or objectives.

Chapter 9 will be concerned with the definitions of goals and objectives as fundamental parts of the Policing by Objectives (PBO) process. Within PBO, Goals are applied across the police force to co-ordinate the efforts of all officers. Objectives are applied to the basic operational units which are usually sub-divisions. By setting objectives at this level, freedom is given to accommodate the variations which may occur in priorities between sub-divisions. Some limited improvements can be made in police effectiveness without adopting the PBO process, but no progress will be made in the absence of precise statements defining the purposes of police activities. Therefore the definition of targets, goals or objectives are fundamental to the measurement of effectiveness and efficiency and the management process. In the chapters which precede Chapter 9, the terms goals and objectives will be used in their general sense to denote the definition of desired results or targets, in the later chapters which describe Policing by Objectives the terms will be used within the strict definitions established in Chapter 9.

Defining Performance Measures

All the elements of a performance measure have been described and they can now be used to define measures related to specific policing goals. The elements should be used in a sequence which will lead from the goal to an appropriate measure. The process starts by stating the goal under consideration because this identifies the purpose of the police activities and the desired results. The next stage is probably the key to the process. Performance measures must be related to the goal and therefore the starting point is to look in detail at the specific police responsibility.

The fundamental feature of the performance measure is its ability to be measured. Therefore the next stage in the process is to ensure that the indicator identified as being the reason for police action is capable of being measured. At this point the distinction should be made between quantitative and qualitative measures. When this distinction has been made, the measure must be examined to ensure that it can be applied consistently to the factor to be measured and that the measures obtained will be an accurate representation of the facts. This step tests the reliability of the measure. The next step is to test the validity of the measure by ensuring that it actually measures what it is required to measure. When the proposed performance measure has passed through all these stages successfully it will be appropriate to use. If it fails any one of the steps it should be redefined. A summary and sequencing of the steps is shown in Figure 3.1.

Figure 3.1   Defining performance measures

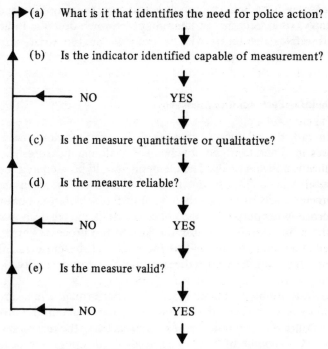

GOAL – What is the purpose of the police activity?

PERFORMANCE MEASURE –

(a)   What is it that identifies the need for police action?

(b)   Is the indicator identified capable of measurement?

NO   YES

(c)   Is the measure quantitative or qualitative?

(d)   Is the measure reliable?

NO   YES

(e)   Is the measure valid?

NO   YES

Define Appropriate Performance Measures

Examples Of The Application Of Measures Of Effectiveness

To illustrate some performance measures which can be used to establish police effectiveness, police responsibilities in crime control, the promotion of road safety and traffic flow, and the enhancement of feelings of public tranquillity, will be explored. The purpose is to demonstrate the practicalities of performance measurement and the limitations which must be acknowledged.

Crime Control

Goal:-
To reduce the occurrence of crime.

The definition of the goal identifies the purpose of police action. The next stage in the process of defining performance measures is to identify the exact nature of the problem, quite simply, what indicates there is a problem to solve? Unfortunately, this simple question has a far from simple answer. An examination of the nature of crime, reveals it takes a wide variety of forms and motivations. If the police are to be responsible for reducing crime, then clearly it must be established which forms of crime are amenable to preventive action by the police. A significant number of assaults take place in people's homes where police officers do not generally patrol, therefore it may not be reasonable to include such cases in general crime statistics which are then used to measure police effectiveness. Other crimes may be preventable by police action, but the police may take a conscious policy decision not to become involved in the prevention of these crimes. Shoplifting is a crime which the police do not make direct efforts to prevent by patrols but restrict their actions to the provision of a service to facilitate the prosecution of offenders detected by private citizens. Once again it is not reasonable to include these crimes which are only recorded upon detection, in crime statistics which are used to measure police effectiveness.

Police performance measures in relation to crime should:-

1   identify those crimes likely to be prevented by police action;

2   discount those crimes which the police, as a matter of policy, do not actively seek to prevent.

It may also be necessary to identify a number of specific

33

performance measures based upon individual categories of crime which recognise the various degrees of difficulty associated with crime reduction. By undertaking this process the force will arrive at a definition of a *preventable* or *suppressible* crime. The force can use the definition as the basis for the subsequent measures of police effectiveness.

Having established the concept of a preventable crime we can move to the next stage in the process to ask the question "Is the indicator capable of measurement?". Reports of crime are quantifiable measures, but they are not always reliable. Police statistics are widely acknowledged to record only those instances of crime which the public report to the police which may leave substantial numbers of certain crimes unrecorded. Different groups within the community will report crimes to the police at differing rates and furthermore the reporting rate varies by category of crime. Therefore in communities where vandalism and minor theft are a relatively frequent occurrence, the number of cases reported to the police are likely to be less than in communities where these crimes are less frequent. Where the public have confidence that reporting a crime to the police will have a positive result, for example the recovery of their property, they are more likely to make a report than in cases where they believe there is little action the police can take. Thus, almost 100 per cent of the incidents of thefts *of* cars are reported to the police, whereas probably less than 50 per cent of thefts *from* cars are reported. Where performance measures are to be based upon reported crime figures then it is essential to establish a reliable base for these measures. Unless all crimes are being reported to the police it will be necessary for a force to undertake a public survey to establish the proportion of crimes reported, based upon what is known as the victim rate. Public surveys can establish the number of occasions when crimes actually occur and this rate can be compared with the number of crimes actually reported. Unless the victim rate is established, then reported crime statistics will remain a suspect performance measure.

Another factor directly affecting the reliability of reported crime figures is the way in which a police force may define some incidents as crimes. Probably the most significant difference in definitions of a crime is the use by the police of an arbitrary financial value placed upon the damage of property which places a case of vandalism either in the crime statistics or outside. This does not prevent these figures being used but it may be necessary for a force to modify its recording procedures for the purpose of establishing performance measures.

The final question that should be asked in this process of defining performance measures concerns the validity of the measure. In the case of reported crime statistics their validity is linked closely to the issue of reliability which has been examined in the previous paragraph. If the process of definition of a preventable crime has been performed and the reliability of the figures established through the use of additional sources of information such as victim surveys, then the subsequent results should provide valid performance measures based on crime rates.

Following this process a performance measure can now be defined:-

The number of preventable crimes committed in year 'x' compared with the number of preventable crimes committed in year 'y'.

Goal:-
To increase the number of offences detected.

Before performance measures can be attached to this goal, the same process of analysis must be performed to determine the exact nature of the police responsibility and the means by which offenders are detected. It is unreasonable to compare the detection rate on a sub-division where less than one per cent of the detected offences are shoplifting, with another sub-division where that particular crime represents more than 10 per cent of the detected offences. Therefore, it is necessary to examine how offenders are detected. The examination will establish the contribution made by citizens who identify and name the offender, the number of detections achieved through the admissions made by persons arrested for another offence, and the contribution made by other sub-divisions or police forces who arrest offenders who admit offences in the police area under consideration. It is also important to establish the contributions made by various sections of the force. For example, the quality of the initial police response to the call from the public to the scene of a crime is a very important factor in determining whether or not the offence will be subsequently detected. Similarly the role of detectives and criminal intelligence must also be examined to provide a sound basis on which their effectiveness can be assessed. Therefore, in relation to this goal, it might be appropriate to establish a number of performance measures in relation to categories of crime and the methods by which the detections occurred.

Two performance measures can be considered:-

(i) The number of crimes of burglary in dwelling houses detected by arrest or summons in year 'X' compared with the number detected in year 'Y'.

(ii) The number of crimes detected by arrest or summons through routine checks by patrolling officers in year 'X' compared with the number detected in year 'Y'.

Promoting Road Safety And Traffic Flow

Goal:-
To reduce the number of road accidents.
To improve the flow of traffic.

The first step the manager must take in his search for appropriate performance measures is to review and analyse the exact nature of his responsibilities. Road accidents like crimes, take a variety of forms. The operational police issues raised by a minor collision which takes place in a slow moving line of traffic are of a different order to the issues relating to an intoxicated motorist driving on the wrong side of a motorway at 70 miles per hour. The causes of accidents can be seen on a continuum of preventability which range from the momentary error of an individual driver, inadequate road construction, vehicle defects, dangerous driving, to drunkenness. The categories of accident which can be affected by police actions and the strategies most likely to be effective, must be identified. The police can undertake enforcement, education, such as drinking and driving campaigns, or traffic management where they seek to influence other agencies to improve or modify road construction. It is clear that some accidents will continue to occur in spite of police action, thus it seems unreasonable to measure police effectiveness based on all accidents. The principles

36

of analysis used in relation to crime control are equally applicable in relation to road accidents. There is a need to define a preventable accident as the standard criterion on which police effectiveness should be assessed.

When a preventable road accident has been defined, then it is capable of direct measurement as a quantitative performance measure. Its reliability will be directly related to the skill with which it has been defined, however it should be remembered that not all road accidents, and in particular damage only road accidents, are reported to the police. The possible difference between the number of accidents that occur and the proportion actually reported to the police has to be acknowledged and strategies developed to ensure the reliability of the performance measure. The goal relates specifically to road accidents and therefore the validity of the measure is achieved through its reliability.

Two performance measures can be defined in respect of the reduction of road accidents:-

(i) The number of road accidents attributed to the violation of road junction controls in year 'X' compared with year 'Y'.

(ii) The number of road accidents involving drivers who had a blood alcohol level beyond the legal limit in year 'X' compared to year 'Y'.

The police also have responsibilities for improving the flow of traffic. However not all of the factors which affect the movement of traffic are under the control of the police. When he is asked to respond to this goal the police manager will have to establish those factors which he can influence though police patrols, the deployment of traffic wardens and the enforcement of parking regulations. The definition of performance measures for this goal will require some innovation because it is unlikely that there will be existing measures which can be used. Performance measures for this goal could be established by measuring the time taken to travel between two locations at various times of day and night. Comparisons could be made between the travel time when there was little or no traffic on the road and the time taken for the same journey during peak traffic hours. When a number of standard journey times have been established throughout the force area, then the effects of police traffic control strategy or road improvements can be objectively measured.

The reliability and validity of the measures will depend upon the care that was taken when the standard measures were obtained. It is essential that the type of vehicle used and the times of the day are the same on each occasion.

A performance measure can be defined as follows:
The difference between journey times at low and peak traffic hours in year 'X' compared with year 'Y'.

Traditionally specialist traffic departments have been given the responsibility for promoting road safety and traffic flow and they have tended to justify their contribution to these goals on the basis of the enforcement of traffic legislation. With the exception of relatively few examples, there has been an assumption without evidence to substantiate it, that there is a direct link between the number of motorists reported for offences and improvements in road safety and traffic flow. The definition of performance measures provides an opportunity for this aspect of police operations to be examined to produce evidence to demonstrate a link.

Enhancement of Public Tranquillity

Goal:-

To enhance public tranquillity.

We have seen the need to have a careful analysis leading to a definition of a preventable crime or a preventable road accident. In the case of public tranquillity there may not be a shared consensus within the community as to the definition of public tranquillity. However, research has consistently shown the quality of people's lives is directly related to such matters as their general feeling of safety and security both at home and in public places. The public's fear of crime is apparently more influenced by their perceptions of the general state of their neighbourhood than the actual crime rate. People who are concerned about the amount of litter on the streets, children causing nuisances and vandalism, are more likely to fear becoming the victim of a crime than people who do not have these concerns. These issues of public tranquillity also affect their satisfaction with the police. People who see these matters as a problem in their neighbourhood expressed less satisfaction with the police than citizens who do not see them as problems.

The definition of performance measures in respect of public tranquillity is complex. It is in this area where the police manager's skill at consulting with his local community and the ability of the officers under his command will be tested. In answer to the question, "What is it that identifies the need for police action?", it is likely there will be a number of indicators. For example, the police receive letters from concerned citizens, residents associations and politicians complaining about the lack of police attention to some problems of disorder or nuisance. These complaints may concern drunkenness outside certain public houses at closing time, children cycling in pedestrian shopping precincts, and damage to public amenities such as parks and gardens. Although all these matters can be counted and thus appear to be quantitative measures, the real nature of measures of public tranquillity are based upon people's attitudes and feelings which are essentially qualitative performance measures. It will be for the manager to decide whether he has sufficient information on which to proceed to define performance measures. If he is uncertain, public attitude surveys will provide a valuable insight into the level of the public's satisfaction with their local police and the priority for police action which should be assigned these order maintenance problems.

Despite the inexact nature of the concept of public tranquillity, the process of defining performance measures must start with a definition of the police responsibility. The definition will almost certainly vary from one sub-division to another and there may also be some variation within a sub-division. Therefore performance measures may be specific to a problem and to an area. The residents of a housing estate may be concerned with the nuisances caused by children in the street, children cycling in the pedestrian shopping areas and damage to telephone boxes. Therefore, it will be these issues which will form the basis of the definition of public tranquillity in that neighbourhood. The reliability of the measures will be directly related to the skill with which they have been defined, recognising the limitations of the data which are available. It is recommended that more than one measure is used to evaluate the results of actions directed towards improving public tranquillity. Three performance measures can be defined as follows:–

(i) The number of complaints of general nuisance received from the public on housing estate 'A' in year 'X' compared to year 'Y'.

(ii) The number of persons observed cycling on pavements and pedestrian areas in year 'X' compared to year 'Y'.

(iii) The number of incidents of damage to telephone boxes in year 'X' compared to year 'Y'.

With practice performance measures are relatively easy to define. It is essential to define the exact nature of police responsibility and then identify those aspects which can be used as measures of police effectiveness. By following the sequence shown in Figure 3.1, distinctions can be made between measures of quantity and quality, and the reliability and validity of the measures will not be overlooked. Performance measures are a key of the management cycle and will be raised during other stages of the cycle.

4   Measuring Police Efficiency

Effectiveness is concerned with measuring achievements towards an objective, efficiency is concerned with the cost incurred in pursuit of the objective. Thus efficiency is also based on a measure. The annual cost of a police force can be found in its budget which can be examined to show the individual cost of vehicles, stationery, uniform, petrol and wages. It is the last item which represents more than 80 per cent of the typical police budget. Another way of looking at costs is to see them as resources which have to be managed to give the best return for their use. It is simple to understand how reducing the waste in stationery or petrol can increase efficiency by reducing costs. In the context of the entire budget these savings are fairly small compared to the cost of human resources represented by wages. Therefore, when a police force talks about improving its efficiency it is concerned with the ways in which it uses its officers and civilian staff. The diverse nature of police work and the variety of tasks that are performed make it necessary when considering efficiency, to direct attention to the time officers or civilians spend on these tasks. A police officer represents, for the purpose of this analysis, 40 hours of available time each week. Irrespective of how this time is used, it can only be used once. If time is wasted in unproductive activities then it is lost. To keep this idea in mind the term *consumed time* will be used to represent the use of human resources.

The learning objectives of this chapter are:-

1   To be able to define 'efficiency' and 'improved efficiency'.

2   To understand how the concept of efficiency fits into the planning stage of the management cycle.

3   To understand how efficiency is related to the use of resources.

4 To understand why human resources should be seen in the context of consumed time.

5 To understand that a management review to establish the strengths and weaknesses of the force must include measures of the use of resources.

6 To understand the concept of mandatory tasks and mandatory time.

7 To understand the concept of discretionary tasks and discretionary time.

8 To understand the concept of maximum theoretical available time and how it can be calculated.

9 To understand the concept of the actual available time and how it can be calculated.

10 To be able to calculate the consumed time for specific police activities.

11 To be able to measure the use of time by an operational unit and thereby establish workload.

12 To be able to calculate the minimum number of officers to complete a given workload.

13 To be able to calculate the establishment figure for officers from a given workload.

14 To understand the concept of unit costs and their application to calculations of efficiency.

Definition

A police force can be effective without necessarily being efficient because it can pursue and achieve its goals without any consideration of cost if it has unlimited resources. It is theoretically possible for the reverse to be true, however it would be pointless for a police force to cost almost nothing but to come nowhere near achieving any goal. Therefore efficiency should *not* be defined without reference to effectiveness.

Efficiency is the cost of achieving a specific result.

Improved efficiency is the *reduction* in the cost of achieving the same or a better result.

Resource Measures

When reviewing the present performance of the force, the police manager should assess whether he is using his resources to the best effect and consider alternative means of achieving the same results. Therefore when measures are being taken to establish the effectiveness of the force, it is useful to measure the amount of time which is being spent by officers on the activities directed towards the objective. Later in the planning stage the resources which will be required in the future to improve the effectiveness of the force must be identified. There is no point designing a policing plan to combat a particular problem if there are no resources available to implement it. The review may also identify some officers who have time available which might be used for new tasks. A useful place to start to examine the way officers spend their time is to identify those tasks which are fundamental to the responsibilities of the force. These tasks will be called the *mandatory* tasks to signify that the policy of the force demands that they must continue to be performed. A manager must know the time that is used by his officers to complete all the mandatory tasks that occur. On some sub-divisions it is possible that the officers who respond to calls from the public reach the point where they do not have enough time to complete all the calls that are received. Other officers on the sub-division may find they can complete all their mandatory tasks using only three hours out of their eight hours on duty. They use the five hours to perform tasks which they decide should be done. In fact they exercise a degree of discretion over the use of this time. The time during which the officers exercise some choice as to their tasks, will be called *discretionary time*. If it is decided that improvements should be made in police effectiveness then discretionary time may be the resource which can be used to implement new policing methods. The typical eight hour shift can be divided into two parts comprising the time used for mandatory tasks and the remaining discretionary time. This calculation is sufficient for day-to-day needs, however for longer term planning a manager must know the man hours which will be available from a given number of officers.

By taking the total number of police officers on a sub-division it is possible to calculate the theoretical maximum number of man hours that they will work in a given period. In reality the number of man hours that are available for ordinary duty are less than the theoretical maximum because time has to be subtracted for annual leave, sickness, training and many other tasks which take officers away from the sub-division. The man hours which remain after these commitments have been subtracted will be called the *available time*.

Analysis Of Activity Times

There are many reasons for analysing the time consumed by police activities. A change in priorities may give rise to the need to find some additional time to implement a new policing initiative. This time has to be found from somewhere and a useful place to start is to look at existing activities which seem to take a substantial amount of time but do not seem to produce many tangible benefits. A force may be considering transferring the responsibility for some work from one group of officers to another. However, before transferring that work it is essential to ensure that the officers who are to take on the responsibility have sufficient time at their disposal. To measure the time needed for specific activities it is useful to start by identifying the individual constituent elements. The method can be illustrated with reference to a road accident which is progressed from the police attendance at the scene to completion with the prosecution of a driver for careless driving. The principles which are described can be used for most police activities.

Response Stage

The response stage is divided into four specific activities. The police officer spends time travelling to the scene of the accident after he receives the call. He uses more time at the scene, travelling to the police station and completing the initial report. These four activities are listed in Figure 4.1 where some times have been allocated to give an example of the method of calculating the total time. If there is a need to look at ways of finding time to do additional tasks this method is useful because it is possible to identify the parts of the task which takes the most time. Thus a 30 per cent improvement in the efficiency of travelling to the scene of the accident would only reduce the overall time by a few seconds. However, a similar improvement in the efficiency of the paperwork procedures would make a significant reduction in the time used in the final part of the incident. Therefore, any attempts to improve efficiency should be directed at the activities which consume the largest amounts of time.

Figure 4.1   Initial phase

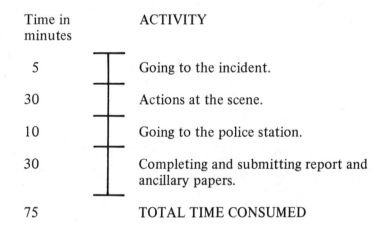

Time in minutes	ACTIVITY
5	Going to the incident.
30	Actions at the scene.
10	Going to the police station.
30	Completing and submitting report and ancillary papers.
75	TOTAL TIME CONSUMED

Completion Stage

The enquiry stage of the incident takes the initial report and progresses the case to the prosecution of the offending driver. For the purpose of this example it will be assumed that a specialist accident enquiry squad has the responsibility for these tasks. When the accident report is received further enquiries are made, witnesses interviewed and statements obtained, and plans are prepared of the scene. A report is prepared, a prosecution authorised and the summons procedures implemented. The case is heard at the magistrates court and the papers are subsequently filed. The sequence of these activities is shown in Figure 4.2, where times have been allocated for these tasks as illustrations. Road accidents comprise a significant volume of work for the police and therefore there are considerable advantages to be gained by improving the efficiency of the enquiry procedure. Once again it is wise to examine the activities which consume the most time as the place to start improving efficiency. The further enquiry stage concerned with witness statements takes most time. The presentation of the case at court is also time consuming, however the police may be able to exercise little if any control over this part of the process, therefore it will be more profitable to examine the enquiry and reporting procedures.

Figure 4.2 Completion phase

Time in minutes		ACTIVITY
120		Further enquiries, witness statements, plans of the scene.
40		Preparation of reports.
30		Preparation of court documents.
50		Presentation of case at court.
10		Documentation of result.
250		TOTAL CONSUMED TIME

Experience shows that the vast majority of cases of careless driving are resolved without the need to call witnesses to court to give evidence. Some cases are filed without taking proceedings and in many others the defendant pleads guilty. Therefore the need to take detailed statements in all cases must be questioned. Another system could be considered. A questionnaire designed to elicit all essential information could be sent by post to the witnesses named in the initial report and returned to the accident enquiry squad. A summary could be prepared on the basis of these responses to provide sufficient information on which to base the decision to prosecute. In cases where a prosecution was to proceed, the case could be given a preliminary hearing on the facts in the summary. Where the defendant chose to contest the case the witnesses could be interviewed on the basis of their questionnaires and statements obtained. The time saved by this change in procedures would be considerable.

The principles of analysing tasks into their constituent parts is the first stage in the measurement of time. Methods will have to be chosen to enable time to be measured and assigned to these parts. The degree of sophistication and hence accuracy required for these measures must be determined by individual managers based on their needs. In police forces with computerised command and control systems these measures of time may be collected as a by-product of the system. It is wise to assess the accuracy of these figures where they exist before they are used. This can be done simply by taking a sample from the data and obtaining the times by some independent measurement system. However, in most cases these data will be confined to the response stage of the incident and therefore some other means will have to be developed for the completion stage.

In cases where there are no existing sources of data to provide measures of consumed time they will have to be developed. To give a representative picture of the number of mandatory tasks and the time needed to service them it is likely that a fairly substantial survey will be required covering a number of officers over several days. To illustrate one method of collecting these data an incident recording card is shown in Figure 4.3. These cards would be completed by officers who attend incidents.

The card identifies all the elements of a typical incident. The first section of the incident card enables the sub-division, shift, beat, date and the type of incident to be recorded. The following section, which records times on a 24 hour clock, enables the response time and the time at the scene to be calculated. There is a section which covers a report, if appropriate. The number of prisoners and charges can also be shown. Following sections allow the type of patrol to be identified and to establish whether the officer went immediately to the scene, thus identifying those occasions when a response will be delayed. The final part identified

Figure 4.3   Incident Card

MANAGEMENT SERVICES	DO NOT WRITE IN THIS COL.
Sub-Division ☐☐ Shift ☐☐	☐☐☐☐
Incident Location Beat ☐☐	
Date ☐☐☐ Day _____	☐
Incident _____	
_____	☐☐
Time Message Received by you _____	☐☐☐☐
Time of Arrival at Scene _____	☐☐☐
Time Departed from Scene _____	☐☐☐
Report YES/NO*	☐
REPORT TYPE:- Crime, accident, offence*	
Other (specify)	
Time spent on Report	☐☐
	☐☐☐
Prisoner YES/NO*	☐
Number of Prisoners	☐☐
Main Charge	☐☐
Time spent with Prisoner (Booking in, Interview, Documentation etc.)	☐☐☐
PATROL TYPE: First Response Panda, Foot Patrol (Unit), Area Constable*	☐
Did you go immediately to the Scene? YES/NO*	☐
Were you *(a) The first officer at the Scene? *(b) Sent to assist other officers?	☐
Number	
Circle as appropriate	

48

incidents where an officer has attended to give assistance to another officer. This section enables the cards from all officers who attended the incident to be added together to give an overall consumed time for each incident.

The card has been used to establish consumed times for various incident categories, the frequency with which reports and arrests were made, and to establish if variations occurred in the consumed time between different types of police patrols. Officers wishing to establish similar data may well find this incident card an appropriate means, but the format should not be assumed to be suitable until it is tested against the specific information requirements of the sub-division. Before undertaking a survey consideration should be given to the way in which the data are to be analysed. In the card illustrated, the boxes in the right-hand column have been designed to assist computer analysis.

Unfortunately, the second or completion stage of the incident does not lend itself so readily to one simple measurement system. As far as follow up enquiries are concerned, a pro forma could be attached inside the file on which individual amounts of time could be recorded as the enquiry progresses. In the absence of direct observational measurement by a project team, it is probably the only means at a manager's disposal to measure the time required for this process. Where the report is passed to a specialist unit, such as a court administration department, it would be possible to establish the number of items processed by individual members of the department. For example, if two members of staff are employed exclusively on the preparation of the documentation for the application, the checking and despatching of summonses, then the time expended on each individual item can be calculated by establishing the volume processed in a particular time period and dividing that number into the total hours used. If a clerical officer had a working day of 7 hours and processed 42 files, then the average time per file would be 10 minutes.

The Use Of Time By A Productive Unit

Methods have been described which measure the time used to perform various police functions. The use of time can also be seen from the perspective of the people who perform the tasks. The distinction has already been made between the time which is spent by officers performing tasks which must be done, mandatory tasks, and those where they can exercise some choice, discretionary tasks. Of course the amount of time they have to devote to discretionary tasks will depend upon their mandatory workload. A manager may wish to direct his officers into specific activities during this discretionary time and therefore he must know how much time is available. By adopting the procedures illustrated in the previous section the amount of time spent on specific mandatory tasks can be measured. This figure can then be subtracted from the total time available to the officer or group of officers to give the number of man hours available after these tasks have been completed. However, there are other tasks which these officers are obliged to perform, such as attendance at court, providing cover in the enquiry office for other officers to have meal breaks and other ancillary tasks. This time must also be measured to give the full workload of the officers.

The next stage in the calculation of the use of resources is to take a group of officers, which will be called the productive unit, and calculate their actual available time.

The annual available time represented by one officer is calculated by taking the theoretical maximum number of working days and then subtracting fixed abstractions and variable abstractions to give the net annual availability. This calculation is shown in Figure 4.4, with fixed abstractions of annual leave and public holidays accounting for 28 days and variable abstractions, such as training and sickness accounting for a further 30 days, leaving a net annual availability of 202 days. In some forces it may be necessary to include other variable abstractions within this calculation, such as the provision of support from one division to another in connection with football matches, public demonstrations, attachments to various departments for specialist training and so forth. It would be for individual managers to measure the amount of variable abstractions and ensure they were included within the calculation. When the net available days have been calculated, it is possible to determine the manpower necessary to cover a beat for 24 hours a day, 365 days a year:-

$$\frac{365 \text{ days} \times 3 \text{ shifts}}{202 \text{ shifts per man}} = 5.42 \text{ men.}$$

Figure 4.4   Annual available time

Theoretical Maximum Time

     52 weeks x 5 days = 260

Fixed Abstractions

Annual leave	20 days	
Public holidays	8 days	
	28	232

Variable Abstractions

Training	15	
Sickness	15	
	30	
Net Annual Days		202

Net Available Days = Theoretical Max − (fixed abstractions + variable abstractions)

    The above calculation assumes the net available time of 202 days per year for an officer and thus it would be necessary to provide an establishment of 6 officers for each beat on a sub-division to provide a 24 hour cover.

    The calculation of net available time enables the manager to establish the resources that are represented by a given number of officers and he is then able to calculate the officers required to provide a constant 24 hour cover to a beat. These calculations however do not give any information on the workload that can be accommodated by those officers. A method has been described to calculate the time needed for specific police functions but this may not give the complete picture of the workload represented by all mandatory tasks. In cases where the most important information is to establish the total workload represented by mandatory tasks another system can be used where the unit of analysis is the officers themselves.

A simple example of the way in which these calculations could be made is shown in Figure 4.5. A maximum daily available time of 480 minutes is reduced to a net discretionary time of 230 minutes, when subtractions are made for meals, report writing, administration, attending calls for service and so forth. The discretionary time in the example given is approximately 48 per cent of the officers' maximum available time.

Figure 4.5 Daily available time

Theoretical Maximum

8 x 60		480 minutes

Fixed Abstractions

Meals	45	435 minutes

Variable Abstractions

Preparation for patrol	15	
Report writing	50	
Administration	20	
Attending calls for Services	120	
	205	230 minutes

DISCRETIONARY TIME = 230 minutes (48%).

The daily available time can be used as a means of determining the absolute minimum manpower required to cover all the mandatory tasks the officers are required to perform. The constable represented in Figure 4.5 has a total commitment of 250 minutes per 8 hour shift. If he was one of 10 constables on a shift, then the total mandatory workload for that shift would be calculated as follows:-

$$\frac{250 \text{ minutes} \times 10 \text{ (constables)}}{480 \text{ minutes}} = 5.2 \text{ men}$$

If discretionary time was eliminated and officers worked on mandatory tasks from the moment they came on duty until the moment they completed duty, then six constables would be required to complete the average daily workload. Therefore it would be theoretically possible to use the other four officers to perform tasks which were specifically planned by the supervising officer.

This calculation can provide a measure of workload which can be translated to manpower requirements. However there are a number of problems with the practical application of the calculation. There is an implicit assumption that workload can be calculated to provide accurate averages. This assumption is valid provided a large sample of data is taken and accurately measured. Average workload also assumes that police work occurs in predictable patterns, this is correct over long periods, but may be very inaccurate on a day to day basis. Therefore it is essential to build into the calculation a reserve or buffer of manpower which will be able to deal with the unexpected. Research has shown that this reserve should be sufficiently large to give officers an average discretionary time of 50 per cent per shift. Therefore on the basis of the mandatory workload established in Figure 4.5, the realistic strength would be six times two constables, giving a figure of twelve officers. Assume for the purpose of the next exercise that the workload on the sub-division is equally distributed throughout the period of 24 hours, then based on the net available time which has been calculated, each of the twelve beats will require an establishment of six constables to ensure continuous manning. Therefore the establishment of this sub-division to service the mandatory tasks will be 72 uniformed constables. The assumption that workload is equally distributed over a 24 hour period is not valid and therefore it is necessary to measure workload linked to the time of day. In the past, simple counts of the numbers of calls on the police for service have caused some managers to assume there is scope for reducing the number of officers on duty between 2am and 6 am. However, a count of calls received is not a valid measure of workload because it does not take account of the time that is used at incidents, which may be longer at night because more serious crimes and road accidents can occur during those hours. However, the apparently lower workload during those hours is a useful point to start examining improved strategies for manpower deployment to ensure resources are available to meet the predicted demand.

Methods of Measurement

The incident card was used to measure the time spent on a range of activities which can be specified by the manager. To calculate workload the method must concentrate on the officers who are engaged on the tasks. Techniques of work measurement such as those used by Organisation and Methods (O and M) specialists may be examined but care must be taken because some methods are wholly inappropriate for measuring police patrol workload.

The widely used O and M technique of activity sampling, where individuals are asked to mark a grid at pre-determined time intervals indicating the category of work they are performing, can only hope to give a vague indication of the general workload of a police officer. The substantial variation in tasks which are being performed by uniformed patrol officers, together with the relatively short time some of these tasks take to complete, makes this method of establishing workload singularly inappropriate for all but a few limited functions within the police. The most accurate method is to select a number of competent and reliable officers and obtain their co-operation in the completion of daily diary sheets which give an almost minute by minute account of the activities they perform. An example of a suitable diary sheet is shown in Figure 3.6. Although this is a very detailed method, it is probably the best point from which to start such an analysis. This will give a detailed picture of the activities which are being performed by the group of officers and also the amount of time consumed. When these data have been analysed it will be possible to take a more detailed look at specific areas of activity such as report writing for example, which may suggest the introduction of new methods to provide an opportunity to improve efficiency.

Figure 4.6

UNIT: DATE: TOUR OF DUTY:

POSTING: OFFICER:

| TIME | | TYPE OF ACTIVITY | TIMES IN MINUTES | | | |
Start	Finish		Station	Free Patrol	Response	Other
		Total				

The Relationship Between Time, Resources And Efficiency

The chapter has illustrated the means of measuring the time used in specific police activities, the theoretical maximum time and the net available time for an officer or a group of officers. Outside any considerations of efficiency this information is vital for the planning stage of the management cycle because a manager must know the resources he has at his disposal and the way in which they are being used at present. He cannot plan changes in policing methods or deployment if his officers are totally committed on tasks which policy has made mandatory. His first concern will be to try and find ways of performing those mandatory tasks more efficiently and thus create some 'spare' time. In fact he is looking for improvements in the productivity of his officers.

Time has been used to provide a means of measuring the use of resources. Efficiency is ultimately based on the cost of achieving a goal and therefore these times should be translated into costs. The simplest way of using costs in this context is to reduce them to individual or *unit costs* . To calculate the unit cost of a uniformed constable it is necessary to add together his wages and the overheads which are incurred by the force, such as National Insurance contributions, the cost of uniform, rent allowance and compensatory grant. The result is the total annual cost of the constable. To relate this cost to time, the total annual cost can be divided by the theoretical maximum time available. On current figures the unit cost of a constable with eight years service is about eleven pounds per hour. The same simple calculations can be used to establish unit costs for other officers and civilians. Not all unit costs are based on time, for example the average cost per mile for traffic patrol cars or casual user car allowance. These unit costs will also be needed in some calculations of efficiency.

To illustrate how the unit costs can be used to measure improvements in efficiency by reducing cost, the example of the completion stage of the road accident given in Figure 4.2 can be used. For this exercise assume there is an average of 100 accidents per month which are investigated by the accident enquiry squad. This represents a workload of 200 hours per month for the obtaining of witness statements and plans. The system of questionnaire is adopted which reduces the average time for this part of the procedure to 15 minutes for each case, which means a workload of 25 hours per month. Based on a unit cost of eleven pounds per hour for a constable there is a reduction in the cost of this procedure from £26,400 to £3,300 per year. There may be a possibility for other savings because the work now has a large clerical element which could be done more cheaply by civilian staff.

The Relationship Between Effectiveness and Efficiency

In Chapter 3 methods were developed to define performance measures which could be used to establish the extent to which a police force was achieving its objectives. In this Chapter efficiency has been related to the use of resources and the costs of police operations based on the amount of time which is consumed in the pursuit of an objective. In the future police managers will be asked to demonstrate not only the extent to which they are achieving their objectives but the cost of the operations, in other words, effectiveness and efficiency. Therefore there will be a need to combine the two measures. To illustrate the process we can consider the traffic congestion being experienced in the centre of a small town. The problem is brought to the attention of the sub-divisional superintendent by the bus company who are experiencing serious delays in their timetables on routes which pass through the centre of the town. The timetables had been set on the basis of journey times measured by the company. These times are now being exceeded with a journey which should take 30 minutes taking between 45 and 60 minutes at certain times during the day. The analysis of the problem shows that there is a substantial disregard for the parking restrictions in the town centre. Cars are being parked in contravention of parking prohibitions in streets where it is difficult for large vehicles such as buses to pass. The problem appears to be caused by people shopping and occurs between the hours of 10.00 am and 4.30 pm. The analysis provides a measure of effectiveness, namely the journey times of buses, which are monitored by the company, However, it is always useful to have secondary measures which can help establish the results of police action, although they are not performance measures in themselves. A secondary measure in this case could be the number of vehicles parked in prohibited areas at a particular time of the day. This would not be a performance measure because it is the journey times which will give the real measure of the improvements to the traffic flow.

The sub-divisional superintendent has examined the problem and has developed a performance measure for which he has objective data to measure the effectiveness of his policing methods. He has a secondary measure which will enable him to establish the impact his policing method is having on what he believes to be the cause of the problem. However, he recognises that even if he prevents all parking in prohibited areas he may not necessarily increase the speed of traffic through the town centre. For similar reasons it would be nonsense to use the number of people reported for parking offences as a performance measure related to traffic flow. The widespread disregard for the parking prohibitions can be addressed by a directed enforcement policy. It is at this point that the superintendent has a choice concerning the resources he will deploy to solve the problem. He can use uniformed patrol constables or traffic wardens. The decision will have implications for the cost of the policing method. A constable will cost at least twice as much per hour as a traffic warden, although the latter is likely to be equally effective at solving the problem. Therefore, the use of traffic wardens will be twice as efficient as using constables. Of course there would be other benefits because the constables would be available for work more fitting to their skills and powers.

When the plan is implemented the superintendent has a measure of effectiveness and a secondary measure to assess the impact of his plan. He can record the man hours used in the plan and calculate the cost of the exercise based upon the unit cost of a traffic warden. He is also able to demonstrate the relative efficiency of traffic wardens against constables. When the bus company report a return to normal journey times the plan can be scaled down to reduce costs by deploying the traffic wardens on other duties. However, the situation can be monitored using the journey times and remedial action taken when the situation appears to be deteriorating.

5   Developing Policy

The two preceding chapters have been concerned with internal examinations and assessments of the force. Although the quality of police services has been discussed there has been no in depth consideration of how data can be obtained to measure this important aspect of the manager's considerations. In Chapter 4, it was suggested that a police force must first seek to be effective and then consider its efficiency, because there seems to be little point in having a very efficient force which is totally ineffective. This chapter raises another important consideration. The values of our society would suggest that a police force should not strive for absolute effectiveness and efficiency without considering the wishes of the community. To achieve these two goals but to lose the support and confidence of society would be too high a price to pay. Community involvement and influence on policing policy are fundamental pre-requisites of the style of policing which has developed in Britain. The task of the manager is to establish the means by which the diverse and sometimes contradictory demands of groups in society can be identified and assessed. Police forces must have formal mechanisms which include the consideration of these demands, in their process of defining strategic policy. The process offers advantages to the members of society as they become formally recognised as part of the planning stage of the management cycle and their wishes are included in the monitoring and evaluation process. There are also advantages for the police because the process allows them to identify the responsibilities of society and also to point out the limitations placed on the police by legal obligations and limited resources.

The learning objectives of this chapter are:-

1   To understand how the community's needs and wishes should be included in the process of policy formation.

2   To recognise the limitations of traditional methods of assessing community needs.

3   To understand the management requirements for objective methods of assessing community needs.

4   To recognise the means by which the quality of police services can be measured.

5   To understand the uses of public surveys as an aid to police management.

6   To have a knowledge of the basic requirements of public survey techniques.

7   To understand how survey techniques can be adapted to suit particular information requirements.

The need for more formal consultation methods with all sections of society was recognised by Lord Scarman who recommended the nationwide introduction of the consultation committees. The Home Office encouraged chief constables to establish local consultation arrangements (Home Office Circular No 54/1982) and gave guidelines to assist them. There are many reasons for forming local consultation committees, but it is their role in assisting with policy making which will be discussed.

The success of these arrangements will depend upon a number of factors, not least, the extent of the quality of police/public relations and the ability to achieve a consensus on solutions to local policing problems. It is clear these committees do represent another challenge to the skill and professionalism of police management. A number of management questions are raised by the formation of the committees:-

(i) Can the information which is obtained through the consultation process be seen as reliable and valid for the purposes of making policy?

(ii) Can this information be used as a basis upon which improvements in police effectiveness can be measured?

(iii) What influence should the committees be able to exert on the policy of the police?

(iv) The Home Office Circular says the arrangements should be 'effective in practice'. How will this be ensured? What characteristics will identify an effective consultative arrangement when compared with an ineffective arrangement?

(v) Do the committees represent the views of the people they purport to represent?

These questions concern three main themes, first the matter of the reliability and validity of the issues raised by the consultative committees, the utility of these data as performance measures, and finally, the quality of the internal police policy making process. A case study will serve to illustrate the first two points.

Case Study

A housing estate had been identified by a sub-divisional superintendent as having serious crime problems and as a response he formed a group of eight constables, supervised by a sergeant, to give added police cover to the area. After the first year of its operation a progress report claimed some success in dealing with the problems. The report recommended extending the policing method by forming a similar group of police officers, to provide special policing cover for another area of the sub-division known as Foleshill. His recommendation was supported by the views of local community leaders and politicians, from whom the sub-division enjoyed considerable support and mutual co-operation. The Foleshill area was said by the community leaders to have a serious crime problem, a lack of confidence in the police, police visibility was said to be low and there was said to be racial tension. It was claimed these problems were more serious there than in other areas of the city. The enthusiasm of the local council could be measured by their proposal to provide several thousand pounds to assist with the provision of a police section station to accommodate the police officers posted to the proposed team.

It is worth examining the evidence available to the senior officers for them to decide on the most appropriate course of action.

61

In common with many policing initiatives at the time, the review of the performance of the initial policing project on the housing estate was based exclusively on subjective perceptions. When apparently objective measures were included, such as crime and vandalism figures, these relied entirely on the assumption that either *all* such incidents were reported to the police or the proportions being reported before and during the life of the project remained unchanged. Neither assumption could be supported on the evidence of research into these matters. Thus it was impossible to measure the improvements achieved in crime control by this additional police manpower. Any claims to have improved the public's awareness of the increased presence of police officers, or to have reduced their fear of crime or improved their satisfaction with the police, could not hope to be sustained in the total absence of objective evidence. Thus a replication of the policing project in a different community could not be justified simply by the results achieved on the housing estate.

If previous experience did not provide information on which to make the managerial decision, how could the arguments made by the local community leaders and politicians be viewed? Did they provide a sound basis on which to proceed to deploy several police officers at considerable cost to the force? The questions could not be answered. The case for change was being made on personal opinions and beliefs. The chief constable decided that before the proposals should be implemented some questions should be answered with objective evidence:-

(i) What was the true nature of the policing problems?

(ii) How did these problems manifest themselves, what were the measures of police effectiveness?

(iii) What policy options did the analysis suggest?

(iv) If changes were to be made to the policing methods, what specific objectives were to be pursued?

(v) After the changes had been implemented what measures could be used for evaluating the results?

We can again see the cyclical nature of this problem solving exercise. The performance measures identified in (ii) are readily available to be measured in the evaluation stage (v).

The views expressed by the local leaders provided the starting point for the objective investigation. Two officers within the force examined the views expressed by the community leaders and prepared a means of testing these issues with the residents. Of the four issues identified, only one, the crime problem, had a data source within the force. However, the problem of unreported crime made the use of police statistics unreliable. If it was true there was a lack of confidence in the police, then a large amount of crime might not be reported. Improved confidence in the police might apparently generate more crime by increasing the proportion of crime being reported to the police.

To obtain the necessary information a direct survey of the residents of Foleshill was suggested to measure their experience of crime and the police, and their attitudes to crime and the police. A similar survey was suggested for the remaining area of the city to make some comparisons between the two groups of people. A questionnaire was developed and a random sample of a thousand residents of Foleshill were approached by interviewers who recorded their responses on the questionnaire. A similar survey was made of a random sample of 300 people from elsewhere in the city. The survey and the data were collected and analysed by the internal resources of the force.

The questionnaire obtained information from the residents to provide an assessment of the present effectiveness of the policing of Foleshill compared with the rest of the city. The survey was also designed to provide data which could be used as a means of evaluating any improvements that had been achieved in the event of changes being made to the policing methods. Data on the following topics were obtained from the survey:–

1   The frequency of the occurence of a range of crimes and the proportions which were reported to the police.

2   The frequency of sightings by the residents of the police and contact between them and the police.

3   General attitudes towards the police and satisfaction with

various aspects of the service which they provided.

4   Public perceptions of the seriousness of a range of crime and social problems which were mainly concerned with issues which influenced the resident's perceptions of public tranquillity in their neighbourhoods.

The data obtained from the survey in Foleshill questioned the conclusions drawn by the community leaders. When these data were compared with the responses obtained from the citizens living elsewhere in the city, there were few differences in the experiences and attitudes. In fact on some issues the allegedly "deprived community" of Foleshill was more satisfied with the police service it was receiving and perceived a greater police presence than residents in other areas of the city.

When the results of this survey were presented to police management and conveyed to the community leaders, it was obvious to all concerned that the problems apparently afflicting this community were no more severe than those afflicting other communities throughout the city. Furthermore, in some respects the police enjoyed more confidence in Foleshill than elsewhere. These results should not be taken as concluding there were no problems in the community, however it is management's responsibility to ensure resources are used equitably throughout the force on the basis of the priorities identified in the chief constable's policy. Thus, the proposal to establish a group of police officers with an exclusive responsibility for this area, based in a specially built section station, was abandoned in favour of a less radical proposal.

Policy Implications to be Drawn From the Case Study

The local politicians and community leaders' views of the policing problems of Foleshill were not supported by the opinions of the residents. Therefore, it would have been unwise to act solely upon information obtained through consultation with the local representatives, because it was not an accurate representation of the policing problems. Furthermore, the opinions of community leaders could not have been used as a reliable and valid means of measuring subsequent police performance, because the police, by changing their methods, would have been trying to solve problems which did not exist.

The case study illustrates the importance of making a careful analysis of the existing situation before making plans to change. The process of gathering data on which to make the analysis also provides the opportunity to obtain data on which effectiveness measures can be based and used later in the management cycle. Consultation has an important part to play in police/community relations and the process of developing strategic policy but it has some significant limitation which cannot be ignored.

Public Surveys As A Source Of Management Information

Public surveys are gaining greater acceptance as a source of information to aid the decisions which police managers have to make. It is essential that the information they provide should be reliable and valid. Therefore such surveys should not be undertaken without a clear understanding of the problems and pitfalls. A full description of the techniques and practical considerations of public surveys is outside the purpose of this book. Attention will be restricted to the consideration of the management aspects of surveys, such as the reasons for conducting a survey, the administration and logistics and the advantages of various survey methods.

Defining the Management Information Requirements

Before any decisions are made concerning the need to commission a public attitude survey, the specific information requirements of the police management problem should be carefully defined. The manager should ask himself why he needs the information and what purpose it will serve when he has obtained it. Consider the simple example of a sub-divisional superintendent who is being asked by his local consultative committee to use more officers to patrol on foot. A simple response to this demand would be to reduce the number of mobile patrols and deploy the officers on foot. A more thoughtful response would be to consider the advantages to be gained from such a change. Local community representatives might claim advantages with such comments as, 'It will reduce public fear of crime', 'It will improve public satisfaction with the police', 'It will reduce crime by the deterrent effect of more visible police'. A manager must recognise it is also possible that negative consequences could occur. Reducing the mobility of the police could produce complaints about delays in responding to calls from the public and reductions in detection rates for crime because of slower responses to crimes in progress. The proposal to increase the number of foot patrol officers also identifies the range of information which may be required to evaluate the results of the change.

Before responding to the demands to deploy more officers on foot patrols, a survey could be conducted to obtain data to describe the existing levels of police visibility and public satisfaction with police patrol deployments. These data would fall into the category of descriptive data. There are two other principle categories of data. Surveys can provide information which can diagnose the reasons for an existing situation. In the case study, the descriptive data might have revealed that certain sections in the community in Foleshill were less satisfied with the police than others. A further survey could have been commissioned, if this had been the case, to establish the reasons for this difference in public attitudes. The third purpose which can be served by survey data is to provide the means of evaluating the consequences of changes to policing methods. 'Before and after' surveys are one of the most powerful qualitative performance measures of changes in police effectiveness.

Identifying Existing Sources of Data

It is unlikely that a public survey will provide all the information required by a manager. The range of information needs identified by the issues raised in the previous paragraphs should initiate a review of existing data sources. Before changing the methods of deploying uniformed officers, information concerning the number of calls received by the sub-division and the response times to these calls would be important information for future evaluations. Existing sources of data should not be overlooked as they can at the very least provide a background to the preparations for public surveys.

The Administrative Requirements For a Public Survey

When the need for a direct survey of the public has been established, practical considerations must be addressed. The force must have someone who understands the technical requirements of conducting surveys, or they must have direct access to a person who is prepared to give the necessary support to the force throughout the process. There is no point receiving technical assistance in preparing the survey, if that help is not continued to assist in the interpretation of data. One course would be to hand the technical aspects to a commercial organisation or an academic institution, this has some advantages but may be expensive and it also has a number of other disadvantages. If the project is referred to external experts, the force will need to retain careful control of the management of the project to ensure the data are suitable for their purpose.

The survey will require a project leader or co-ordinator and an assistant or office manager. The administration of a survey involves the technical knowledge which is required at various times throughout the project, and the continuing day to day administration. These tasks should be split between two people. Depending on the survey method there will be a need for people to distribute, collate and analyse the responses. Unless the survey is very rudimentary and on a small scale, some computer facilities will be required to analyse the questionnaires. The availability of these resources, manpower and technical aids, will determine the timescale for the completion of the survey.

Public Survey Methods

There are two principle methods of conducting public surveys. The less expensive method is the postal survey, but it has more disadvantages compared to the more costly personal interview method.

In the postal survey method, questionnaires are despatched to a sample of the public. The recipients are asked to complete the questionnaire and return them in prepaid envelopes. This avoids the cost of employing interviewers to undertake the person to person collection of data. There are a number of disadvantages with this method. It requires a very careful construction of the questionnaire to ensure it can be understood by the people who are asked to complete it, because they do not have an opportunity to clarify ambiguous questions with a trained interviewer. Another substantial disadvantage is the sometimes high proportion of people who fail to respond to the survey. The person selected by the sampling procedure can never be guaranteed to be the person who actually completes the questionnaire which can lead to distortions in the sample.

The alternative method is to use a questionnaire as a structured interview format which is taken by interviewers who interview the person selected by a random sampling procedure. The questionnaire is then completed by the interviewer on the basis of responses given by the subject. Using this method there is less opportunity for the sample to be contaminated because it is the selected person who responds to the questionnaire. The questions can be relatively more sophisticated and complex as the interviewer can guide the subject through the procedure by careful questioning and probing. The interviewer is also available to clarify any ambiguities or misunderstandings which may arise from time to time. Finally, when a person declines to take part in the survey, it is possible with the use of an interviewer to determine the reasons for the refusal. It can never be assumed that the reason people do not take part in surveys concerning the police is because they do not like the police.

The decision concerning the type of method to be used will have implications for the questionnaire design and the pilot study which must be performed before the questionnaire is used in the main survey.

Questionnaire Design

If there is one area to be singled out as having a critical requirement for professional advice and expertise, then it is the design of questionnaires. If the data have been obtained using inadequately designed questions, then the whole process is a wasted effort. The basic rules for questionnaire design follow a simple pattern. The subject areas for questions can be identified through the process of the defining policing objectives and performance measures. The researcher has to translate those objectives and performance measures into suitably phrased questions which will reliably and validly produce data related to the objectives. No questionnaire should be used without undertaking an appropriate pilot study. The value of pilot studies cannot be over emphasised, because it is the only way in which a questionnaire design can be tested before it is used in the main study. As much care should be taken with the pilot study as with the main study, for example it is not adequate to invite colleagues in the office to complete a questionnaire which is going to be used to measure school children's attitudes towards police officers. Furthermore, if a survey is to be used to sample the opinions of all sections of the community then it will be pointless conducting a pilot study only in a middle class residential area.

In addition to questions related to a direct measurement of the objectives of the study, the researcher must consider the influence on the subjects' responses caused by social and demographic variables, such as the age and sex of the respondent, and the type of housing in which he or she lives. These demographic variables are important for subsequent analysis because people's opinions may vary according to the area in which they live, and there also may be differences between men and women or between young and old, or between people who live in their own house and those who live in rented accommodation. A further purpose of these data is to test the sampling method used.

A final consideration in the design of a questionnaire is to consider the means by which the data will be analysed. In most circumstances a computer will be used to perform this task and therefore it is essential at the design stage to ensure the questionnaire is also suitable as a computer input document. It may be the survey is to be conducted within the force, but the data input and analysis are to be performed by some other agency. If this is the case, then liaison must be made at an early stage between the project director and the agency who will undertake the data input and analysis. If this does not occur the agency may refuse to input the data directly from the questionnaire and require the force to transfer thousands of items from questionnaires on to some approved input document.

There are a number of computer programs available for analysing data. One of the more widely used programs should be chosen for this purpose, such as Statistical Package for the Social Sciences. [1] Before choosing the computer program consideration must be given to the size of data base which the program is capable of handling, and the statistical routines which the program can perform to ensure not only are frequency counts and averages produced, but the data is also capable of being examined for underlying trends and predictive relationships.

The Sample

The purpose of a public survey is to establish data which are a true reflection of the whole population's attitudes or opinions. The term 'population' is used to describe the total number of people who comprise the group of people who are under examination. Thus if the police are interested in the attitudes of all the adults living on a particular housing estate comprising 10,000 people, then the survey population is the 10,000 adults. The most accurate means by which that population's opinions and attitudes could be measured would be to interview each person and give them the opportunity of responding to the questionnaire. Even with a population as small as 10,000, it would not be practical to obtain questionnaire responses from every single person. Therefore, the survey has to sample the population. A sample is the number of people taken from the total population, in such a way that the attitudes and opinions of the sample reliably reflect the opinions and attitudes which would have been expressed if all the people within the population had been questioned. Therefore, when considering sampling there are three overriding criteria which must be determined. First, identify the target population, second, establish the means of selection and third, determine the size of the sample which will be required to ensure their opinions and attitudes reliably reflect those of the total population.

To a certain extent the size of the sample is a compromise between the need for reliable and valid data and the practical considerations of time and cost. The extent of sampling error which can be tolerated within the survey can be obtained from standard texts on the subject. [2] As a general rule a sample of more than twelve hundred persons drawn randomly from the population can give a relatively accurate representation of the community's views. However, if specific matters, such as the crime reporting rate is to be measured, it may be necessary to increase the size of the overall sample, particularly if the number of crimes committed in the community is low.

When deciding the size of the sample it should be recognised that the survey will not achieve a hundred per cent response rate. If the Electoral Register is used as a source of names and addresses a certain number of people will have moved away from the district, or will have died, or may have become unavailable for some other reason, such as long term hospitalisation. These factors will reduce the overall number of completed questionnaires. Persons approached to take part in the survey will also decline to take part for a variety of reasons and therefore there will be a refusal or non-response proportion within the sample. Experience suggests in police surveys that beween 8 and 10 per cent of the sample may refuse to take part and a further 15 per cent will be unavailable for interview for the reasons stated. In the case of those who refused to take part in the survey, records should be kept of the reasons why they declined to take part and the demographic data such as age, sex, ethnic origin and so forth should be noted and subjected to subsequent analysis to establish if there were more refusals from one group or section of the population.

There are a number of methods for sampling and these should all be explored in order to find the one which is most appropriate to the survey under consideration. Whichever method is selected, it is essential the process is undertaken in a professional and systematic manner to reduce sample bias which may damage the reliability of the entire survey.

The Collection of Data

When the personal interview method is used, a group of interviewers will be needed to obtain the data. If a force is undertaking the survey using its own resources, then the interviews can be done by women police constables working in plain clothes.

These officers should be from areas of the force that are not going to be the subject of the survey. The number of interviewers depends on the size of the sample and the desired time scale of the survey. It has been found between 7 and 10 questionnaires can be completed per officer per day. Therefore, to complete a survey involving 1,500 subjects within six weeks it is necessary to have 10 interviewers.

The officers who will conduct the survey should be carefully selected for their sense of responsibility, and their ability to approach members of the public and encourage co-operation with the project. When the officers have been chosen they must be given a thorough briefing as to the purpose of the survey and their role within it. They should also be given training in interview techniques. At first sight this may appear to be unnecessary but the style of interviewing which is used in a survey is substantially different to the style of interviewing usually used in day to day police work. In fact it may be necessary to demonstrate to the interviewers their relative lack of skill in this particular type of interviewing and this may be best achieved by requiring them to perform trial interviews in a classroom situation.

The supervision and administration of the fieldwork is an important element in maintaining the overall quality of the survey. Therefore, it is necessary to have a full-time office manager to maintain records, to answer queries from interviewers and code and collate the completed questionnaires. It would also be the responsibility of this person to conduct random re-visits to persons already interviewed to ensure the subject understood the purpose of the survey, to monitor the performance of interviewers and to ensure the survey was being conducted in the required manner. For example, interviewers might misunderstand the instructions in relation to the sample and interview another member of the household when the selected person was not available. If this occurs it will of course contaminate the sampling procedure.

The Analysis of the Data

The precise nature of the analysis to be performed on data will depend entirely upon the purpose of the survey and the nature of the data. A researcher should avoid at all costs the temptation to dredge through data producing masses of statistics in the hope of finding some interesting or significant results. At the data analysis stage the project director should return to the original objectives of the survey and translate those objectives into useful working hypotheses. An objective of a policing method may be a reduction in the fear of crime by increasing the number of uniformed foot patrol officers and thereby increasing public awareness of a police presence. Therefore an appropriate hypothesis to be explored in that case would be as follows:–

"There is a relationship between the citizen's awareness of the uniformed police presence in the neighbourhood and their fear of crime."

When the hypothesis has been established, it is a simple task to identify from the questionnaire those questions relating to police visibility and citizens' fear of crime. The computer can then be used to examine the relationship between the two factors.

Before seizing upon results as demonstrating support for a hypothesis, the significance of the relationship must be considered.

This interpretation involves some knowledge of statistical techniques, and in particular levels of statistical significance. If the researcher does not have this knowledge, then expert advice should be sought.

Other Use Of Public Surveys

The principle techniques of public surveys have been described drawing on the experience gained in the evaluation of an experiment in police deployment methods.[3] The evaluation included two public surveys of 1,500 residents of a sub-division, one before a change in police deployment and another 12 months after the changes had been implemented. Obviously a survey on this scale is a substantial undertaking and would not always be used when changes were made to policing methods. However, some assessments of police effectiveness cannot be made without some measures of public attitudes. Surveys can make a vital contribution to the assessments which must be made of existing police effectiveness in the planning stage of the management cycle and later in the evaluation stage.

The manager has the responsibility to identify his information needs and to decide on the most appropriate means of obtaining the information. If a survey of the public is required, then the research method must be designed to meet the specific information needs. The following headings provide a simple guide to the matters which must be considered in the design process:–

(a) The purpose and objectives of the police activity.

(b) The performance measures.

(c) Sources of data.

(d) Target population.

(e) Sample.

(f) Method.

(g) Analysis.

These seven headings will now be used to illustrate the development of surveys to provide some measures of effectiveness and other information about four police functions. The first two examples will consider the traditional police functions of responding to calls for service from the public and the investigation of less serious crimes. The third example is concerned with one part of the responsibilities of area constables, namely, contact with the community and specifically community groups and organisations. The final example assumes that proposals are being made to implement a schools involvement programme.

Response To Calls For Service

(a) *Purpose of the Activity* – The police respond to calls for service from the public in pursuit of their common law duty to protect life and property, to prevent and detect crime, and in the role identified in the Royal Commission to be a friend to those in need.

(b) *Performance Measures* – The number of calls received and responded to by the force.

The number of calls responded to as a ratio of the officers deployed on uniform patrol.

The average response time to calls for service. The number of arrests made as a result of fast response to calls. Public satisfaction with response time.

Public satisfaction with police action and the result of their call. The quality of police response assessed on the final outcome of the incident, such as the detection of a crime or the resolution of a public order problem.

(c) *Sources of Data* – Response times obtained from incident logs or records.

Analysis of the method of detections to establish the number of arrests as a result of response to calls. Public satisfaction expressed in surveys of persons calling the police for assistance.

Evaluating the long term outcome and resolution of problems referred to the police by the public.

(d) *Target Population* – Records are kept of the persons who call the police for assistance and these names and addresses serve as the source of the target population.

(e) *Sample* – The target population is readily identifiable and a sample could be extracted based on a number of criteria, such as only those people reporting incidents involving crime or those involving order maintenance problems. Sub-samples could also be produced for the time of the day when the call was made or the area of residence. The sampling procedure will depend upon the information needs of the particular survey.

(f) *Method* – It would be inappropriate to expect the responding officer to obtain data concerning public satisfaction and so forth, therefore these data must be obtained in a separately commissioned study. Some form of questionnaire is likely to be the most appropriate means of obtaining these data and this could be distributed either by post or through the use of interviewers calling upon households.

(g) *Analysis* – It is essential the data from the satisfaction survey can be linked directly to the call made by the person to the police.

Investigation of Minor Crime

(a) *Purpose of the Activity* – The traditional police role and duty for the detection of crime.

(b) *Performance Measures – Internal Performance Measures* – The number of crimes detected as a result of follow up investigation. The proportion of minor crimes detected as a result of follow up enquiries.

The methods by which these crimes are detected, such as information from the public or information from other persons arrested. The proportion of detected crime which would have been detected irrespective of follow up enquiries.

The average number of man hours expended per crime investigation. The average number of man hours expended per detected crime. The proportion of follow up enquiries which produced 'NEW' evidence. The relationship between the initial police response, ie tracing witnesses at the scene, and the likelihood of the crime being detected.

External Performance Measures – The public expectation of the police in relation to the likelihood of the crime being detected, the likelihood of stolen property being recovered, psychological support and comfort, the punishment of the criminal and obtaining compensation in court.

(c) *Sources of Data* – Internal performance measures may be obtained from existing records in the force or it may be necessary to obtain new information through specially designed recording methods. The external performance measures can only be obtained by using public attitude surveys, which would be used to measure public expectations of police response, professional competence and the degree of public satisfaction with the service provided by the police.

(d) *Target Population* – The population would be restricted to those people who had reported a crime to the police. If this survey was to be conducted to establish the appropriate police response to the investigation of so called minor or beat crime, then it would be necessary to define such crime and define the sample as people who had reported incidents of crime within those specific categories.

(e) *Sample* – The extent of the sample will be a matter for consideration in the light of the overall purpose of the survey. Once again it could be all the people who have reported a crime within certain categories within a given period, or it could be a random sample drawn from crime complainants throughout the Force.

(f) *Method* – The choice of method will be a matter to be considered in the light of the purpose of the survey and the quality of data required. In most cases it would appear that a structured interview technique employing interviewers would be the most reliable and valid source of information.

(f) *Analysis* – In performing the analysis on the survey data, it will be essential to link the responses to the public survey to factual force data sources such as divisional crime complaints and investigation records.

Area Beat Constables

(a) *Purpose of the Activity* – To maintain contact with community groups and organisations, schools, youth clubs and so forth.

(b) *Performance Measures* – The perceived visibility of the area constable by the public and their knowledge of the officer either by sight or name. The frequency of contact between the public and the area constable, and the public satisfaction with those contacts, the service the officer provides and the fulfilment of their expectation.

(c) *Sources of Data* – Public surveys of perceived visibility and knowledge of area constables, including measures of expectations and satisfaction.

(d) *Target Population* – All known social groups, residents associations, youth clubs, schools, elderly persons' clubs, churches, hostels and all other organisations that would be included as appropriate contacts for area constables.

(e) *Sample* – A stratified random sample taken from the identified target population of known groups that meet the criteria specified
as appropriate to receive regular contacts by their area constable.
The sample would be stratified to ensure a representative sample of all such groups was included. Thus if there were 200 schools and only 50 residents' associations, to achieve a sample of 25 in each category, 50 per cent of residents associations would be included in the sample and only 12.5 per cent of the schools. If a random sample was taken from the entire population, the sample would inevitably be biased in favour of those categories of organisation which had the most numbers.

(f) *Method* – Once again the most appropriate method for obtaining these data would be structured interviews based upon a standard questionnaire.

(g) *Analysis* – There would be a need to count the frequencies of responses within the data and also to establish relationships and patterns of contacts.

A description of a similar study is contained in the report shown in reference. [4]

Schools Programme

(a) *Purpose of the Activity* – The central purpose of police involvement with school children is to improve the image of the police with young people, but these programmes can also have a number of secondary benefits. Exposure to the police in a non-threatening environment may encourage a sense of social responsibility within young people which could lead to a reduction in the amount of crime and social disorder produced by young people. A police-schools involvement programme could also be seen as a method of educating young people in the dangers of such things as drug, alcohol and solvent abuse or in more practical matters such as giving them information concerning road traffic law.

(b) *Performance Measures* – The primary performance measures will be related directly to the primary purpose of a schools involvement programme, namely measurements of the perceptions of the police image by young people. When these measures are taken it would also be useful to attempt to establish
what influenced their image of the police. In response to the secondary purposes of the programme, measures could be taken of their sense of social responsibility, self reports of delinquency, and the probability of them informing the police of suspicious incidents or providing other assistance. The educational aspects of the programme could again be tested through self reports of alcohol, drug and solvent abuse, or in relation to motor vehicle law by direct examination of their knowledge of the subject.

In the three previous examples we have been concerned with existing police practice. In the case of a schools programme it would be imperative to establish the objectives and base data for performance measures during the design stage of a proposed project. Unless such data were obtained, it would be difficult if not impossible to establish the true nature of the problem that existed in relation to young people's image of the police. In the absence of such evidence, there would be a danger of assuming a solution to an unknown problem.

(c) *Sources of Data* – The only feasible source of data would be a survey of the attitudes and opinions of school children.

(d) *Target Population* – The target population would be school children in the age group to be the subject of a schools involvement project. It would also be possible to obtain diagnostic data from a whole range of age groups which could be analysed to establish at which point there were changes in the young people's image of the police.

(e) *Sample* – When the target population has been established, random samples could be taken from the children who were to be exposed to the schools programme. A further sample of children matched on age and educational attainment, but who would not be exposed to the schools programme, could be identified as a control group for comparisons.

(f) *Method* – By taking a control group not only can change over a period of time be established in relation to the group exposed to the schools involvement programme, but influences such as the maturing of the young people could be assessed. A repeated measure method, where the groups are given the same procedures at the beginning and end of the programme would be the most valuable survey method. Depending on the numbers involved, questionnaires and interviews would appear to be an appropriate means of obtaining the data.

(g) *Analysis* – To establish underlying trends and to produce tests of statistical significance on any differences that appear within the measures, it would be essential to use computer based analysis.

References

1 Nie, N. H., Hadlaihull, C., Jenkins, J. G., Steinbrenner, K., Bent, D. H., *Statistical Package for the Social Sciences* , New York: McGraw-Hill Inc. (1975).

2 Hoinville, G., Jowell, R., et al *Survey Research Practice,* London: Heinemann Educational Books Ltd (1977).

3 Butler, A. J. P. and Tharme, K., *Chelmsley Wood Policing Experiment,* West Midlands Police, Birmingham (1983).

4 Tharme, K., *Survey of the Role of Permanent Beat officers in Social/Community Organisations,* West Midlands Police, Birmingham (1982).

6 Organisational Structures and Systems

The second stage of the management cycle is concerned with the organising of resources, which in a manpower intensive organisation such as the police, makes human resources the most important concern. Before a manager can consider changes in the organisation of his human resources he must establish the existing use and effectiveness of those resources. Thus two general issues will be discussed in this chapter, the means of reviewing the present use and effectiveness of human resources and second, methods of reorganising those resources to achieve improvements in effectiveness and productivity. Both these management concerns are part of the planning stage of the cycle, because the organisation of human resources has to be analysed and changes planned. It is only when these plans are implemented to change the organisation structure or procedures that the manager has moved to the organising stage of the cycle.

The learning objectives of this chapter are:-

1   To understand why the planning stage of the management cycle requires an examination of the way in which the organisation of human resources influences police effectiveness and efficiency.

2   To be able to define the purpose of organisational structures.

3   To understand the need to examine the organisational structure within the framework of the methods of supervision and management, the co-ordination of resources, the procedures and systems in use, the clarity of the responsibilities and authority of individuals, and the knowledge and skills of individuals.

4   To be able to analyse an organisational structure, identify its components sub-systems and the relationships between the sub-systems.

5   To recognise the need to relate the organisational structure to the goals of the police force.

6   To understand how police systems and procedures influence the effectiveness and efficiency of the force.

7   To understand the contribution organisation and methods techniques can make to the analysis and improvements of systems and procedures.

8   To understand the need to identify the constituent tasks of police work.

9   To recognise the contributions made by the knowledge, skills and attitudes of police officers to the performance of their tasks.

10 To understand the compiling, use and value of job descriptions for individual postholders and managers.

11 To understand methods which can be used to determine the appropriate level of human resources and their organisation to respond to a given workload.

12 To be able to relate these methods of analysis to a range of policing activities.

A Definition And Purpose Of An Organisational Structure

The purpose of the structure is to organise the members of the force, police and civilians, to optimise their performance in pursuit of the stated strategic policy of the force. It is the means by which the human resources of the force are arranged to the greatest advantage, judged against their ability to achieve the stated goals of the force. Therefore the appropriateness of the organisational structure of a force should be judged on the *results* it produces and no other criteria.

The effectiveness of the organisational structure can only be evaluated by reference to the policy and the goals of the police force. A manager must assess the contribution the human resources under his command are making to the achievement of the goals. The organisation of these resources and the procedures they follow will have a significant effect on the results that are produced. To bring a framework to the analysis of the organisational structure five areas of managerial concern can be identified and used by the manager to examine his own situation:-

1   Supervision and Management – the methods of day to day supervision and control, and the quality of the wider strategic considerations of management planning, organising and evaluating.

2   Co-ordination of resources – the methods of ensuring all officers are aware of, and are pursuing, common objectives.

3   Procedures and System – are compatible with the objectives of the organisation and do not take more time or resources than is absolutely necessary for the effective control of the organisation.

4   Clarity of Responsibilities and Authority – officers are aware of the limits of their powers to make decisions and their authority over others in the organisation.

5   Individual Knowledge and Skills – are matched to the tasks which individuals are called upon to perform.

The five points summarised above are the key elements which underlie the quality of the organisational structure. They must be the focus of the manager's attention as he examines the effectiveness of his organisational structure using the techniques to be described in this chapter.

Sub-divisional Organisation: A Case Study

The sub-division serves as a good example to illustrate the issues which have to be addressed when looking at the influence of the organisational structure on effectiveness and efficiency. The structure of the sub-division which will be used is shown in Figure 6.1. There are three sub-systems; the uniformed patrol officers who provide the 24 hour police function, some investigative tasks, preventive patrol and community contact; the criminal investigation department (CID) who are responsible for the investigation of more serious crimes; and the support and specialist sub-system which is comprised of a plain clothes squad, collator and clerical and administrative support. An organisational diagram is a very useful means of identifying the component parts of an organisation, the relationship between the parts and the numbers of staff who are available to the manager.

Figure 6.1 Sub-Divisional organisation diagram

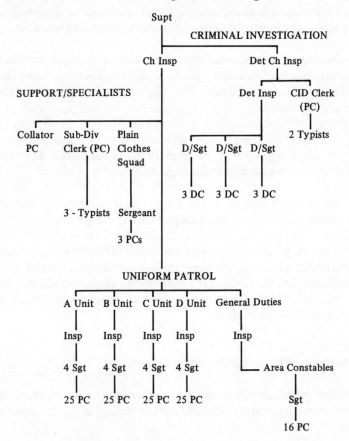

The purpose of the organisational structure is to make optimum use of available resources. Therefore in the planning stage of the management cycle the organisational structure has to be examined in the context of existing effectiveness and efficiency, and the need for changes to improve one or both of these performance criteria. Once again the analysis must start with a definition of the policy of the force which will be translated into specific duties and responsibilities for the sub-division. The next stage of the analysis is to establish the workload which is represented by these duties and responsibilities. Methods for measuring workload were described in Chapter 4. In this context it is also important to examine the managerial workload which is carried by the officers with supervisory responsibilities. As an example, the work of the patrol sergeants could be examined. They are nominally responsible for supervising the work of constables on the streets, however, the instructions of the force require the station officer and the sub-divisional radio controller to be a sergeant. Therefore when the station officer or the radio controller are absent or need relief for their refreshments, the patrol sergeant is taken from his primary duties to provide cover for these tasks. The growth in paperwork and administrative procedures has also created a supervisory workload which has reduced the time the patrol sergeant has available for outside patrol and supervision.

When the range of tasks and the workload have been established for the sub-division, attention must be turned to the way in which the work is organised. In this examination the sub-divisional superintendent will be concerned with the methods of supervision and management; the means by which resources are co-ordinated; the procedures which are used; the clarity of the definition of the responsibilities and authority of individual officers and the skills and knowledge that they require to be effective in their roles. These points will be examined using the sub-division shown in Figure 6.1 to illustrate the matters which the manager must consider in his review.

1 Supervision and Management

An immediate problem for the supervision and management of the area constables is the lack of compatability between the hours they work and those worked by the sergeant and the inspector. There will be times when area constables will be on duty and they will have no immediate supervision from their own supervisors because the sergeant and inspector will either be on a leave day or will have completed their tour of duty and gone home. The area constables will receive supervision from the unit sergeants who are on duty but this is less satisfactory than their own officers.

The ratio of supervisors to constables varies between the CID and uniformed officers. The ratio of sergeants to detective constables is one to three, compared to one sergeant to six constables on the units and one sergeant to sixteen area constables. Sergeants have responsibilities in addition to supervision, however, the apparent imbalance might be a matter worth exploring as a means of improving the quality of supervision for the less experienced uniformed constables on the units.

2 Co-ordination of Resources

A major problem for all managers is the task of co-ordinating the efforts of all his resources towards common objectives. For the police manager problems of co-ordination can be caused through shift patterns which reduce the opportunities for officers to meet and discuss policing problems, and to devise common approaches to deal with these problems. This point has been made concerning the supervision of the area constables. In an ideal world all the unit inspectors would have common objectives which would guide the deployment of their officers; the information gathering activities and crime intelligence role of the area constables would be co-ordinated with the investigative needs of the detectives; the policing problems brought to the attention of area constables by the residents of their beats would be used to direct the deployment priorities of unit constables.

The use of civilian staff should also be considered in this review. There are two separate typing services provided on the sub-division, one for the CID and the other for the remaining officers. The nature of police work causes variations in the demands that are made upon typing services and therefore there will be times when the CID typists will have less work than the other typists and at other times the reverse will be true. These peaks and troughs in work can cause inefficient use of resources, therefore combining the two groups of typists in a common service to the sub-division would enhance the efficiency of the service they provide.

3 Procedures and Systems

The administrative procedures used on the sub-division will not be immediately apparent from the examination of the structure, however it is probably a useful place to start to look for the ways in which the various parts communicate with each other and are co-ordinated through the administration processes. Procedures and systems can have a significant impact on the effectiveness and efficiency of the sub-division and therefore should not be overlooked in the analysis of the organisation.

4 Clarity of Responsibilities and Authority

Although people are organised in a structure such as the one shown in Figure 6.1, it cannot be assumed that they have a clear understanding of exactly what is expected of them and the authority they have over other people or to make decisions. These are all matters which would be included in job descriptions, which may be available for some officers and civilians. Where job descriptions exist they should be reviewed to ensure that they are still relevant to the tasks being performed by the postholder. Where job descriptions do not exist serious consideration should be given to developing them. Individuals must know how their tasks fit into the total efforts of the organisation. They must have a point of reference for them to identify their responsibilities and the limits of their accountabilities. All work involves decision making, therefore individuals must know the limits of their authority to make decisions and those matters which must be referred to a higher authority. Where confusion exists over responsibilities the usual consequence is the passing of problems and decisions further up the hierarchy until someone is prepared to make the decision.

5 Individual Knowledge and Skills

Another assumption which a manager cannot make concerns the competency of his staff. A manager has the responsibility to ensure the knowledge and skills of his human resources are appropriate for the tasks they are expected to fulfil. Consider the role of the collator, there are different levels of knowledge and skill for this work depending upon his job description. If the role is seen as recording and indexing reported crime and information from operational officers, then the work is less demanding than a role which requires an integrated crime analysis service where information is extracted and interpreted to indicate crime trends, patrol deployment strategies and avenues for investigation. When the role has been defined, it is the manager's responsibility to ensure the postholder has the necessary skills and knowledge.

This consideration is true for all posts, furthermore a manager should also try to predict the future human resource needs of his sub-division and train people before they are given the responsibilities. Of course this may involve the force training department or other specialist who would be given notice of the training requirements to enable them to plan ahead. This process can provide the impetus for career development programmes in the force.

Implications To Be Drawn From The Case Study

The brief examination of the sub-division set out in the previous section has identified some important management issues which the superintendent must address in his review of the existing effectiveness and efficiency of his command. To conduct this review he must have a strategy and understand how the various issues relate to each other. The starting point has to be the consideration of the way in which work is done, namely the procedures and systems. It would be shortsighted to organise and assign people to tasks without establishing if there are more efficient methods which, if adopted, would use less people. Therefore the superintendent should ask why tasks are being done and procedures followed. If they are essential then other ways of achieving the same results should be explored. There is a limit to what he can achieve on his own, therefore he should consider calling on the services of organisation and methods officers from the management services department or its equivalent at force headquarters.

When the superintendent is satisfied that he cannot make any further improvements to the way work is organised, then he has to turn his attention to the specific tasks of the individual officers and civilians under his command. It is essential to have a clear understanding of what people do and how this affects the work of other people. This task analysis will also enable the skills and knowledge of each task to be identified. It is also essential to establish the measures which can be used to evaluate the effectiveness of the individual's performance in the post. Another important part of this analysis is to establish the relationships between tasks. To examine a person's work in isolation to the organisational context in which it is located will miss some essential parts of the analysis. It is this latter part of the analysis which will define the responsibilities of the post and the authority the postholder exercises over other people and his authority to make decisions.

The information provided by organisation and methods, and task analysis are essential to the next stage of the process which is the building of the organisation structure or the modification of an existing structure. The process of building will be described in the section relating to establishment review techniques, which is also known as staff inspection. The establishment review process takes the procedures and the tasks identified for individual postholders, and builds a structure which will provide appropriate supervision and management, and enable the efforts of all parts of the organisation to be co-ordinated towards achieving common objectives.

Organisation And Methods

The planning stage of the management cycle demands that a manager should establish the current state of his organisation. Therefore, before any changes should be proposed to the ways in which work is to be done it is essential to examine existing procedures. The discipline of organisation and methods can be used in this examination. Systems analysis is one of the primary skills which can be used.

To illustrate a simple system, the procedures followed by the submission of an offence report can be analysed. In Figure 6.2 an offence report is submitted by a constable and reviewed by the sergeant who decides if it should be returned to the constable for additional information or submitted to the chief inspector. When it is received by the chief inspector he must decide if he has sufficient information to make the decision to prosecute or return the report to the constable for amendments. In cases where the chief inspector returns the report to the constable there is the possibility of two procedures being followed when the report is resubmitted. The report could once again be seen by the sergeant before being sent to the chief inspector, or it could be sent direct to the chief inspector. The latter procedure, which is represented by the dotted line in Figure 6.2, will save time and therefore will improve efficiency.

Figure 6.2 A schematic representation of the administrative procedures associated with an Offence Report

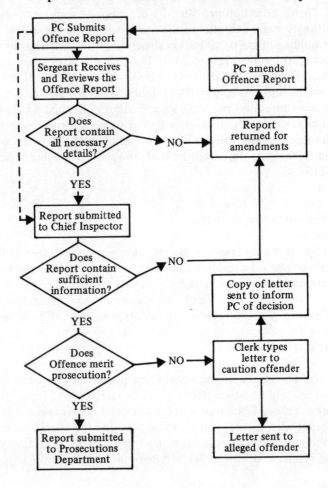

By analysing the procedure in this way it is easy to see who is or is not involved in the process. The unit inspector does not have a role in the present procedure. The decision to prosecute has been delegated from the sub-divisional superintendent to the chief inspector. The caution letter for the alleged offender is prepared by the sub-divisional clerk.

The analysis will also identify the documents which are used in the process. There are obvious ways in which changes to forms or form design can radically affect the efficiency of a procedure. Furthermore, unnecessary procedures and forms can be identified and eliminated.

Work measurement is another technique which can contribute to the management analysis. This is a matter which was raised in Chapter 4, when efficiency measures were discussed. The uniformed sergeant has had a traditional role as the first line supervisor for the review of the paperwork submitted by constables. Some sergeants may feel this task has now reached a point where it occupies too much of their time. Figure 6.2 gives an example of just one source of paperwork but there are many others. The time consumed by reading each item, making written comments, and entering a reference in the officer's work record could be measured to calculate the average time spent by a sergeant on the review of an offence report. This standard time could be used to calculate the total time consumed by this activity based on the number of items examined. The number of submissions of reports and repeated submissions could be counted. An increase in efficiency might be achieved by improving the training of constables to reduce the number of reports that are returned for correction and then resubmitted for review.

Work measurement can establish:-

(i)   The time each part of the process takes to complete.

(ii) The total time for the entire process.

(iii) A count of how often the process is performed in any given period.

(iv) The total time needed to complete a specific workload.

Systems analysis can be an important aid to a manager in his understanding of the interrelationship between the component parts of a procedure or policing method, for example the classification of calls for service into those requiring an immediate response and those where a delayed response could be used. Some police officers would argue that an immediate police response to all calls for service from the public is unnecessary. This view has given rise to the introduction of the use of graded response to calls. The concept appears to have some benefits provided it is introduced for the right reasons, however there are some important aspects of the system of the receipt of calls and the despatching of police officers which must be reviewed before the procedure can be introduced. Two factors become critically important when this procedure is adopted. First, the radio controller has to make a decision on which calls can be safely delayed and those which must have an immediate despatch of a police officer. Of course the controller has policy criteria for guidance, however the usefulness of the criteria depends on the second key factor, which is his access to information. The quality of the decision the controller makes is directly related to the amount and quality of information he has from the caller describing the incident. In cases where this information is poor, the controller takes a greater risk of being wrong in his decision as to the most appropriate mode of police response.

Therefore before making changes to the policy for police response to calls, a systems analysis will provide a detailed picture of the methods of information transmission and the decision making process involved. The system illustrated in Figure 6.3 compares the process when the citizen making the request for police action speaks directly to the radio controller who makes the decision to despatch the police officer and the situation where the information comes to the controller through a third party. In Mode A shown on the left, the radio controller can interrogate the caller until he has received sufficient information on which to make the decision as to the most appropriate police response. In Mode B shown on the right, the message is received by the constable in the enquiry office and passed on a form to the controller. In these circumstances the controller is entirely dependent on the information he receives. If the information is incomplete then the controller has a choice to give the call an immediate priority or to delay the response.

Figure 6.3 Two methods of receiving a call for assistance from the public

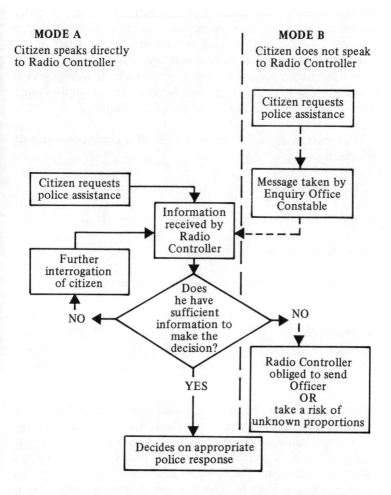

The latter choice involves taking a risk of unknown proportions. In police forces with a central control room which receives calls and passes the information to a sub-divisional controller to despatch police officers, a third mode is introduced. It is dangerous to introduce a graded response system without understanding the relationship between access to information and the quality of decision making, which are both related to the methods of information receipt and transmission. The systems analysis illustrated by this example provides the opportunity to plan the introduction of graded response to calls and also identifies those issues which must be resolved before implementation.

To summarise: an O and M analysis of a system provides an opportunity:-

(i)   To identify the component parts of a system.

(ii) To identify the relationship between parts of a system.

(iii) To identify the people involved.

(iv) To identify the documents and equipment used.

(v)   To measure work as individual items or as composite workloads.

Task Analysis

The organisation and methods analysis establishes the systems and procedures associated with the work. The role of task analysis is to examine these component parts and identify the knowledge, skills and attitudes which must be possessed by the person who undertakes the work. The value of task analysis increases as the complexity of the work increases. A useful way of understanding the role of task analysis is to imagine the process of instructing a completely naive person to perform a task. The starting point of the teaching process would be to provide all the necessary knowledge to the person. In the case of a constable who was being instructed in the enforcement of road traffic law he would have to have a detailed knowledge of legislation; he would require information concerning the procedures and forms to be used in the process of reporting a motorist; and he would require a knowledge of the rules of evidence. Knowledge alone would not be adequate to ensure effective performance, the constable would have to have the skills to identify violations of the law. There would be skills of interrogation, skills in the use of speed detection devices and the examination of the technical aspects of brakes and steering. Finally, to ensure the professional discharge of this work the constable would need to have the appropriate attitude to the task. His attitude would be shown in the exercise of his discretion to either report the offender or give a verbal caution, and in his approach and treatment of the offender.

The relative importance of each of the three elements of the task will vary according to the work and these variations will be reflected in the training which officers receive before they are employed on the work. Task analysis is a very important part of the design stage of training courses. Without a statement of the knowledge, skills and attitudes which are necessary for each task, a training course cannot be properly designed or evaluated.

When a manager has to review the effectiveness of his sub-division task analysis can be used to build job profiles for the officers and civilians under his command.

These profiles can be used to compare jobs and establish the knowledge, skills and attitudes which are required by each postholder. The sub-division which was described in the case study has a constable employed as a collator and another constable providing clerical and administrative support to the CID. For illustration, imagine that both posts were subjected to a task analysis. The job profiles which were produced showed some duplication of work, both officers maintained indices which held identical information on the type and location of crimes, and complainants and offenders indices. The analysis also showed that the officers spent more than half of each working day typing index cards. Furthermore, it was clear the work of both posts did not require any police powers or skills unique to a police officer.

This analysis described the present situation, before recommending any changes a manager has to consider if it is necessary to improve the effectiveness of the service provided by these posts. One of the reasons for the indexing of crime information is to provide information which may guide the deployment of uniformed officers and to aid the investigation and detection of crime. Therefore the task analysis of these two posts has to be reviewed in the context of performance measures which have been set for crime analysis objectives. Where the existing service falls short of the desired performance, the additional knowledge, skills and attitudes which are required to improve the effectiveness should be identified and included in the job specification which will be compiled for the posts.

Task analysis involves job evaluation which brings a number of benefits to the manager. It provides him with performance measures for tasks and subsequently a means of evaluating the individuals who perform those tasks. Thus task analysis is closely linked to the development and use of staff appraisal systems. Without objective performance criteria staff appraisal systems will be less than perfect.

Establishment Review

The primary role of systems analysis and task analysis is to establish the component parts of work. Establishment review in this context also involves some analysis but its primary use is to build appropriate organisational structures which maximises the effectiveness of the human resources used by the most efficient available means.

Establishment review procedures are the means by which the organisation controls the cost of its human resources. The establishment of a section of the force or the entire force should define the minimum numbers of police officers and civilians by appropriate rank or grade, which are required to complete the work necessary to achieve the goals of the force.

The establishment review procedure starts with a statement of the goals of the force or objectives of the sub-division under review. Using the information which has been provided from the syster and task analysis, the need for changes in working practices should be addressed. There is no point setting an establishment figure for a given workload, if the workload could be halved by the introduction of some new procedure. The manager should also consider any anticipated increase in workload which may be caused by changes in legislation or the introduction of new working methods.

The first level of analysis for the establishment review is to determine those tasks which must be performed by a police officer and those which can be performed by a civilian employee. On the sub-division described in the case study, clerical, administrative and typing work was done by civilians and police officers. It should not be assumed that after a review, police officers would cease to be involved in administrative or typing work. If a work measurement exercise reveals a constable on a unit spends an average of less than 15 minutes per shift typing reports, then this might not justify the employment of a typist on shifts to perform this work. However, if the clerical and administrative work of the unit sergeants were also included in the calculation, then a combined post of clerk/typist might be justified on each of the four units, to relieve police officers of this inappropriate work. However, where a police officer was engaged solely in typing and administrative work this work should be transferred to a civilian.

The next level of analysis will make the distinction between the actual tasks performed in pursuit of an objective and the management tasks of planning, co-ordinating, controlling and monitoring. Both aspects of work have to be considered to determine the qualifications, experience and authority required for each task. These considerations will determine the ranks required to perform the work. On the example sub-division, an analysis of the work of detective constables and detective sergeants might show there was no distinction between the complexity or seriousness of the crimes they were allocated to investigate. The supervisory activities of sergeants might account for less than 10 per cent of their work. If the level of supervision detective constables were receiving was judged to be adequate, consideration should be given for a reduction in the number of detective sergeants and replacing those officers with detective constables, reducing the amount of investigation work done by the remaining sergeants and increasing the time they spend on supervision and management.

The review will determine those jobs which can be performed by police officers and those which can be performed by civilians. The content of the work will be defined as the actual job to be done and the management tasks which enable responsibility and authority levels to be assigned. At this stage, using the total workload measures, the appropriate numbers of staff can be calculated. The establishment review officer takes these posts as building bricks and constructs the organisational structure by grouping people performing similar tasks to form sections. Each section will have an appropriate level of supervision and management. The sections will then be built into a departmental structure which will be rationally linked to the force structure. By this process the provision of clerical, administrative and typing services which was fragmented across the sub-division as shown in Figure 6.1 could be rationalised to give the structure shown in Figure 6.4.

Figure 6.4 Sub-Divisional organisational diagram

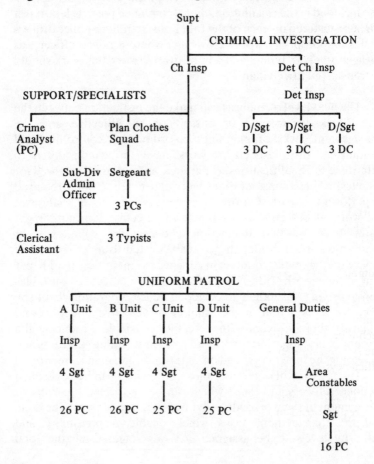

The organisational review of the administrative support of the sub-division removed unnecessary work, set human resources to workload demands by making them more capable of dealing with peaks and troughs in typing work and allowed three police officer posts to be returned to operational policing by replacing those officers with two less costly civilian employees.

One of the most important results of an establishment review exercise for the manager is the preparation of job descriptions, which are a basic requirement of proper human resource management. A typical job description will contain the following items:–

(i)   The location of the post, the title and the rank or grade.

(ii) A statement and description of the job purpose.

(iii) A list of main duties and responsibilities.

(iv) A statement of the qualifications and experience that are required on entry to the post.

(v)   The supervisory responsibility of the post.

(vi) The supervision to be received by the postholder and by whom the supervision will be given.

(vii) The contacts the postholder may have with persons inside the force or outside.

Summary Of Case Study

A number of issues from the sub-division described in the case study have been used to illustrate the application of these techniques of analysis. Some modifications to the organisation of the sub-division have been suggested to improve effectiveness and efficiency. These can be summarised as follows:-

(i)   The administration and typing service has been rationalised, restructured and the productivity improved. During the exercise two police officers have been returned to operational policing.

(ii) The review of the collator identified the need for a more sophisticated approach to crime analysis. The changes gave all the clerical work to a civilian, allowing a police officer to concentrate on providing a crime analysis service to both uniform and detective officers on the sub-division.

(iii) The problems of access to information for the controller's decision making were identified in a review of a system of message handling and the despatching of response units.

(iv) The system for the submission of offence reports was analysed and changes proposed to reduce the workload of the sergeant in respect of examining re-submitted reports.

(v) The supervisory role of the detective sergeants was enhanced by reducing their commitment to routine investigation and increasing the time they had available for supervision and management, further questions could be asked about the need for three detective sergeants.

Investigation Of Crime

There will be occasions when a manager will need to consider the effectiveness of a major aspect of his responsibilities to review the means by which the efforts of his officers are co-ordinated, the quality of the management processes involved, and the skills and the knowledge of his personnel. The investigation of crime is one such major police responsibility and therefore will serve as a good illustration of the organisational and management aspects which should be included in a management review. The purpose of a review is to establish the existing situation and relate this to the improvements which are desired.

For the purpose of this exercise we can use the sub-division which has been illustrated in Figure 6.4. The first step for the manager is to identify what is already known about the issue under review, namely the investigation and detection of crime:-

1   Uniformed constables are almost always the first and only

officers to visit the scene of most crimes at the time when they are reported.

2   Further investigations of crime are done by all operational officers on the sub-division.

3   The decision to allocate crimes to an officer for investigation is done on the basis of the type of crime and the value of the property stolen or damaged.

4   Force policy dictates that all crimes with the exception of very serious offences receive the same level of investigation irrespective of the clues established at the scene.

5   The quality of the information obtained by the officer responding to the scene of the crime is the most significant factor influencing the detection of the crime.

6   The number of crimes detected through further enquiries is a relatively small proportion of the total investigated.

7   A survey of public opinion has established that the public do not expect the police to pursue fruitless investigations provided they, the victims, are informed of the police procedures and are kept informed of developments when they occur. (The survey is a hypothetical example, but the conclusions which have been drawn for this exercise are a reasonable reflection of the findings of actual research).

The second step for the manager is to establish those matters which he will accept and not subject to further consideration. In our case the superintendent believes that force and public policy dictates that certain categories of crime will always be investigated irrespective of the objective likelihood of them being detected. Therefore such crimes as rape, serious woundings, armed robberies and offences against children would be outside the scope of this review. The process of identifying matters outside the scope of the review reduces the work involved and thus makes the process more efficient.

The third step is to identify the key variables in the investigation process. Without doubt the most important determinant of the success of an investigation is the quality of the information gained by the officer who responds to the call from the victim or witness. If information is available for investigation then it follows that the next important variable is the amount of time available to the officers who conduct the enquiries. Therefore, improvements in the effectiveness of crime investigation should be achieved by improving the quality of information which is obtained by the officer responding to the call and by increasing the time available to officers who conduct investigations. The review must now proceed to identify the means of improving the initial response and make more time available for officers conducting investigations.

At this stage it is only necessary to make broad suggestions to obtain the larger picture to identify those matters which will require an indepth assessment. Additional training for officers attending the scene, giving the responsibility for response to crime calls to detectives, or changing the format of the crime report form to provide more detail are some of the suggestions which might be made. The second key factor to provide more time to officers engaged on enquiries cannot be achieved by additional establishment, therefore the aim must be to use existing officers more productively. The opportunities to use officers more productively are suggested by the public's expectations which apparently do not require an investigation of all crimes, and the small number of detections achieved by investigations. These two factors challenge the wisdom of the force policy to investigate all crimes with the same vigour. A system of screening crimes to identify those worthy of investigation would appear to be a means of achieving an increase in productivity. At present crimes are categorised for the purpose of allocating an investigator on the basis of the type of crime and the value of the property involved. These classifications are not appropriate for determining those which could be usefully investigated and those which should be filed. A more sensible basis for making those decisions would be the amount and quality of evidence obtained by the officer responding to the scene. In cases where there were no witnesses, no physical evidence at the scene, no identifiable property stolen, and the method of committing the crime was not unusual and did not fit a distinctive pattern, then there would seem to be little point pursuing further investigations. Where crime case screening has been adopted these factors have been called solvability factors. [1]

The decision to file the crime or allocate it for further investigation should be done on the apparent likelihood of the investigation leading to the detection of the crime. This judgement is based on the information which was obtained by the officer responding to the scene of the crime and his initial enquiries. The choice of which officer to conduct the investigation should also be based on the knowledge and skills needed in the investigation. A relatively complex enquiry covering a series of burglaries which were probably committed by a travelling criminal, would suggest the need for the skills and time of a detective. However, burglaries in a confined neighbourhood which appeared to be the work of juveniles, are more likely to be detected through the local knowledge and contacts of the area constable. Therefore, there appears to be a case for revising the criteria on which crime reports are allocated for investigation. Local knowledge and access to information from the community are as equally important as the more advanced training of detectives, when considering the officers most qualified to conduct investigations.

The review of the investigation of crime has identified the key factors which must be addressed to make improvements. The central issue is the quality of the information obtained by the officer responding to the scene because it will enable the officer who has the responsibility for managing criminal investigations to decide whether the crime should be given a further investigation and second, which group of officers are best qualified to conduct the investigation. Attention must now be turned to the form which is used as the crime report to establish its suitability to provide the level of detail that will be required in the future.

Using the existing forms it is impossible to distinguish crime reports on the basis of those where a significant investigation has been done by the responding officer although it produced no tangible evidence, and other crime reports where the officer had not conducted any preliminary investigation. It would be possible of course to issue an instruction to officers who respond to crime incidents to itemise all the investigations they conducted at the scene, irrespective of the results achieved. A more profitable proposal might be to change the format of the crime report to indicate the existence of evidence based upon the solvability factors and to ensure the responding officer reported the investigative action and the results achieved. An example of a modified format is shown in Figure 6.5. The boxes on the right-hand side would contain a cross if that solvability factor was not present.

Case screening will reduce the number of crimes to be investigated and therefore reduce the amount of time spent on this activity. It is true that the cases which are allocated for investigation may take more time, but if something of the order of 80 per cent of crimes are not given a follow-up investigation, then there will be additional time released to be used for other activities. The uniformed patrol constable will have more time available for directed patrol activities. Detectives, however, may find they have more time than is required to pursue investigations. If this is the case, the number of detectives could be reduced. Alternatively, their role could be expanded to include a responsibility to respond to the scene of crimes when they are reported. This could be a very effective use of their time by improving further the quality of the information obtained at the scene.

The review of the crime investigation process has involved a consideration of the five issues raised during the case study of the sub-division. The supervision and management issues have been examined leading to a more objective system of making decisions, first concerning the crimes which should be investigated and second, the officers who should conduct those investigations. The investigating officer will be chosen on the basis of the knowledge and skills required in individual cases rather than the previous blanket criteria of the type of crime and the value of the property involved. The procedures and forms have been designed in response to the needs of the organisation rather than methods being made to fit existing practice. Finally, the new system will provide a greater co-ordination of resources with all officers having a greater awareness of their responsibilities and their contributions to the investigation and detection of crime.

References

1 Eck, J. E., *Managing Case Assignments: The Burglary Investigation Decision Model Replication*, Washington D.C.: Police Executive Research Forum (1979).

Figure 6.5 Investigation Report

Was there a witness to the crime? ☐ If No place an X in the Box

Name of Witness	Address	Age	I'viewed YES/NO	Result*

* S = Statement obtained   N = Interviewed but no relevant information
NI = Not interviewed   Obtained

2. Can Suspect be named? ☐   Located? ☐   Described? ☐
Identified? ☐
Tick appropriate box

Enter details in Section 8, page 1   If No place an X in Box ☐

3. Can Suspect vehicle be identified?   If No place an X in Box ☐

Regn No.	Make	Type/Model	Colour	Identifying Characteristics

4. Is stolen property identifiable?   If No place an X in Box ☐
If Yes — enter details in Section 10, page 1

5. Was there any significant physical
evidence found at the scene?   If No place an X in Box ☐
If Yes — describe in the narrative

6. Was it likely that this crime was
committed by a person with a
limited opportunity? eg, an employee   If No place an X in Box ☐
If Yes — give details in the narrative

7. In your opinion is there sufficient
evidence either available, or likely
to become available to make further
investigation worthwhile?   YES ☐   NO ☐
                                      Tick as appropriate

105

7 The Individual and the Management of the Force

In this chapter the concern is for the people who perform the work. Ultimately the effectiveness and efficiency of an organisation depends on the commitment the workers have to the achievement of the goals of the organisation. Motivating staff and encouraging compliance with the policy and procedures of the organisation are fundamental management skills. The Hawthorne Experiments in the late 1920s, demonstrated the apparent irrationality of men and women at work. It was found to be impossible to predict the productivity of workers by the apparently rational management of the number of employees, reward systems and changes in the physical working environment. Observations of everyday life provide examples of the apparently perverse nature of the human condition. A manager has to recognise the possibility of a non-rational response to his managerial plans and furthermore transform this apparent difficulty into a strength and benefit. In some circumstances it is possible for a committed work force to continue to be effective despite inept management. If a manager is aware of the strengths and weaknesses of those under his control, he will be able to delegate those matters which can be most competently performed lower in the organisation and closer to the actual work problem.

The problem of ensuring compliance with management policy is a common feature of all work situations, however for the police there are special difficulties. The police force as an organisation is able to make and enforce all kinds of administrative and bureaucratic rules, however it is far more difficult to control the actual delivery of the police service to the community. The constitutional independence of the office of constable severely restricts the force's ability for making rules which limit the exercise of a police officer's discretion in law enforcement activities. In addition to the theoretical legal limitations, the nature of policing on the streets makes close supervision of police work very difficult.

In many circumstances supervisors have to rely entirely upon the reports of their officers for their information about incidents. In many cases police officers are the sole source of such information and even where two officers are present, a consensus description may emerge as to what has occurred. Peer and group solidarity are powerful features of the police occupational culture. The invisibility of police work to supervisors makes it particularly difficult to monitor and control. Unfortunately a common response by police managers is to introduce more administrative and bureaucratic rules. When this strategy apparently fails a typical response is to produce yet more rules and procedures, and it is this circle which tends to increase the alienation of operational police officers from their supervisors.

The learning objectives of this chapter are:-

1   To recognise the human dimensions of work and management.

2   To understand the practical limitations of managerial control in police work.

3   To be aware of the possibilities of conflict existing between constables and officers with management responsibilities, and to appreciate the consequences of this conflict.

4   To recognise the need to have a management system which is appropriate to the needs of police work.

5   To recognise the need to have a management system which involves both 'top-down' and 'bottom-up' communications.

6   To understand the management issues associated with the perceived low status of the uniformed constable.

7   To understand the meaning and implications of the climate of the organisation.

8   Within the context of the climate of the organisation, to understand the influence of communications, decision making, the allocation of work, the integration of individuals and

orders and regulations as being less relevant to the *real* world. Two groups, the control/rewards system, and conflict and competition.

9   To be able to review an organisation and establish its climate and the implications for its existing effectiveness.

Police Officers' Attitudes To Work And Supervision

Applicants to the force have attitudes and opinions which comprise their mental image of the police and police work. Police selection procedures stress the need for personal integrity, self reliance and self discipline on the premise that an integral part of police work is the need to think and act decisively, using individual initiative. Selection procedures endeavour to recruit officers with these qualities and training procedures seek to reinforce their importance. A questionnaire survey of police recruits suggested these procedures were relatively successful in selecting candidates with opinions which reflected these principles of police work. The questionnaire contained a number of statements concerning police work and the recruits were asked to respond on a four point scale, indicating their agreement or disagreement with these statements. Between sixty six and ninety per cent of the recruits agreed with the following statements:-

"The tradition of the police service is based on individual action and responsibility."

"In the final analysis, a police officer is personally responsible for his actions."

"The more freedom of action that an officer has, the better he will be able to perform his work."

"Police work experienced in practice is vastly different from the work that is described in the various orders and regulations."

"Your past experiences are the best guides to your actions in most circumstances."

The two latter statements suggested recruits anticipated placing reliance on past experience to guide their actions and saw other statements were related to rewards within the force and their perceptions of senior officers. Nine out of ten recruits believed that 'individual initiative was rewarded in the police' and 'senior officers were in touch with the needs of police officers on the ground'.

The same questionnaire was given to a group of police constables who had been in the force for five or more years. Their opinions in respect of individual action and responsibility, the need for the freedom of action in order to be an effective police officer and experience being a critical guide to decision making, were identical to those expressed by the recruits. However, less than 20 per cent believed individual initiative was rewarded in the police and only 14 per cent believed senior officers were in touch with the needs of police officers on the ground. The differences in the responses to these questions by the more experienced constables compared with those of the recruits were quite remarkable, given the similarity of the responses to the other statements. The image these constables had of their own responsibilities and the requirements to be an effective police officer appeared to conflict with their perceptions of the rewards system of the force and their belief that senior officers did not understand operational police work.[1]

In another questionnaire survey, data were obtained from police constables as part of an evaluation study of changes in policing methods on the sub-division. Before the change in policing methods there was a group of ten constables who were known as permanent beat officers. Each officer had specific responsibility for a beat and was expected to be the link between the police and the community. To pursue this role they were given a considerable degree of freedom concerning the hours they worked and the specific activities they performed. During the experimental period these officers became part of a group of constables who were responsible for a much larger area. They tended to lose an identity with their small section of the community. They were given responsiblity for responding to calls from the public and were expected to investigate more than two thirds of all the crimes reported on the sub-division. In short, they changed from individuals who could plan and manage their police activities based on their knowledge and needs of the community, to become part of a group controlled by matters outside their influence. A comparison of the responses of the permanent beat officers to the questionnaire before and one year after the implementation of the system, showed dramatic declines in their satisfaction with their freedom to choose their working methods, the amount of responsibility they were given, their opportunities to use their abilities, working relations between senior officers and constables, and the way in which the force was managed. These results clearly demonstrated that the experiment achieved a reduction in job satisfaction for the officers who took part. They also illustrated that management can change the level of job satisfaction experienced by constables through changes in the work environment.[2]

The Management System And The Constable

The root of the alienation experienced by constables appears to be the result of operational officers, constables and probably some first line supervisors, believing they have different objectives to their senior officers. The constables' orientation is towards the street police philosophy of action, relatively unimpeded discretion, with experience of the past as a guide for decision making. This is seen to conflict with the apparent objectives of senior officers for administrative orderliness and adherence to rules and procedures as ends in themselves. It is a conflict between the inherent risk taking of street policing with the ultra caution of the bureaucrat.[3] This alienation between the street police culture and senior officers appears to occur relatively soon after a recruit joins the force.

Police organisations have had a tradition of centralised control with decision making the prerogative of the highest level. The development in recent years of larger police forces has had the effect of moving the authority for decision making further away from constables who perform the operational tasks. In many large police forces, operational officers have no apparent influence on the policy making process and may rarely see the person who makes the decisions. It is interesting to note the comments made by a Royal Commission fifty years ago. At the time of their report, police forces were considerably smaller than they are today, however the Commission was concerned that as police forces increased in size, the instructions issued to subordinate officers became more elaborate. This tendency to increase the issuing of rules arose in "some cases from insufficient personal contact between subordinate ranks and their responsible chiefs and from the natural desire of the latter to shield themselves from blame for any mistakes on the part of their subordinates by the issue of instructions setting out the proper course to be followed in every foreseeable emergency". (Royal Commission on Police Powers and Procedure, 1929, paragraph 4). It is impossible for remote, centralised decision making to reflect accurately the needs of operational personnel, therefore field personnel tend to question the validity and competence of the centralised structure in achieving the goals of the police force. [4]

For a service organisation such as a police force, the organisational philosophy is of crucial importance in shaping the behaviour of its members. A management text by Heaton examined two organisational models:- [5]

(i) *Established Models,* are hierarchical and authoritarian; communication goes from the highest level downwards, with the behaviour of individuals being ordered and coerced in ways determined by the higher authority. This organisational philosophy suits the individual who prefers directions and control, and who avoids responsibility, McGregor's Theory X individual. [6]

(ii) *Target Models,* have communications from the top to the lowest level, and include mechanisms for feedback from below back to the top of the structure. The management patterns are more complex in this model, requiring the organisation to be sensitive to the ideas of its members. This model has the capacity to enable organisations to learn and adapt. Achievement tends to be seen in organisational terms rather than in terms of individuals. Individuals suited to this type of organisational structure can be designated as Theory Y individuals, who accept responsibility, are self directed, capable of learning and direct their energies towards self accomplishment.

Heaton contrasted the two models thus: "In the established pattern, organisation is imposed from the top down and is managed or administered". In the Target Model, "organisation evolves in a circle and the function of leadership is to catalyse, not to impose". Despite some enlightened man-management, the police force remains a predominantly hierarchical, authoritative, bureaucratic organisation which, as Heaton suggests, is a more suitable work environment for Theory X individuals. Paradoxically, the evidence from the social-psychological research which has examined constables shows quite clearly they are predominantly Theory Y individuals, who are self assertive and have high levels of self esteem and seek self actualisation. [7] Furthermore, constables develop "Theory Y" attributes as a necessary response to their work environment. Therefore police officers can be in a continuous state of psychological confusion, attempting to compromise the demands of the organisation on the one hand, with behaviour demanded by the very nature of the tasks they are called on to perform on the other hand. The process of compromise leads to the disillusionment with supervisory officers, and to strategies to neutralise the punitive aspects of the organisation's control, as illustrated by Cain [8] in her description of "easing behaviour". The socialisation process is essentially a 'learning' experience, in which police officers learn how to go beyond the organisational rules and procedures, whilst maintaining a facade of conformity which facilitates the 'illusion of control'.

There appears to be strong evidence to conclude that the management system of most police forces is the reverse of that which is required for effective police management. Police work demands a system which will encourage initiative, discretion and decision making and not a system which tends to inhibit or destroy those qualities. The police management system must seek to balance the need for an appropriate degree of control to maintain accountability with the greatest possible freedom of action and discretion for officers to plan and control their work.

The Status Of The Uniform Constable

The conflict between freedom of action and organisation control affects all operational officers throughout the force. Another major management problem affects a substantial proportion but not all officers. This problem is the apparent paradox between the espoused philosophy of the force, which asserts the primacy of the uniform beat function, and the practical reality of the treatment uniformed officers believe they receive. As a generalisation, the uniform beat patrol section of the force contains the least experienced constables, sergeants and inspectors.

It is the section to which specialists are returned for indiscretions or after disciplinary action. It is the section of the force from which manpower is taken to respond to short term or even long term resource needs elsewhere. Officers seeking promotion are encouraged to leave uniformed patrol work to become specialists. Most damaging of all, uniformed constables themselves tend to perceive their work and consequently themselves, as having low status in the eyes of the rest of the force and the public. [9]

For the manager, the heart of the matter is the perception of low status by uniformed patrol officers. Low self esteem will inevitably produce a lowering of morale, motivation and commitment among these officers. Officers in this condition cannot be expected to provide the best possible service to the community. It would be dangerous to over state this problem but it is a vital issue for modern police management and apparently has not been resolved at least since 1967, when a Government sponsored report discussed it at length. [10]

Apart from the personally damaging consequences of low morale, motivation and commitment, there are wider organisational consequences. The perceived low status of uniformed patrol work encourages officers to seek transfers to other specialist assignments. The cost of turnover of staff, both constables and supervisors, works against the achievement of a pool of expertise, knowledge and skills within the uniformed patrol force. The constables in the uniformed patrol force have a high proportion of inexperienced officers compared to other sections of the force. On promotion, sergeants and inspectors tend to be transferred to uniformed work to serve their apprenticeship as supervisors, and then take their knowledge and skills into specialist branches to be replaced by other recently promoted officers. The training for uniformed patrol officers has tended to be unimaginative and repetitive, reinforcing the perceptions of the low status of this work. If uniformed patrol officers are the 'backbone of the force' then it is unfortunate that the levels of expertise and knowledge are constantly being diluted by the transfer of experienced officers from this work to be replaced by inexperienced constables and supervisors.

Before a solution can be proposed to the problem of the perceived low status of the uniformed patrol officer, the nature of the problem must be identified. The importance of uniformed patrol work is not disputed, the difficulty appears to be the absence of a means of clearly establishing the achievements of the uniformed patrol force and the skills which are required for these activities. In our society, status is something which is given or acquired mainly through achievement.

Thus there appears to be two matters which must be resolved if the problems associated with the status of the uniformed constable are to be resolved. First, the role of the uniformed patrol force must be examined, performance objective established and the various aspects of their work clearly defined. They are workers without job descriptions who believe they perform the residual tasks after everyone else has decided what they would prefer to do. Second, the uniformed patrol force must be managed in a manner which will enable officers as individuals and as a group to measure their achievements. When they have knowledge of the results they achieve, they will have a sense of personal achievement and the opportunity of achieving public recognition and status.

The Climate Of The Organisation

Management text books often refer to the 'climate of the organisation' when discussing employees' perceptions of their working environment. Climate is a useful analogy for describing the results of the interaction between the work environment and individuals. In the same way that most people feel better on sunny, warm days, so there are certain climates or atmospheres at work which are preferred by the majority of workers. The perceived status of uniformed constables is a matter which affects the whole organisation. To return to the meteorological terms, this is an aspect of the macro-climate. There are also issues of a smaller scale which can be influenced by individual managers within sections of the force, these are aspects of the micro-climate. The micro-climate of the sub-division is obviously intimately influenced by the climate prevailing in the force. However, it is possible for a sensitive manager to generate for himself and his staff a working environment which encourages the best results.

The skill of the manager is shown by the way in which he is able to identify the climate of his organisation and relate it to the effectiveness of his sub-division or department. The relationships which exist between him and his staff and between other groups in the organisation can either promote or inhibit the achievement of the common objectives. When he has identified and defined the relationships that exist, he must ask himself if they are conducive to the goals of the organisation. If they are inhibiting effectiveness and efficiency, then remedial actions should be planned and implemented.

It is human relationships which will determine the climate of the organisation. The complexity of the manager's problem is as broad as the nature of relationships in other spheres of human activity. There is almost certainly no right or wrong approach to human relations, the key variable will always be the specific situation in which the manager is obliged to perform his role. The overriding consideration will be the results achieved by the use of the resources for which he has responsibility. To this end, human relations issues will be managed to achieve a consensus and shared perceptions amongst staff of the objectives of the organisation, the means of achieving those results, and an understanding by everybody of their own and others' contribution to the objectives. Key concepts determining the degree of success or failure of achieving a coherent and integrated organisational approach, will be the quality of communication and decision making, the means by which work is allocated, the degree of integration of individuals and groups, the control and reward system, and the management of conflict and competition. Each concept will be examined in turn to provide a definition, an explanation of its importance, and some examples of positive and negative aspects of its influence on the organisation.

Communication

The function of communication is to make all members of the organisation aware of their responsibilities and tasks in pursuit of the goals of the force. Unfortunately, it is not always easy to achieve a good communicating system in organisations. There are factors which can inhibit communications and the passing of information. A manager who relies on using written methods is unlikely to achieve the same degree of understanding among his staff of their role as a manager who prefers a face to face style of communication.

Communication methods should be:-

(i) Open – say what they mean, people trust the information and do not have to "read between the lines".to get some hidden message.

(ii) Flexible – the communication methods change to suit the information needs. Simple information can be transmitted on paper but more complex matters use direct face to face contact.

(iii) Responsive to the needs of the organisation – large organisations need to adopt methods which reflect their size and may be significantly different to smaller less complex organisations.

All communications systems are based on passing information and instructions from the top to the bottom, however, it is essential that they should also be able to transmit information in the opposite direction. A communications system with feedback loops will enable senior officers to test their subordinates' understanding of the instructions passed down. In the absence of this feedback it is dangerous to assume officers interpreted the instructions in the way the author intended. A second function of the feedback loop is to provide a means by which senior officers can use the knowledge and experience of subordinates in the management strategy. To obtain the maximum benefit from this upward communication the manager must have the confidence to allow his subordinates to be constructively critical. If he is not able to encourage this openness then he is only going to hear what his officers believe he wants to hear.

The value of the top-down and bottom-up communication systems is obvious, however, the need for communication between officers on the same level can be overlooked. If, for example, communications between area constables and detectives is poor, then the information gathered by the former officers may not be available to the latter officers and consequently crimes may remain undetected.

The most damaging characteristic of a poor communications system will be confusion amongst the officers as to their role and contribution towards the goals of the organisation. Confusion and uncertainty are the hallmarks of poor communication within the organisation and the predominant means of information dissemination becomes rumour and speculation. Some communications system will exist in all organisations, but if the manager issues written instructions, with no explanations and without ensuring the instructions are received or understood by subordinates, then the results are unlikely to improve the achievements of the organisation. This style of management is almost exclusively one way and consequently the manager becomes increasingly remote from the problems of the world and his instructions can become unrealistic.

Decision Making

When a problem occurs decisions have to be made and the choice to ignore the problem actually means the decision is made by default. In the organisational context decisions are made for the purpose of directing the efforts of individuals towards achieving goals. The decision making process is the means whereby the organisation makes modifications to its strategy in response to new information or changes in the environment. Therefore the quality of those decisions will be significantly affected by the information which is available to the decision maker. Thus as a guiding principle, decisions are best made closest to the problem and the source of the information. Unfortunately with a centralised control and decision making policy, the chances of the most appropriate decision being made becomes less likely as the problem is passed up the hierarchical structure.

An organisation with a good decision making system will have clearly defined policy and authority levels whereby all individuals have formal guidelines which clearly establish the boundaries of their responsibilities and accountability. Policy guidelines will be set within the context which recognises that the most appropriate place to make decisions is closest to the problem and the point in the organisation which has access to all relevant information. This ideal system has a number of implications for the organisation. The need to have access to information implies the need for appropriate communications systems where people are able to be open and honest with each other. If good communications systems do not exist both vertically and laterally then there are likely to be implications for the quality of the decisions made. Reward systems will be discussed later, but it is essential to recognise that the quality of the decision making process will be significantly affected by the rewards system in operation. If the organisation encourages and rewards risk taking amongst managers within preset policy, then it will reduce the likelihood of managers abdicating their responsibilities and passing problems up the organisation. Furthermore, it will produce a climate in which managers will be able to develop and expand their skills and expertise. Probably the most important aspect of organisational climate which will affect the quality of decision making is the degree of trust existing between managers and their subordinates and between individuals within the organisation. Subordinates should believe their managers can be trusted with information and will not use it against an individual. Supervisors should be willing to trust the judgement of individuals and accept that occasional mistakes are inevitable. In a climate of mutual trust the decision making process should not only be more responsive and therefore of a better quality than in other organisations, but there will also be the opportunity for managers to learn and develop. To encourage commitment by all officers the management strategy should enable officers of lower rank to contribute to the decision making process. The bottom-up communication flow should be structured to give this opportunity and should be formally recognised through consultative machinery. It is very easy for staff associations and trade unions within the force to be critical of police management. However, if they are to be involved in contributing to the decision making process, then they must be constructive and provide alternative solutions to those they criticise.

Allocation of Work

The allocation of work can have an important influence on the organisation climate on the sub-division. The trend of increasing specialisation of police tasks has been said to have reduced job satisfaction among uniformed officers by narrowing the scope of their work or by preventing them from taking an incident from the initial report through to its conclusion. Many of the issues are familiar to the social psychology of work in industry, where production line methods were claimed to have caused similar problems. Some reversal of the trend has been attempted recently, for example with the transfer of responsibility for the investigation of less serious crimes to the uniformed branch. However, the issue is not whether to increase specialisation or decrease it. The question for the manager is to establish the tasks which must be performed and then determine the people who are best qualified to undertake the work. The allocation of work will affect the organisation climate. There is almost no likelihood of the job satisfaction of uniformed constables being enhanced by the transfer of a task which everyone believes is a wasteful use of resources. Constables who have been given the responsibility for the investigation of less serious crime may complain about the additional work, but they are also likely to feel more aggrieved about having to do a task which is very unproductive.

Before tasks are allocated their purpose should be seen in the context of the goal and objectives of the organisation. The tasks should be compatible with the other work performed by the officers. Although tasks may be compatible with the goals of the force, they should be seen in the context of the established priorities for the allocation of resources. Tasks should not simply be imposed on existing organisational structures because they may have profound consequences for supervision and administrative support. All these issues must be considered and changes made to the organisation and structure where appropriate. Finally, the allocation of tasks should be preceded by any training which is necessary to prepare the officers for their new work.

Integration of Individuals and Groups

The principal reason for the organisation of resources was said to be the need to combine the energies and skills of a number of people to achieve goals which would be unobtainable through the efforts of one individual. The statement may appear so obvious it seems unnecessary to make. Unfortunately one of the major factors inhibiting the improvement of productivity in organisations and particularly the police, is the lack of co-ordination and integration of the efforts of individual officers and the various sections of the force.

Individuals need to have an identity with others who perform the same tasks. Studies of the police have shown that small group membership is an important aspect of police work and particularly relevant to job satisfaction. Feeling part of a group provides an opportunity for learning the job and provides mutual support at times of difficulty or emotional stress. The manager must provide the circumstances in which a group identity can develop. A constable may nominally be the member of a group of officers, but if shift patterns mean he regularly meets only one other constable, sees his sergeant once or twice a week and work arrangements mean he always patrols and works alone, then there is little chance of a team identity being established by the group, although nominally they comprise a team.

A sense of belonging to a group can be important to individuals and is essential for the organisation. By belonging to a team individuals are able to share a desire to achieve common objectives, and thus their work is co-operative and co-ordinated. In complex organisations such as police forces, integration occurs on more than one level. Constables are members of small teams, such as a group of area constables, or detectives. The next level is the sub-division and it is essential the various teams of officers also accept their membership of the larger team and share sub-divisional objectives. The team concept extends through a series of building blocks where several small groups form a single large team. The organisational structures already exist in the form of sub-divisions and divisions. It is the manager's task to give these groupings a purpose and identity for them to be used as part of the management system.

Initially the team is used as a means of promoting the commitment and motivation of officers towards the goals of the force. Then the team concept can be used to show individuals the importance of their contribution to the work done by others. The uniformed officer who responds to the scene of a crime should be aware that the officer who will continue the investigation relies on the responding officer's skill and work in his attempts to detect the offender.

In some forces a rift can develop between operational officers and their colleagues in headquarters departments. In principle, headquarters are established to help and support the work of operational officers, however occasions can arise when the opposite appears to be true. The co-ordination of effort must embrace headquarters departments for them to reflect their supporting role. Methods must be established for these departments to be sensitive to the work of operational officers and respond accordingly.

There may appear to be a paradox in the title of this section. An important goal of management strategy is to encourage the behaviour of employees to be compatible with the goals of the organisation. Two simple strategies can be used, first, appropriate behaviour can be rewarded and second undesirable behaviour can be punished. The difficulties associated with direct supervision of officers on the streets makes the simple application of these two strategies something of a problem. The most appropriate means of control would seem to be an organisation climate in which constables *want* to comply and conform to the instructions and policies of the force and deliver a professional service to the community. Therefore the police should use a means of managerial control which exemplifies a positive attitude towards the behaviour of officers. A control system compatible with the professional goals of the force will encourage compliance by high professional standards of leadership.

This philosophy of management control which emphasises the positive or rewarding aspects of work should be extended to include a learning approach to control. The police Discipline Code has the problem of making individuals culpable for mistakes and therefore the shortcomings or failings of the force organisation may be overlooked. This is not an argument for the repeal of the code. However, in the long term, more will be achieved if officers and the force are able to learn from the errors of the past. Thus a goal of the control/rewards system should be to lead to improvements in the performance of officers and the force. Before an officer can learn by his experience he must have a means of receiving comment about his work from his supervisor. Therefore opportunities must exist for officers to have this feedback as soon as possible after events. Giving feedback and counselling are skills which must be learned if they are to achieve the maximum benefits. It is very easy for the recipient of feedback to feel threatened by potential criticism and take a defensive stance. If this does occur the opportunities for learning and self development are substantially reduced. Therefore feedback mechanisms must be sensitive to the feelings of individuals.

Some research in a police force in the United States showed how the rewards system was in contradiction to the policy of the force. [11] The policy stated that the force was committed to community involvement priorities and encouraged officers in the community relations aspects of their work. However, when the records of transfer of officers on request, commendation for good work and promotions were examined, it was found that it was law enforcement work which was rewarded. Furthermore, when police officers were observed in their work, it was law enforcement activities they saw as priorities. The lesson is simple, rewards given to police officers should be compatible with the goals of the force.

Conflict and Competition

Competition and friendly rivalry between groups of officers can be a source of motivation and encourage officers to achieve better results. Unfortunately, the dividing line between the positive aspects of competition and the negative consequences of conflict is not always recognised. Where competition is based on unequal opportunities, a danger exists for damage to the team spirit of the working group. Uniformed officers achieve satisfaction from detecting crime, however if they believe they are given only those crimes with little chance of detection because crimes with more chance are kept by the CID, then competition turns to conflict. The uniformed officers feel they are being denied opportunities for success. Information received by area constables can be important in the detection of crime by other officers, however, the chances of information being passed to other officers is reduced when area constables believe they will receive no recognition for their contribution to the detection of a crime. Thus conflict of individual interests can lead to a reduction in the overall achievements of the force. Therefore competition will be positive when all officers believe there is an equal distribution of resources and opportunities.

Competition can motivate the achievements of officers when it is managed within a context which is constructive. If competition is used to show the weaknesses or inadequacies of individuals or groups, or being better than another group becomes the only goal to be achieved, then competition will become destructive and change to conflict. People will become anxious and defensive. They will not co-operate with each other in case the other group takes advantage of the situation and claims the achievement on their own work. Competition when it is constructive can lead to innovation and promotes the use of imaginative solutions to policing problems. Conflict, however, can suppress innovation because individuals or groups fearing failure will continue to use existing methods.

Review

It is unlikely any force will be suffering from all the problems of organisational climate which have been described. Furthermore, it would be dangerous to make the assumption that the problems do exist within the force or the sub-division. The manager's task is to review his own situation, determine the quality of the organisational climate and establish its impact on promoting or inhibiting the achievement of the organisation's objectives. The aspects of organisational climate are summarised in Fig 7.1, and can be used as a means of reviewing the climate of the force or a part of it. Each aspect has two alternatives, both must be read as a pair and then scored on the five point scale as shown in the instructions. When the list has been completed the manager will be able to see a broad picture of his own perceptions of the climate of his force or sub-division. As a further exercise he could ask other officers to complete the questionnaire and compare their perceptions with his own. At all costs the manager must guard against assuming there is an a problem with the climate of his organisation and seek to change individual elements before he is aware of all the implications. When the questionnaire has been completed each item should be reviewed:-

1   Why does this aspect of the climate apply to my sub-division/department?

2   If I am sure it applies, then is it helping or hindering the effectiveness or efficiency of the sub-division/department?

3   Is it important?

4   Is it something I should change?

5   Can I do anything to change and improve the situation?

6   What are the likely consequences if nothing is done to change the situation?

The answers made by other members of the sub-division will help to answer the first question. When the element has been identified, its consequences for the sub-division's effectiveness must be assessed. If it helps and promotes the sub-division's achievements then it should be preserved; if it makes no difference then it is probably safe to ignore it. If it is believed the performance of the sub-division is being inhibited, remedial action should be considered, but before tremendous efforts are exerted the importance of the change should be considered. Some problems may be relatively minor and do not justify the efforts which would need to be made to change. Finally, the manager must always be realistic and not assume he can change the world, some things are beyond his control or influence.

When the review has been completed the manager will have a clearer picture of the climate of his organisation and the consequences that ensue from it. Any proposed changes will have a purpose and a context. Furthermore, if other members of the sub-division have been involved in the review a commitment to change will have been generated.

References

1 Butler, A. J. P., *A Study of The Occupational Perceptions of Police Officers* , Doctoral Thesis, Faculty of Law, University of Birmingham (1979).

2 Butler, A. J. P. and Tharme, K., *The Chelmsley Wood Policing Experiment* , Birmingham: West Midlands Police (1983).

3 Reuss-Ianni, E., and Ianni, F. A. J., "Street Cops and Management Cops: The Two Cultures of Policing", in Punch, M. (ed), *Control in the Police Organisation* , Cambridge, Mass: The M.I.T. Press.

4 Butler, A. J. P. (1979) op cit.

5 Heaton, M., *Productivity in Service Organisations* , New York: McGraw Hill (1977).

Figure 7.1 Organisational climate review

Instructions

Summarised below are paired descriptions of features of the climate of the organ-isation. They have been related to a sub-division but they are equally applicable to a department or the force as a whole. Read each pair in turn and then show the extent to which either or both apply in your opinion to the people who work for you by circling the figure based on the scale shown below.

1 = the statement on the *left* nearly always applies.
2 = the statement on the *left* applies more than the statement on the *right*.
3 = both statements are equally likely to apply.
4 = the statement on the *right* applies more than the statement on the *left*.
5 = the statement on the *right* nearly always applies.

1	All members of the sub-division share a common view as to their objectives and the results to be achieved.	1 2 3 4 5	Groups within the sub-division have different views on the objectives to be achieved.
2	There is agreement about the means by which objectives will be pursued.	1 2 3 4 5	Groups within the sub-division do not agree on the means to be used to achieve the object-ives.
3	Everyone understands and appreciates the contributions being made by other officers on the sub-division.	1 2 3 4 5	There is no recognition of the efforts of other officers on the sub-division.

Communications – the ways in which information or instructions are passed to individuals

4	Individuals and groups are aware of their responsibilities and tasks.	1 2 3 4 5	Individuals and groups are confused and uncertain of their responsibilities and tasks.
5	Communication channels and methods are open, flexible and responsive to the needs of the organisation.	1 2 3 4 5	Communication channels and methods are administrative, bureaucratic and closed.
6	The communication systems include feedback loops to test understanding.	1 2 3 4 5	Communications are one way from top-down with little or no opportunity for feedback.
7	Opportunities for lateral communication between individuals and groups are developed and encouraged.	1 2 3 4 5	There is little or no lateral communication between groups.

Decision Making – who makes decisions and how?

8	Problems are actively identified and decisions made to resolve them.	1 2 3 4 5	Problems tend to be ignored and decision making is a last resort.

9 Decisions are always made in the context of the goals and objectives of the organisation.	1 2 3 4 5	Decisions tend to be arbitary and unstructured with little or no reference to the long term consequences.
10 Wherever possible decisions are made closest to the source of the problem.	1 2 3 4 5	Decisions tend to be passed up the structure away from the location of the problem.
11 Individuals can make decisions based on their clearly defined roles and responsibilities.	1 2 3 4 5	Individuals are uncertain of their responsibilities and roles in the decision making process.
12 Clearly defined policy is available for reference in the decision making process.	1 2 3 4 5	Policy for decision making is ambiguous and vague.
13 The rewards system of the organisation encourages individuals to be prepared to make decisions.	1 2 3 4 5	The organisation discourages individual initiative and risk taking by punishing errors in decision making.
14 All individuals in the organisation have access to, and an opportunity to influence the decision making process.	1 2 3 4 5	The decision making process is a closed system in the hands of an individual or small group of individuals.

Allocation of Work – who does what and why?

15 All tasks that are performed are rationally linked to the goals and objectives of the organisation.	1 2 3 4 5	Tasks tend to be performed through historical precedence with little or no reference to goals and objectives.
16 Tasks are undertaken with due regard to the priorities of resource allocation.	1 2 3 4 5	The priorities of resource allocation are not considered in determining which tasks should be undertaken and by whom.
17 The organisational structures are determined by the tasks to be performed and the allocation of work.	1 2 3 4 5	Tasks are simply superimposed on existing organisation structures and working practices, with no regard to the possible needs for modification.
18 The allocation of work recognises the need for appropriate levels of skills and knowledge and includes the provision of training.	1 2 3 4 5	Work is allocated with no regard to the levels of skills and knowledge which must be required and without providing training.

Integration of Individuals and Groups – how much team spirit exists?

| 19 Individual officers feel part of a team with shared objectives. | 1 2 3 4 5 | Individuals feel isolated and may not recognise the objectives of other officers. |
| 20 Working groups which form, operate on the basis of shared objectives. | 1 2 3 4 5 | Working groups operate without reference to the objectives of other groups. |

127

21 Individuals perform their tasks 1 2 3 4 5 Individuals see their tasks as
   as part of a collaborative and   separate and distinct from
   corporate strategy for the   the procedures which contrib-
   completion of a whole piece of   ute to a whole piece of work.
   work.

22 Headquarters departments 1 2 3 4 5 Headquarters departments are
   are seen as a responsive and   seen as having objectives
   vital support to the work of   which are not consistent with
   operational police officers.   the needs of operational
                                                    police officers.

Control/Rewards Systems − how are achievements recognised and rewarded?

23 The control systems are con- 1 2 3 4 5 The control/reward systems
   sistent with force goals and   are seen as ends in themselves
   objectives.   and are not necessarily com-
                                                     patible with force goals and
                                                     objectives.

24 The control/rewards systems 1 2 3 4 5 The control/rewards systems
   are seen as a means of enabling   are seen as a means of
   individuals to improve their   identifying and punishing
   performance.   mistakes.

25 The control/rewards sytems 1 2 3 4 5 Feedback is mainly through
   promote the use of sensitive   indirect means such as annual
   feedbacks loops to provide   staff appraisal and discipline
   direct knowledge of results.   enquiries.

26 The rewards system is com- 1 2 3 4 5 Rewards are not compatible
   patible with the goals and   with the espoused goals and
   objectives of the force.   objectives of the force.

27 The predominate form of 1 2 3 4 5 Control is seen as a discipline
   control is through self-   to be imposed and enforced
   motivation and internalised   from the top.
   standards.

Conflict and Competition − is it friendly and productive or aggressive win/lose?

28 Competition between individuals 1 2 3 4 5 Competition is viewed as a
   and groups is seen as a means   means of showing the weak-
   of motivation.   nesses or inadequacies of
                                                    other individuals or groups.

29 Competition is seen to be based 1 2 3 4 5 Competition is seen as a means
   on the equal distribution of   of exploiting the benefits of
   resources, skills and knowledge.   an unequal distribution of re-
                                                    sources, skills and knowledge.

30 Competition occurs within the 1 2 3 4 5 Competition is based on
   context of a shared sense of   overt win/lose relationships
   achievement.   without regard to the organisa-
                                                    tion's goals and objectives.

31 Competition is seen as energy 1 2 3 4 5 Conflict suppresses the pro-
   to be harnessed to promote   posal and implementation of
   new and imaginative solutions   innovative solutions to prob-
   to problems.   lems, individuals or groups are
                                                    not prepared to risk failure.

The question could be answered again by your officers or by your colleagues in
the same rank. The answers could be compared. Where differences exist it may
tell you quite a lot about your style of management.

6 McGregor, D., *Human Side of Enterprise* , New York: McGraw-Hill Book Co.

7 Butler, A. J. P., and Cochrane, R., "An examination of some elements of the personality of police officers and their implications", *Journal of Police Science and Administration* 4, 441-450 (1977).

8 Cain, M. E., *Society and the Policeman's Role* , London: Routledge and Kegan Paul (1973).

9 Jones, J. M., *Organisational Aspects of Police Behaviour* , Farnborough: Gower Publishing Co. Ltd.

10 Home Office, *Police Manpower, Equipment and Efficiency* . Reports of Three Working Parties, H.M.S.O. (1967).

11 Nadel, S. W., Measurement Systems and Organisational Goals in a Large Metropolitan Police Department, *Police Studies* , Figure 1, (3), 3-45 (1978).

8 Implementing Changes in the Organisation and Management

Introduction

Predicting the future of an organisation carries an implicit assumption of a commitment to change to meet the challenge of a changing world. Unfortunately changes in organisations may create more problems than they solve. The need to establish the 'here and now' in the planning stage of the management cycle has been a theme of the previous chapters. Its importance cannot be overstated. Without this knowledge the process of change may damage or even destroy successful working practices. Progress is unlikely if for every step forward there are one or two steps backwards. In the future the police will be asked to review the results they achieve when expending the community's rates and taxes. There is no doubt the issues raised by these demands will cause problems for police managers. Some may even claim the measurement of effectiveness and efficiency is impossible. It is certainly difficult but *not* impossible, policing is not a random and arbitrary response to social problems, but a more or less directed strategy towards identifiable goals. At present the strategies may be based more upon experience than an objective assessment of the likelihood of success. In the future police management will need to have a more formal foundation than 150 years of history without rejecting the value of past experience.

A second, but equally important, perspective of modern policing is the public demand for accountability. In reality the two issues of the economical use of resources and accountability have the same fundamental consequences for the police manager. Unless he can demonstrate results, how can he be seen to be using his resources to the best effect. He will certainly not be able to be held accountable, because the word implies some form of evaluation. Without establishing results he cannot be judged and thus be held accountable. To achieve and demonstrate accountability the force must have a systematic and circular management process, proceeding from planning and organising to controlling the implementation of the strategy which will then be subject to an evaluation process. [1]

The review of Unit Beat Policing suggested management problems contributed to the criticisms which were made of the system. The implementation of Unit Beat Policing did not follow the system described in the management cycle (Figure 2.1). Therefore, it was argued, there was an inadequate knowledge and understanding of the problems which Unit Beat Policing was trying to resolve, and there were no data on which to base objective examinations of the progress of the system. The planning phase described in Chapter 2 can be summarised thus:-

Establish strategic policy; gather and analyse facts on the present situation; review options and choose the best strategy.

Chapters 2 to 7 have been addressing the issues of determining policy, and gathering and analysing facts on the current situation. The next stage is to describe how the techniques which have been described can be used in a management review of the force. The management review will be the completion of the planning phase of the management cycle and will establish the foundation on which the force will proceed in the future. Two methods of conducting this review will be described later in the chapter. When the review has been completed, a management system will be required to enable improvements in operational effectiveness and organisational developments to be achieved. A suitable management system is also described later in the chapter.

The learning objectives of this chapter are:-

1   To understand the present day demands that are being made on police managers and the need to improve management practice.

2   To understand the relationship between accountability and the measurement of results.

3   To understand the concept of the 'ideal police organisation' and recognise its constituent elements.

4   To know the basic elements which must be reviewed in the planning stage of the management cycle.

5   To understand the distinctions between two methods of organisational review, namely the review of functions and procedures, and the operational management review.

6   To know the basic principles and requirements necessary to undertake a force review of functions and procedures.

7   To know the basic principles and requirements necessary to undertake an operational management review of the force.

8   In the context of the operational management review, to understand the role and functions of the Review Agenda.

9   To understand the role and functions of the reports that are produced through the review processes and how they relate to the preparation of the chief constable's Policy Statement.

10 To understand the role and function of the Policy Statement.

11 To appreciate the need to address in the Policy Statement both improvements in operational effectiveness and efficiency, and the organisational and management development needs of the force.

12 To understand the need for a co-ordinated management system to provide a coherent framework to organise, implement, control and evaluate the future strategy of the force.

13 To understand the basic elements of the Policing By Objectives (PBO) model.

14 To understand the use of the Linking Pin communications model within the context of PBO.

15 To understand the role and functions of the PBO Co-ordinator.

The Ideal Police Organisation

The management review will be primarily concerned with operational issues within the force, however, the importance of the force organisation and its climate should not be overlooked. The review provides a unique opportunity for the force to measure itself against the "ideal organisation". Ultimately, any improvements which are made to the operational effectiveness of the force will depend on the work and co-operation of all officers. Therefore, before describing the review process it is worth summarising the elements of an ideal police organisation which will facilitate the improvement of operational effectiveness and efficiency.

Policy

Police executive management, the community and operational police officers share a consensus about the duties and responsibilities of the police, the desired levels of effectiveness, the police's share of public resources, and the methods and criteria to be used to evaluate police performance.

Executive Management

The force have common planning, organising, implementing and controlling/evaluating policy and methods. The force uses a systematic approach to problem solving. The executive management plan and make decisions directed towards achieving goals which are directly linked to force policy. Performance standards for effectiveness and efficiency are objectively established and based on force policy. Budgets are formulated on the basis of the resources required to achieve an agreed level of effectiveness in pursuit of force policy. The force organisational structure is compatible with the tasks to be performed.

Executive management and headquarters functions provide a supporting role in response to the needs identified by operational officers.

Operational Management

The basic operational unit has a clear understanding of its responsibilities and tasks, and the objectives for which it is accountable.

The operational unit controls all the resources necessary to achieve those objectives.

The efforts and achievements of each operational unit are co-ordinated to form a coherent strategy to achieve the goals of the force.

Decisions are made as close to the problem as possible by the person or persons who have the greatest knowledge of all its aspects. The management of the operational unit provides opportunities for a flexible response to any changes or new situations which arise. Communications systems operate top-down and bottom-up and provide opportunities and encouragement for lateral communication.

Human Resource Management

The deployment of human resources is designed to achieve maximum results in relation to the units objectives. All officers know and understand their duties, responsibilities and tasks, and their contribution to the overall achievements of the force.

All officers have a clear understanding of their boundaries of decision making.

The predominant management philosophy is compatible with the self directed, self reliant requirements of police work. Communications, both vertically and horizontally have appropriate feedback mechanisms.

All officers understand the criteria upon which they will be evaluated, which are based on achieving results compatible with the goals of the force.

Individuals and sub-groups have access to, and make contributions to, the policy making process.

Individuals are provided with opportunities to expand their knowledge and skills, and develop in their work.

The Planning Phase

The nine elements of the planning phase can be seen in Figure 2.2 and are described in Chapter 2. When a manager is faced with the task of planning for the future he has to relate the concepts to his own circumstances. This chapter will provide a guide to this task. A useful starting point is to translate the concepts to a series of simple questions and basic requirements which must be satisfied:-

Questions

As an organisation, what is our present performance? In terms of performance, what do we wish to achieve in a year from now?
What resources are available?
What strategies are available?
What constraints exist?
What are the negative consequences of each strategy?
Which is the preferred strategy?
How will we know when our target has been reached?

Basic Requirements

There must be a statement of policy which is capable of being translated into measurable objectives.
Resources must be measured and the time currently being consumed in mandatory tasks must be identified.
Performance measures must exist or be developed to establish objective levels of effectiveness and efficiency. Constraints preventing improved performance must be identified.

There are a number of ways the management review can be undertaken but we will be concerned with describing two:-

(i) *The review of functions and procedures*. This method is concerned with examining specific functions and procedures within the force. A typical example of this method is the formation of working parties to examine the traffic division, the prosecution system, the police response to calls from the public, and the investigation of less serious crime.

(ii) *Operational management review* . This method gives the task of the management review to individual operational units. The chief officer sets an agenda of policing priorities, then he asks sub-divisions and departments to identify their individual contribution to achieving these priorities.

There are advantages and disadvantages with both methods and the choice must be made on the specific needs of the force. The choice of method is a matter which the chief officer should carefully assess before deciding the review process his force will adopt.

The Review Of Functions And Procedures

The usual reason for the review of functions and procedures is a preparation for major structural and administrative reorganisation. The chief officer initiates the process by asking the force to examine the present structure, organisation and procedures with a view to improving effectiveness and reducing costs. The chief officer should take care to set the terms of reference for the review by identifying issues to be examined and establishing a context which is directed towards a problem solving approach rather than an exercise in modifying current practice without regard to the results being achieved. To illustrate this point, consider a working party formed to review the traffic division. The terms of reference could be set thus:-

"To review the traffic division and make proposals for its reorganisation to improve its effectiveness."

The working party are obliged to recognise the continued need for a traffic division which may not necessarily be the most effective means of providing a service to the public. The terms of reference require a review of the activities of the traffic division with little regard for alternative means of solving problems associated with road traffic. Alternative terms of reference could be set as follows:–

"To review the contribution made by the traffic division to the improvement of traffic flow and promoting road safety, and explore alternative means of achieving or improving the current effectiveness of the force and reducing costs."

The terms of reference require a review of performance based on policy targets. The working party are free to provide any solution, including the elimination of separate traffic patrols, providing the overall effectiveness of the force is not impaired. The terms of reference for working parties therefore cannot be set unless a preliminary assessment has been made of key problems facing the force.

The advantages of using working parties enables work to be spread across a number of people and in the process these people become involved in questioning the activities of the force. The proposals made by each working party should reflect the range of knowledge available to the group. During the process of the review those involved start to appreciate the problems which are facing the force and as they proceed from analysis towards making proposals for solutions, a commitment is generated to a consensus view as to the changes which should be implemented. Thus the very process of analysis starts to generate a climate which is likely to be more receptive to organisational change than in circumstances where a small group of highly placed officers formulate plans which appear to be imposed upon the rest of the force. Unfortunately, working parties are not always the fastest means by which analysis and proposals are achieved. A compromise has to be struck between the value of prolonged debate and wide ranging discussion, and the need to produce an end product. Where the working party technique is adopted, it is essential that a small team of officers should be appointed to co-ordinate the activities of the working groups and translate their proposals into a coherent summary of the issues and problems facing the force.

The summary report of issues and problems facing the force is the foundation upon which future development will be based and can be used to develop the Policy Statement of the force. The report serves a number of functions; it identifies the need to consider the restructuring of the force to make it more compatible with the tasks to be done; it identifies where there are gaps between desired performance and actual performance; it identifies where there are deficiencies in the amount of management information which is available to the force; and it identifies the need for additional knowledge and skills amongst officers – training needs. There is a great danger at this point, of the force embarking upon a reorganisation of its resources, additional training and investment in computerised management information systems without establishing a purpose for these actions beyond a feeling that change has some inherent value in itself. The purpose of the changes to the force must be described in a Policy Statement which will provide the guiding principles for the future development of the force.

When the Policy Statement has been published the process of preparing the force to undertake the necessary changes can be commenced. Every member of the force must be aware of their individual duties and responsibilities, and receive appropriate training for any new skills which may be required. The relationship between parts of the force must be clearly stated, for example, the relationship of headquarters support departments with operational officers must be clear. The basis on which success or improvement will be judged must be defined and the evaluation processes decided. In short, the force must strive to achieve the characteristics of the ideal police organisation described in the previous section of this chapter.

The force must now consider how the long term improvements which are desired, can be sustained into the future. It is the answer to this question which the remaining chapters of the book will address. In essence, there is a clear need for a management process which will ensure the continuing focus of attention on results and the effective and efficient use of police resources in a changing world.

Operational Management Review

A force-wide reorganisation is probably more easily achieved in smaller and less complex police forces where they are not experiencing excessive pressures from the environment. In larger, complex forces in an urban environment, there may not be the same opportunities to withdraw many officers to review the force or to undertake radical organisational change programmes. In these forces a progressive step-by-step approach may be a more acceptable and practical method of improving effectiveness and efficiency.

The Stages of the Management Review Process

It should be remembered that the review process is concerned with the "here and now".of the force. Data will be gathered during this review but it will be used as a basis of determining present performance and subsequent evaluation, and *not* as an evaluation of past performance. This is an important distinction. The review should be a candid and thorough assessment of current performance, uninhibited by the feeling that past actions should be justified. The questions to be posed in the planning phase use the term "strategy".to describe the proposals for improving effectiveness. There is a distinction between strategy and policing methods. As an example, co-operation with the education department and the social services is a strategy which might be used to reduce crime. A policing method would be to establish a liaison officer on each division to review the decision to prosecute juveniles with representatives of the social services and education welfare departments. The management review will need to consider both policing methods and the broader issues of strategy.

Before describing the details of the management review process the stages can be summarised as follows:-

Stage 1

The management review process is initiated by the chief officer producing an agenda of problems and issues facing the force.

Stage 2

Using the agenda as a starting point, sub-divisions and departments will review their effectiveness, by assessing their work against performance measures. Management review reports will be prepared and submitted to chief superintendents to be co-ordinated across divisions.

Stage 3

The reports will be collated at headquarters on behalf of the chief officer to produce an assessment of the state of the force. The analysis will identify:-

(i) the means by which improvements in operational effectiveness can be achieved almost immediately;

(ii) the need for further organisation or management development, or additional resources before improvements in operational effectiveness can be achieved.

Stage 4

When the analysis has been completed, the chief officer can define his Policy Statement for the forthcoming year, stating the aims of the force.

Stage 5

The force will then use a co-ordinated management system to proceed to achieve the aims defined by the Policy Statement.

A summary of the stages of the management review process are shown in Figure 8.1.

Figure 8.1 Management review process

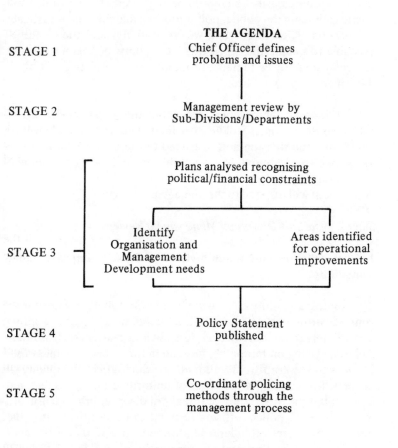

STAGE 1

THE AGENDA
Chief Officer defines
problems and issues

STAGE 2

Management review by
Sub-Divisions/Departments

Plans analysed recognising
political/financial constraints

STAGE 3

Identify
Organisation and
Management
Development needs

Areas identified
for operational
improvements

STAGE 4

Policy Statement
published

STAGE 5

Co-ordinate policing
methods through the
management process

The agenda set by the chief officer will identify the strategic policy issues. Issues related to crime, public tranquillity and road traffic will be relevant to territorial sub-divisions and some specialist departments. The priorities for specialist departments will also be identified in the agenda.

It is important to understand that the agenda identifies priority areas where special efforts are to be made to improve the effectiveness of the force, anything not mentioned in the agenda should not necessarily be ignored or neglected. The force will still attend calls from the public, police football matches and investigate cycle thefts. Therefore, when we come to consider the resources available to pursue these priorities, care must be taken to ensure sufficient manpower remains to maintain the effectiveness of all those mandatory activities.

To describe the practical process of the management review two separate examples will be explained. The first example will be based on a sub-division and restricted to the priority "to improve the public's perceptions of tranquillity in their neighbourhood." The second example will be used to describe how a headquarters department will respond to the management review.

Stage 2 – The Sub-Divisional Management Review

1 What activities does a sub-division perform to improve public tranquillity?

Public tranquillity has a wide definition. Obviously disorderly youths, drunkenness, prostitution and noisy parties spring immediately to mind. However, less obvious matters such as litter, children cycling on footpaths, football in the street, solvent abuse, vandalism and graffiti, are all matters which affect the quality of peoples' lives. Much of the work of uniformed officers is directed towards this priority. When outbreaks of disorder or vandalism are reported to the police, officers respond to these calls to stop the disorder or detect offenders. Uniformed officers patrol the sub-division in cars and on foot to deter outbreaks of disorder and to enforce the law when problems occur. Officers use their time, when not responding to calls, to pay particular attention to likely trouble spots on their beats. Some outbreaks of disorder or vandalism require follow up investigations, which, once again, are the responsibility of uniformed officers. When particularly serious problems occur, special steps can be taken to reduce the nuisance, for example, plain clothes patrols or observations, or intensive uniformed patrols. Any other actions which are taken on the sub-division to solve these problems should be identified and listed.

2 What means does the sub-division have to measure the results it has achieved in pursuit of the chief constable's priority?

The evaluation of policing methods is going to become increasingly important in the future and it is one of the primary reasons for undertaking the management review. Sub-divisions are being asked to improve public perceptions of tranquillity. Therefore it is essential that measures are identified which can be used to establish if improvements have been achieved. Obviously some police actions are more effective in improving public tranquillity than others, and performance measures can help to identify policing methods on which more effort should be made and those which are less worthwhile.

The public's perceptions of tranquillity are based more on qualitative judgements rather than hard facts. However, their perceptions can be translated into facts, such as the number of incidents of nuisance, disorder and so forth that are reported to the police. Other indicators can also be counted, such as:-

(i) The number of persistent complaints which are resolved.

(ii) The number of incidents of damage to public amenities, eg, telephone boxes, bus shelters and so forth.

(iii) The amount of graffiti.

(iv) The number of offenders detected for acts of damage.

(v) The number of letters of appreciation received about nuisances which have been resolved.

(vi) The number of comments in local newspapers about nuisances.

Some of these measures are more precise and reliable than others, but nevertheless they do provide some means of measuring the results of police methods. However, not all measures are applicable to all the activities which are listed in response to question '(1)' above. To clarify the relationship between measures and policing methods a matrix can be used such as the one shown in Figure 8.2.

The activities have been listed on the left hand side and the performance measures are across the top. Each activity is then examined to determine if the performance measure is appropriate. The effectiveness of responding to calls in terms of improving the public's perceptions of tranquillity might be measured by the number of letters of appreciation and the number of offenders detected for acts of damage. The effectiveness of preventive mobile and foot patrol can be assessed by all the performance measures illustrated. This method summarises the analysis and can be developed later when other factors are taken into account. At this stage preventive police patrols appear to be the most likely means to achieve the improvements, however, it is not clear which type of police patrols are most useful. This point illustrates the need to look carefully at the benefits of developing better methods of measurement in the future. This is not an easy task, but the evaluation process will be easier where performance measures are more precise. Performance measures given in the example should not be seen as the only ones available or the most appropriate. The definition of performance measures is one aspect of the review where all ideas should be considered. In the first review, sub-divisions will have to use measures which are available at present. The number of nuisance or disorder calls can be obtained from the management information produced from command and control incident logs. Process and crime statistics may provide information on persons detected for acts of damage. The bus company and British Telecom can provide information on incidents of damage to their property. All useful sources of information should be explored because the sub-division must identify the measures in the review report, on which its future performance can be evaluated.

3 What manpower is used on the sub-division to improve public perceptions of tranquillity?

The officers who work on the sub-division will be controlled either from the sub-division or from divisional headquarters or from force headquarters itself. For example, area constables are a sub-divisional resource, the plain clothes squad is a divisional resource and the task force and the traffic division are force resources. All the resources deployed on the sub-division should be examined in turn to see what they contribute. Although the traffic division represents a uniformed presence, their role does not include matters relating directly to the enhancement of public tranquillity, therefore they can be discounted from the sub-divisional review. As a second step the work of other resources should be examined to determine the proportion of time they spend on activities relating to maintaining public tranquillity. For example, what proportion of time is spent by officers in cars on patrol, specifically directed towards preventing nuisances or disorders. In most cases this figure will be substantially less than for example, area constables or members of the special constabulary. In some cases officers are given specific responsibility for combating nuisances and disorders and thus they will spend a significant proportion of their time on these matters. The officers of the task force could be such an example.

The important points to consider in relation to manpower are:-

(i) Do all these resources contribute something to the improvement of public tranquillity?

(ii) Who is responsible for controlling these officers?

If it is not the sub-divisional superintendent then it may not be wise to include these officers in later plans, as they can be taken away from the sub-division to do other work.

(iii) What time do these officers spend on tasks related to improving public tranquillity?

A matrix can be used again to summarise the results of this analysis. In Figure 8.3 the activities from the previous matrix have been shown on the left hand side and the manpower resources shown across the top. The activities which had the most performance measures also appear to have the majority of resources. Preventive foot patrols are performed by some unit officers, area constables and special constables. Plain clothes and

Figure 8.2 Activities reviewed against performance measures

ACTIVITIES	PERFORMANCE MEASURES								
	Number of complaints received from the public	Number of persistent complaints resolved	Number of incidents of damage to public amenities	Amount of graffiti	Number of letters of appreciation	Comment in the media	Number of offenders detected for acts of damage	Public satisfaction expressed in public attitude survey	
1 Responding to calls from the public					X		X	X	
2 Preventive mobile patrol	X	X	X	X	X	X	X		
3 Preventive foot patrol	X	X	X	X	X	X	X		
4 Further enquiries/ investigations		X			X		X	X	
5 Plain Clothes patrol/observations	X	X	X				X		
6 Intensive police patrols	X	X	X	X	X	X	X		

Figure 8.3 Activities reviewed against manpower

ACTIVITIES	MANPOWER								
	Sub-Division				Div	Force			
	Mobile Patrol Officers	Unit Foot Patrol Officers	Area Constables	Special Constabulary	Plain Clothes Squad	Task Force	Traffic Division		
1 Responding to calls from the public	X	X	X						
2 Preventive mobile patrol	X								
3 Preventive foot patrol		X	X	X					
4 Further enquiries/ investigations			X						
5 Plain Clothes patrol/observations					X				
6 Intensive police patrols						X			

intensive police patrols are also seen as potentially useful for improving public tranquillity. However, if preventive patrol is to be successful there is a need to co-ordinate the places and times when it will pay greatest dividends.

4 What specific improvements could be made to the public's perceptions of tranquillity?

When considering the question of making improvements in police effectiveness it is a mistake to try to improve everything at once. By looking critically at the performance measures previously described, it is possible to identify those which are most likely to be capable of showing improvements in public tranquillity. Comments in the local newspapers are more likely to be influenced by the policy of the editor than any actions taken by the police on the streets. However, a reduction in the number of persistent complaints is a real indicator of police success. Other useful measures of the effectiveness of policing methods are an increase in the number of persons reported or arrested for acts of damage and a reduction in the number of incidents of damage to public amenities.

When reasonable measures of effectiveness have been identified, the sub-division can seek policing methods which can be employed to improve the public's perceptions of tranquillity assessed on these measures. Therefore, the sub-division would be restricting its ideas to methods which would reduce the number of persistent complaints and incidents of damage to public amenities, and increase the number of persons detected for acts of damage.

At this stage as many officers as possible should be able to contribute to the process. Their knowledge of the specific problems on the sub-division and their experience of dealing with them will assist the planning team to develop policing methods.

The starting point for identifying means of improving effectiveness is to examine existing policing methods to see if they can be improved. Experience has shown the value of responding to calls promptly where there is a possibility of catching offenders at or near the scene. Therefore it is important that the sub-division should ensure it has the resources to respond appropriately to calls of disorder and vandalism. The review of police activities and manpower resources showed the potential value of preventive patrol, but it also appeared there was a need for some co-ordination and analysis to identify the best times and places where patrols should be deployed. Therefore preventive patrols may be better described as 'directed patrols' which are supported by an analysis of incident patterns and a co-ordination of manpower deployment throughout the sub-division.

To acknowledge the assistance which the community can make to police effectiveness, consideration could be given to publicity to encourage the public to report incidents of disorder and vandalism. These reports will improve the analysis of patterns which will provide a better basis on which police patrols can be deployed in the future.

In Figure 8.4 a matrix has been used to compare policing methods with desired improvements in effectiveness. The summary produced by this comparison confirms the value of co-ordinating manpower across the sub-division in a directed patrol strategy, which is based upon an analysis of incident patterns.

5 Are there any constraints which may prevent the improvements to police effectiveness?

We have already identified one constraint in the use of manpower. Although officers from the task force work on sub-divisions, the sub-divisional superintendent does not have control over the day to day deployment of these officers. Therefore, he cannot rely on them being available for use in directed patrol plans. If special constables only work between certain hours or the number coming on duty cannot be predicted in advance, then it will be difficult to rely on their use in directed patrol plans. Restrictions on the use of vehicles or petrol economies, may have placed a limitation on the number of calls to which cars can respond. If members of the public are going to be encouraged to report incidents to the police in the hope of preventing offences or catching offenders, then the sub-division must have mobile resources to respond. The entire policy could fail because the public become disappointed about police response to their calls.

Co-ordinating the use of manpower on the sub-division may be difficult where contact between officers occurs only occasionally. A

Figure 8.4 Policing methods reviewed against improvements

POLICING METHODS	*Reduce* the number of persistent complaints	*Increase* the number of persons detected for acts of damage	*Reduce* the number of incidents of damage to public amenities					
	IMPROVEMENTS							
1 Appropriate response to calls from the public		X						
2 Analyse incident patterns	X		X					
3 Use directed patrol	X	X	X					
4 Co-ordinate use of resources	X		X					
5 Seek public co-operation		X						

Figure 8.5 Policing methods reviewed against constraints

POLICING METHODS	CONSTRAINTS							
	Do not control divisional plain clothes squad	Do not control task force	The number of special constables coming on duty cannot be predicted	Petrol restrictions have limited vehicle use	Lack of contact between area PCs and other uniform officers			
1 Appropriate response to calls from the public				X				
2 Analyse incident patterns								
3 Use directed patrol	X	X	X					
4 Co-ordinate use of resources	X	X	X		X			
5 Seek public co-operation				X				

recent review of area constables suggested the contact between them and other officers was relatively infrequent.

When the constraints and policing methods are summarised on the matrix (Figure 8.5) consideration must be given to the implications for sub-divisional effectiveness. The limitations on the use of vehicles imposed by petrol economies is a matter which must be referred to headquarters as it concerns force policy. The sub-division is in a position to resolve some of the problems associated with the lack of contact between area constables and other officers, and the unpredictable numbers of special constables reporting for duty. The use of the divisional plain clothes squad and the task force is a matter which may be resolved by agreement between sub-divisional superintendents and the divisional chief superintendent. The review of constraints on improving effectiveness may identify the need for additional resources, or the development of better management information systems. All these matters should be included in the management review report.

6 Do headquarters departments provide an adequate support to the sub-division or could improvements be made to the service they provide?

The review of constraints in the last section may raise matters concerning the support provided by headquarters departments. The primary role for headquarter's departments is to support the efforts of operational officers, however, they need to be informed of ways in which they can improve their service. The management review will provide an opportunity for these matters to be raised with these departments.

Management Review Report

When all of the priorities on the agenda have been examined a report will be prepared which will be submitted to divisional chief superintendents for them to co-ordinate the assessment of their division's effectiveness. For each of the priorities in the chief officer's agenda, the reports will contain information on the following points:-

(1) A list of activities which are done at present to pursue the particular priority on the agenda.

(2) Existing measures, including the sources of information, which are used now to determine the effectiveness of the activities listed in (1) above.

(3) An assessment of the effectiveness of each policing activity based on the measures defined in (2).

(4) A description of policing methods which could be used to achieve improvements in the specific priority in the agenda.

(5) A list of the measures which could be used to assess the results achieved.

(6) A description of the constraints which may prevent or inhibit improvements being achieved. Although it may not have been possible to accurately measure the use of time by officers the time which may be available to undertake any additional activities is a constraint which should be considered.

(7) A description of the means of resolving the problems caused by constraints, including the need for headquarters involvement or policy decisions, or the provision of additional resources.

Headquarters Departmental Management Review

Before embarking upon the management review based on the questions defined above, the heads of departments should ask themselves some additional questions:

(i) Does the work of my department contribute directly to the effectiveness of sub-divisions?

If the answer is 'Yes' then the review process described for sub-divisions should be used to determine exactly what contributions are made to sub-divisions.

Obviously where a priority is not applicable to a department this will be stated and not subjected to the detailed review.

If the answer is 'No' then the department should examine its work and define the criteria on which it can be evaluated. The most approach to the management review process is to take each area of activity in turn and examine ways in which the effectiveness and/or efficiency could be improved. The seven items to be included within the review report can be modified where necessary to fit the particular circumstances of the departments.

In departments which contain a number of separate squads or sections it may be appropriate to delegate the responsibility for the review to these squads or sections. However, the reports they submit should be co-ordinated by the chief superintendent before being submitted to be collated for the chief officer.

Stage 3 – Collation of Review Reports

The responses from sub-divisions and departments must be collated for the chief officer to enable a composite picture to be drawn of the present state of the force. Does the force know its present performance levels based upon objective criteria? Are there resources available to accept additional tasks to improve the effectiveness of the force? Is the support provided by headquarters departments helping operational officers achieve their objectives? The process will have caused officers to examine their management responsibilities, their resources and to define their criteria for evaluation. The review will almost certainly reveal management information deficiencies and a lack of knowledge of the results achieved. It is also likely to point to matters where headquarters departments are not responding to the real needs of operational officers. The step-by-step approach seeks to develop simultaneously on two fronts, improving operational effectiveness and providing improved management information and support functions. The skill is to enable the two aspects to develop as complementary.

Stage 4 – The Preparation of the Policy Statement

Whichever method of management review the force undertook there is a need to state unambiguously the policy of the force for the future. The collation of the review reports will provide a broad picture of the strengths and weaknesses of the force. The way ahead will be defined within the Policy Statement which is the foundation of the managerial process and can serve a number of purposes. It may serve as an agreement between the chief officer and his police authority by defining mutually agreed priorities, or as a means of securing financial resources in the annual budget negotiations. It may serve as an agreement between the chief officer and his force as to the joint areas of concern. However, the Policy Statement will always have one primary purpose, it is the guide to the tactical management of resources. All activities performed by constables must be compatible with the purpose and aims of the force declared in the Policy Statement. Every time a constable leaves the police station to go about his duties he should have an understanding of the aims of the force and the contribution he can make to achieving those targets.

When preparing a Policy Statement the following matters and issues should be considered for inclusion:-

1   The Policy Statement will identify to the force that there are certain essential functions and services which are being provided and which must be maintained. There is a danger when organisational change is being implemented that officers through enthusiasm for the change process will neglect essential activities.

2   Areas of special concern and priorities for improvements will be stated. Limitations in resources such as manpower, vehicles and so forth must be identified and any policy constraints such as a prohibition on types of policing methods must be contained within the statement.

3   Levels of responsibility and accountability will be described in the Policy Statement and the autonomous operational unit must be defined. The appropriate autonomous operational unit will almost certainly be the sub-division as it controls sufficient resources to provide a degree of flexibility but it is not too large and remote from the policing problems of small communities.

4   The Policy Statement will define the means by which the community will be able to contribute to tactical policy making and influence police operations.

5   The boundaries of police responsibilities must be established and related to the responsibilities of local highways authorities, social services, prosecuting solicitors departments, the courts

and so forth.

6   The role of headquarters departments will be defined and their contributions towards the operational effectiveness and efficiency of the force will be determined.

7   Where constraints to improvements in operational effectiveness have been identified the Policy Statement must show how attempts will be made to remove them. A short fall in resources may be met through reducing the overtime budget and using the money saved to purchase equipment. Deficiencies in management expertise amongst officers may be resolved by additional training. Inappropriate workloads on uniformed constables may be relieved by taking some crime reports by telephone.

Before the force prepares the Policy Statement the chief officer will have decided what he wants the force to achieve in the year ahead. Almost certainly there will be improvements in operational effectiveness which can be achieved in the short term. However, the management review will identify many problems related to resources, organisation, procedures and administration which the force will have to address before further improvements in operational effectiveness can be achieved. The chief constable will have to decide the extent to which he will commit time and resources to addressing these organisational and management development matters. The commitment of resources can be seen as investments for the future as benefits may not be achieved immediately.

Stage 5 – Implementing Change

So far, facts have been gathered and analysed in relation to the existing situation. The future aims of the force have been defined in the Policy Statement. The really difficult achievement in the management of organisation is the translation of plans into actions and results. At this point the focus moves from the chief officer to the operational units, the sub-divisions and departments. They have their own assessment of their strengths and weaknesses, they have had the opportunity to propose strategies for improving effectiveness and they are aware of the constraints. The time has arrived for them to organise their resources, implement the plans and control and evaluate the work. These three phases of the management cycle were described in detail in Chapter 2 and Figures 2.3, 2.4 and 2.5. At this stage officers responsible for pursuing the chief officer's policy have to ask themselves a series of questions and identify some basic requirements in relation to each phase. These questions and requirements can be summarised as follows:-

Organising Phase

Questions

How will the preferred strategy be implemented?

What resources will be used to implement the preferred strategy?
How will tasks and responsibilities be assigned to individuals and groups?
What are the present procedures, systems and tasks of the working unit and individuals?

Basic Requirements

The constituent tasks of the strategy must be identified.
Having identified the constituent tasks, the persons who will have responsibilities for performing those tasks and for the management and control of the tasks, must be identified.
The people who have been identified must be placed within some formal organisational structure.
The individuals must possess the necessary knowledge, skills and attitudes to perform the tasks.
If individuals are not qualified for the tasks, then training must be available to ensure they are brought to the required standards.
Support required from elsewhere, for example, headquarters support services, must be identified and included in the organising phase.

Implementation Phase

Questions

How should the strategy be started?
Have all the preparations been completed?

Are all the resources available?

Are all the people involved prepared and committed to the strategy?

Basic Requirements

Ideally the people who are going to perform the tasks have been involved in the preparation of plans and the organisation. At this stage all individuals should have been identified, briefed and where necessary trained for their new tasks. Individuals must be aware of their roles, tasks or responsibilities and levels of authority. Individuals must be clear as to the objectives to be achieved. Individuals must understand the criteria on which they will be evaluated.

Controlling/Evaluating

Questions

Who will be responsible for controlling and evaluating?
At what stage and at what frequency will formal evaluations be performed?
What has been achieved?

Basic Requirements

Formal mechanisms must have been established in the planning phase for monitoring and evaluating. The tasks of monitoring and evaluating must have been assigned during the organising phase to individuals or groups. The criteria on which the monitoring and evaluating will take place will have been identified during the planning phase. The implementation will have occurred in a way which encourages control through motivation; people will want to participate and make the strategy a success. Rewards will be allocated on the basis of objective assessment of what has been achieved by both groups of officers and individuals.

The Force Management System

Although the management stages which follow the planning stage have been clearly defined, there is no guarantee that the force will adopt one common and co-ordinated management system. If this does not happen, then the benefits of the review and the planning stage will be lost. It is now time to examine the requirements of a police management system and propose one option. In this chapter no further developments will be made in the management process, the discussion will be confined to the description of the system. In Chapter 9, we will return to consider the practical application of the system to a police force.

Police work and police organisations require a sensitive and flexible management system. The discretionary nature of police work and the diversity of policing problems encourages the use of a system which allows the greatest possible freedom to operational officers. However, the legal accountability of chief constables requires the freedom of operational officers to be exercised within strict parameters. Policing By Objectives (PBO) is a management system which satisfies these needs and provides a framework where sustained organisation development and improvement can be achieved. [1]

Policing by Objectives was developed by Val Lubans and James Edgar following a review of the use of Management By Objectives by police forces in the United States. The principles and definitions used to describe PBO in this text are directly attributable to those authors.

PBO is a process built upon three basic management concepts – planning (including organising), implementation and evaluation. The planning stage is usually the most comprehensive and time consuming as it involves a detailed review and assessment of the present performance of the force, followed by a statement of targets for future development. The result of this process as we have seen is the publication of the Policy Statement. In the next stage, Step 2, the general strategic policy is refined into specific Goals which define the force-wide priorities; in the third stage, Step 3, Objectives are defined which are followed in the fourth stage by Action Plans, Step 4. Implementation takes place in Step 5, which is followed by evaluation in Step 6. The process is illustrated in Figure 8.6.

Figure 8.6   Basic PBO cycle

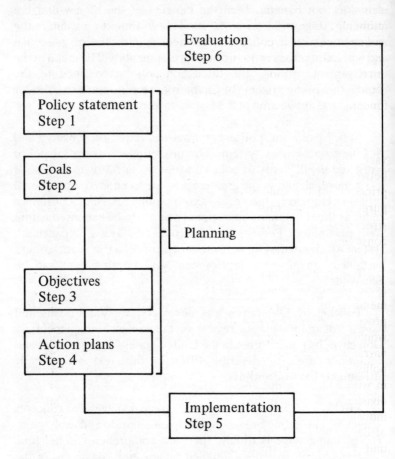

Based on the model at p.23, 'Policing by Objectives', by V.A. Lubans and J.M. Edgar.

PBO is a systematic approach to management in which every element has a specific function to achieve a specific result, and although the model is infinitely flexible the underlying rationale and purpose of each constituent element should not be changed. If and when alterations are made, they should be carefully considered in relation to the model as a whole, as a single structural change could significantly affect changes elsewhere in the model, causing fundamental damage.

The scale upon which PBO is implemented within a force will vary according to circumstances, for example the differences between a force-wide and a step-by-step approach. However, the principles of the concept will remain unchanged and the central purpose will be identical, namely to ensure that Action Plans on the street are a response to the strategic policy established by the chief constable.

The systematic approach of PBO requires the force to be clear as to the duties and responsibilities of the various parts and members of the force. The following chapters will describe the process of implementing PBO from the viewpoint of officers who would actually be engaged in the process. By using this method the narrative can be directly used as an action guide for improving police management. The reader must assume the imaginary force in which this concept is being adopted has designated the sub-division as the primary operational unit. Having made this decision individual and collective responsibilities are based on the principle of decentralised decision making based upon the sub-divisional unit. This style of management attempts to give the greatest degree of independence of action to all members of the force, whilst ensuring the overall control and accountability of the chief constable. Therefore parameters within which this discretion may be exercised can be set, responsibilities clearly stated and management communications systems established.

The crucial role played by the communication systems in an organisation was discussed in Chapter 7. Co-operation and the free exchanges of ideas and information are keys to the successful implementation of PBO. The Linking Pin model shown in Figure 8.7 forms an important element of PBO by providing a structure for top-down and bottom-up communication. Under this system, decisions by management at the top of the structure are made after

Figure 8.7 The linking pin communication and planning model

Based on the model on p.22 of 'Policing by Objectives' by V.A. Lubans and J.M. Edgar

consultation with officers lower down the structure. Commonsense suggests, before setting Goals, chief superintendents should consult their superintendents to help in the analysis of a problem. The community is involved in the planning process, either as individuals or through representatives, and this is shown at the top of the Linking Pin model. The degree of involvement of the community in the preparation of the Policy Statement is a matter for the chief officer but, by including them in the model, a commitment to real police-public consultation is demonstrated.

The Linking Pin model defines a number of groups where discussions occur and where decisions are made. The Policy Statement is produced by the Executive Planning Group following the internal force review and consultation with the community. The senior officers who are involved in the Executive Planning Group attend the Chief Constable's Policy Group where the Goal setting process is conducted with chief superintendents. At the next level, chief superintendents and their superintendents are concerned with establishing Objectives for each sub-division. The forum for this process is the Objective Planning Group. Finally, individual superintendents meet with the officers on their sub-division in the Sub-Divisional Planning Group. In most police forces these forums already exist as the Chief Superintendents Conference, Divisional Superintendents' Conference, and Sub-Divisional Liaison Meetings. Therefore the PBO process is building on existing structures and provides a co-ordinated purpose for these groups.

Overview Of Policing By Objectives

Step 1 – Policy Statement

The Policy Statement is produced following the detailed force review. The results of the review, which reflected the desires and needs of the public as expressed either directly or through their elected representatives, provided the foundation from which the Policy Statement was produced. This document is the ultimate responsibility of the chief constable who is publically accountable for the force.

Step 2 – Goals

When Step 1 is complete, the force has a clear statement of its policy direction and priorities. This is the overall plan, and the following stages, Steps 2 to 4, translate through a refining process general policy into specific actions to achieve the overall result. Goals are the first stage in this process, and their purpose is to co-ordinate the efforts of all sections of the force towards achieving the results which are required by the Policy Statement.

To take the very simple illustration of seeking to improve road safety, it is obvious many officers can do things which may achieve this result, but if these activities are not co-ordinated across the force, the actions of one group of officers may conflict with the actions of another group. For example, one sub-divisional commander might favour a strong policy of enforcing the Construction and Use Regulations, whereas another might prefer to caution offenders for all but the most serious offences. Both strategies have their advantages and disadvantages, but the chances of a person being prosecuted should not be dependant upon the sub-division on which he was reported.

It will be the responsibility of divisional and departmental chief superintendents to prepare Provisional Goals based upon their own divisions or department's problems and priorities. These Provisional Goals will be prepared after an examination and analysis of the particular problems facing the division or department, as related to matters contained in the Policy Statement. When the Provisional Goals are submitted to the Chief Constable's Policy Group, they will be accompanied by a narrative description of the reason for each Goal.

The Chief Constable's Policy Group will review the Provisional Goals submitted. Areas of common interest, overlap of responsibilities, demands for specialist resources, information needs and training requirements, will be identified. During this review, the Goal Statement for the force will be agreed by the Chief Constable's Policy Group. The Goal Statement will then be prepared and contain a narrative description of the reasons for individual Goals, thus providing a greater understanding of the priorities to be pursued at the Objectives setting stage.

164

Step 3 – Objectives

The central purpose of Goals is to provide a framework for forcewide co-ordination of effort and resources. Therefore Goals will always be formulated as a result of an analysis of real problems which affect specific parts of the force, however they will be published in a form which makes them generally applicable throughout the force. It is in the process of setting Objectives that the particular concerns of a geographical area (sub-division) or department are to the fore. When the Goal Statement is published it will include some descriptions of specific problems which may affect one division or department. These general observations should be considered in the detailed analysis which is to be conducted by the person responsible for setting Objectives. The majority of Objectives will be set by sub-divisional superintendents, who will consult with their officers when the force Goals are published.

A detailed description of the Objectives setting process is described later, but it can be briefly summarised as follows; when the Goals are published, the sub-divisional superintendent will assess his sub-division's performance in the light of the Goals, and after consultation with his officers produce Provisional Objectives, which will be submitted to the divisional chief superintendent for confirmation. When the chief superintendent has agreed and confirmed the Objectives, they will be returned to the sub-division for Step 4 to be undertaken.

Step 4 – Action Plans

During the process of formulating Objectives it is recommended that Provisional Action Plans be prepared, as this process allows officers to consider possible courses of action in a practical and realistic way. Abstract plans which cannot be implemented in the real world are less than helpful. A considerable degree of flexibility is envisaged in this part of the process, but it is recommended that some written record of Action Plans be maintained. This will assist in establishing which of the Provisional Action Plans are actually used, and to what success.

In many respects this is the most radically different aspect of police management to be adopted by the force and is probably the most difficult. It will be a test of the combined abilities and commitment of sub-divisional personnel, and in particular, the management capabilities of the sub-divisional superintendent.

Step 5 – Implementation

In many respects the implementation of Action Plans will not radically alter the activities which officers are already performing. PBO is not a magic solution to crime and public disorder. However, the force will become more concerned with why officers are doing these activities and the results they produce. Traffic process will not be done for the sake of it, but rather it will be part of an Action Plan designed to 'reduce road accidents' or 'reduce complaints from the public about speeding vehicles' or 'reduce the annoyance caused by illegally parked cars near a Bingo Hall'. Furthermore, the activities of several officers will be co-ordinated towards the same results, and the impact of these actions monitored and evaluated. It must not be forgotten that all the other police activities of servicing calls from the public, attending court, maintaining public order at football matches and so forth will be continuing as before.

Step 6 – Evaluation

It might be argued by some that Action Planning does not represent a radical innovation in police management. If there is some validity for such discussion concerning Action Planning, the same cannot be said for Evaluation. It is in the area of evaluating results that police management is most vulnerable, and this part of the PBO model does represent significant innovation.

The process of setting Action Plans involves a requirement to monitor the results achieved from their implementation, thus, evaluation is a continuous process in one form or another. The degree of evaluation on the sub-division will be a matter for the sub-division in consultation with the divisional commander, but it should not become an end in itself. In the first instance, a force review will be conducted after the first year of operation. This will involve the submission of an evaluation report from sub-divisions to divisional commanders, who will produce a composite report covering their division for submission to headquarters. This review will form the basis on which the next cycle in the PBO process will be formulated.

Organisation Development

The review process and the Policy Statement made a distinction between the operational issues and organisation and management development (Figure 8.1). The management process which followed the publication of the Policy Statement reinforced the distinction by separating Performance Goals, which concern operational improvements, and Development Goals which draw attention to the need to improve management support, organisation procedures and so forth. Both Performance and Development Goals will follow the basic management cycle (Figure 2.1) but in the case of Development Goals, there may be no reason to specify Objectives and Action Plans. Consider the introduction of word processing to sub-divisions to improve the productivity of existing typists. The implementation will follow an existing procedure within the force and therefore the identification of intermediate steps in the form of Objectives and Action Plans would be superfluous. The result will be achieved when the equipment is installed and taken into use, therefore the outcome measure is obvious. The rationale for introducing the equipment was based on a need to improve the productivity of existing typing staff to reduce the amount of typing done by police officers. In these circumstances a Performance Goal could be defined concerning a reduction in man hours spent by police officers in typing and clerical work. This Goal should have Objectives and Action Plans produced because it will be the responsibility of the sub-division to evaluate the contribution made by the equipment towards improving their use of time. In most cases headquarters departments will have the responsibility for implementing actions in response to Development Goals, but operational officers will evaluate the organisational and management improvements which may be achieved. This distinction is important, just as community relations activities cannot be assumed to be successful without direct evaluation from the public, so neither can changes made in the support provided by headquarters be assumed to be successful without direct evaluation by operational officers.

The PBO Co-ordinator

The review was co-ordinated on behalf of the chief officer by an officer or group of officers who provided a focal point for the process and produced the composite review report. The PBO process requires co-ordination and administration, particularly at the beginning and end of the management cycle. An officer or group must be given the responsibility for overseeing the process and providing day to day co-ordination. This person will be called the PBO Co-ordinator, and he should be able to have direct access to the chief officer to ensure problems can be solved as quickly as possible.

References

1 Lubans, V. A., and Edgar, J. M., *Policing By Objectives*, Hartford, Conn: The Social Development Corporation (1979).

9   Goals and Objectives

Introduction

Chapter 8 considered methods of preparing the police force to adopt methods to improve its effectiveness and efficiency. The management review involved the entire force in a consideration of its existing strengths and weaknesses and formed the basis of the chief officer's Policy Statement.

Experience has shown, for example in the case of Unit Beat Policing, that improvements in police effectiveness do not happen by chance, they will only occur through the conscious efforts of all concerned. Therefore, to make progress from the Policy Statement to implement necessary changes to the force, there is a need which was identified in Chapter 8, for a management process to co-ordinate activities. Policing By Objectives contains all the necessary elements to achieve significant improvements in the cost effective use of police resources. In this chapter the development of Goals and Objectives will be described to enable police officers with management responsibilities to adopt this system.

The Policy Statement provides a description of the overall view of the force. The first requirement is to refine the broad statement of intent into specific targets to be addressed, identifying those matters where immediate steps can be taken to improve performance and other matters where developments will be required within the force before operational improvements can be achieved. Thus Goals identify targets for the force as a whole. The purpose of Objectives is to identify specific measurable improvements which the operational units, sub-divisions or squads, will be seeking to achieve. It is likely that every operational unit in the force will not set objectives for every Goal, but will identify their specific problems and address those rather than seek a broad brush approach.

The learning objectives of this chapter are:-

1   To understand the link between the Policy Statement and Goals.

2   To be able to define a Goal.

3   To be able to distinguish between Performance, Maintenance and Developmental Goals.

4   To understand and be able to apply the Goal setting methods.

5   To understand the role and functions of the Administrative Directions within the context of the Goal Statement.

6   To understand the link between Goals and Objectives.

7   To be able to define an Objective.

8   To understand the need to define a measurable result when setting an Objective.

9   To understand and be able to apply the Objective setting methods.

Goals

The purpose of Goals is to provide more specific direction to police management planners and is the managerial link between the Policy Statement and Objectives. The centre of concern at this stage is to determine the specific targets which are to be developed from the Policy Statement.

Definition

A Goal is defined as:-

a simple, single sentenced expression which indicates, at a minimum, a result or end state to be achieved.

Therefore a Goal will always begin with the word 'To', followed by a declaration of a desired result. For example, a simple Goal might be:-

To reduce the number of burglaries.

In some circumstances, it may be appropriate to add a qualifying phrase to the Goal:-

To reduce the number of burglaries, *without incurring additional overtime costs* .

However, such a qualifying phrase may apply to all Goals set by the force and, therefore, such a qualifier may instead be contained in the Administrative Directions which will be attached to the Goal Statement.

Types Of Goal

An essential pre-requisite of every Goal is that it should be linked directly to the Policy Statement and, by so doing, should achieve some tangible and measurable result. Thus, Performance Goals, such as the Goal 'to reduce the number of burglaries' can be understood and measured. It is possible for the majority of Goals to be written as Performance Goals. However, it is all too easy in management change programmes for the organisation, either through enthusiam or by neglect, to lose sight of the need to maintain particular activities at their current level. For example, a sub-division may produce an innovative and sophisticated Action Plan to combat burglaries in dwelling houses, but to pursue that Action Plan, may require manpower resources that are currently being expended upon other essential tasks, such as responding to calls from the public for police services. Thus, the execution of this Action Plan may severely jeopardise the policing capacity to respond to calls, thereby damaging the service to the public and, as a consequence, public satisfaction with the police.

To safeguard these essential functions of the force, it will be seen as entirely appropriate to clearly specify *Maintenance Goals* with a view to formally establishing throughout the force those tasks and activities which must be maintained at their present level of efficiency and effectiveness. To illustrate, such a Maintenance Goal could be written:-

To maintain the current response times to all calls from the public which are defined as emergencies.

The overview of PBO in Chapter 8 introduced the concept of Development Goals to facilitate the improvements in the management and organisation of the force. The achievement of Development Goals will usually be the primary responsibility of headquarters departments although they could be linked to Performance Goals to be pursued by operational officers. Consider the example of the provision of typing services to sub-divisional officers where it has been established during the review process that constables spend on average one hour per day typing. Officers are obliged to do their own typing because the typing staff cannot cope with the workload generated by the sub-division. As there can be no increse in typing staff the introduction of technology in the form of dictation equipment and word processing could be adopted as a means of improving productivity. Thus a Development Goal could be defined as follows:-

To provide an integrated dictation and word processing facility on each sub-division.

The Development Goal could be linked to a Performance Goal "to reduce the time spent by officers on typing". This Goal would be used to define Objectives to measure the amount of time saved by officers which would vary between sub-divisions depending on workload.

The Goal-Setting Strategy

Goals are anchored to two previous force initiatives. They are linked, in the first instance, to the Policy Statement which was itself directly related to the force review. Thus the Policy Statement and the management review reports should be seen as the cornerstones of the Goal-setting process. It is probably most helpful to conceive Goal-setting as the discipline of asking a series of questions in sequence, proceeding from one question to the next, after having clearly established an answer to the preceding question. This method re-emphasises the disciplined planning which is the base of PBO. It is likely that some of the questions which will be asked in this process will have been raised in the management review process. If this is the case, then the answers given in that review can be used to assist the preparation of Goals.

Question 1

What are the key priority areas identified within the Policy Statement?

The Policy Statement is unlikely to contain any radical departure from the generally accepted notions of police duties and responsibilities. The policy areas which are likely to be identified cover such issues as the control and reduction of crime, improvement of road safety, enhancement of public tranquillity, improvement of community attitudes towards the police, the improvement in skills and personal performance of officers, and a general requirement to increase the efficiency and effectiveness of the Force. Having recognised the broad areas it is necessary to establish reasonable targets, as it is unlikely that resources will be available to pursue simultaneously, and with the same vigour, all matters expressed within the Policy Statement. Thus to assist in determining priorities, the second question can be posed.

Question 2

What is it that tells us we have a problem in this policy area?

It is unnecessary to restate the sources of data available to answer this question, but briefly they have been evolved through the review process, through public consultation and possibly by means of a social survey conducted in the community. Therefore, based upon such data, it should be possible to identify those specific issues which are more critical than others.

For example, in respect of crime, burglary in dwelling houses may stand out as a matter of particular concern, not only to the police but to the public. Consequently, when examining the area of crime control burglary may head the list. In terms of public tranquillity, which is a more general concept, it may be possible to identify such things as football matches, locations of public resort in town centres and municipal housing estates, as places which are sources of public complaint and concern respecting the quality of public order. Thus in setting a Goal relating to public tranquillity, it might be useful to specify particular areas of concern to the force. Care should be taken in making such specifications however, as this approach will inevitably constrain the range of options available to those members of the force who are responsible for Objectives and Action Plans.

It is wise to ask the following questions before concluding discussions on priorities.

Question 3

Are we satisfied we have sufficient information available on which to answer Question 2?

Despite the information that has been produced during the review process, the need for further specific information should not be overlooked. If there are found to be significant shortcomings within the management information system, then consideration should be given to specifying Development Goals which will either be the responsibility of some headquarters' support group, or be delegated to sub-divisions to address on their own initiatives.

Having determined priorities and explored the exact nature of the problem, the next stage can be examined.

Question 4

Are these problems which have been identified likely to be solved either fully or in part by police action?

The answer to this question is almost certain to be 'Yes' as otherwise they would not have formed part of the original Policy Statement. Having established the problems are a matter for the police, it is important to determine the range of police methods which may be appropriate when seeking the solutions.

174

Question 5

What can the Force do to solve these problems?

At this point, the quality of consultation which has been undertaken by the members of the group formed to establish Goals will be shown. In consultation with sub-divisional commanders, who will in turn have consulted their own officers, this part of the Goal-setting process should allow some exploration of particular methods which could be used. This process, however, should not be seen as one which will constrain officers lower in the force at the Objective-setting and Action Planning level, as it will be they who will formulate specific plans. But if these considerations are not undertaken at the Goal-setting stage, Goals may be set which will require the commitment of personnel who are not available, or the use of equipment that has not been provided for in the budget, or requires officers to operate at a performance level for which they have neither the training nor the skills to undertake.

A consideration of possible strategies can be expressed in the Administrative Directions accompanying the Goals, to provide personnel at the Objective-setting and Action-Planning stages with a broad framework within which to operate. It should not be forgotten that PBO is not a recipe for anarchy, nor is it rigid centralised control, but rather a balance between what the policy makers decide is appropriate at the policy level, pursued within a framework which gives freedom for innovation and imagination at the point of action.

The next question is closely linked to the consideration of possible strategies.

Question 6

Do we have sufficient resources?

Once again, without predetermining the Action Plans to be implemented by operational officers, it is important for those officers responsible for setting Goals to have a good understanding of the resources, particularly in terms of discretionary time available for officers to devote to Action Plans.

Present management information systems may not be able to measure accurately the amount of time which is available for use by uniformed and detective officers in pursuing Action Plans. This is a critical deficiency and steps should be taken to provide this information in the future. For the purposes of the first cycle of the goal-setting process, professional judgement must be exercised to ensure the Goals are realistic in terms of probable resources. A further safeguard could be to allow sub-divisions to establish their priorities from the Goals, and set Objectives within the confines of their own restricted knowledge of resources.

An evaluation of performance is an integral part of PBO, the final question must be formed thus:-

Question 7

What will be the measures which show that the Goal has been achieved?

Generally, measures need only be specified for Performance Goals but they may be appropriate in other cases, say in maintaining the standard of public satisfaction to response to calls as measured by an attitude survey. It will be a matter of judgement where performance measures are appropriate and necessary, but it is a factor which the Goal-setting group must address so as to ensure operational officers know the grounds on which they are going to be evaluated.

Having considered all the above questions, Goals can then be set within the context of the Policy Statment. There can be no hard and fast rules as to how many Goals are sufficient or appropriate. This again is a matter for professional judgement. However, as a general guide it is better to have too few Goals than too many. After all, the quality of the force will not be judged on the total number of Goals it produced or was pursuing. Quality will be determined on the *results* achieved towards those Goals, and it is better therefore to have ten Goals and achieve eight rather than twenty Goals and achieve only five.

The process of setting Development Goals can follow a similar sequence of questioning to avoid drawing conclusions about a solution before the problem has been fully understood. To return to the problem of police officers spending time on typing, in earlier references the problem was said to be related to low productivity of typists which could be improved by introducing technology. However, another reason for officers having to type their own reports could be the force requirement to produce certain reports quickly and thus officers are obliged to type their own reports at times when typists are not at work. The solution to this latter problem would not necessarily be achieved through new technology.

Maintenance Goals can serve the useful purpose of ensuring officers do not fail to recognise the importance of, and their responsibility towards, maintaining the levels of service achieved in the past. In subsequent years, such Maintenance Goals may be implicit and not necessarily articulated.

Goals are intended to provide a management link between the Policy Statement and Objectives. Whilst Goals therefore form, in the abstract, targets to be addressed, they also form a vital management function of directing the attention, and subsequently the activities, of the members of the force by co-ordinating efforts in a force-wide commitment towards their achievement.

The Goal-setting process provides a forum in which the co-ordination of various parts of the force, in particular support services, can be achieved. It is at this stage that scarce resources such as speed monitoring equipment, training courses and the like, can be apportioned throughout the force, or set within some framework whereby all sub-divisions have an equal opportunity to share in these resources as and when they are required. Thus Goals must be sufficiently wide to allow flexibility within the subsequent stages of PBO, but they must also be sufficiently clear to ensure the policy makers of the force can bring direction and priorities towards the Objective-setting and Action-Planning process. To this end, Goals should be accompanied by Administrative Directions or general instructions.

Administrative Directions

There are no absolute rules as to what should be contained within the Administrative Directions accompanying the Goal

Statement. However, the following may help to establish some of the more important issues.

It may be useful to specify the *range* of the Goal. For example, some Goals may have a definite life such as one which demands the training of sergeants in Action Planning. When all the sergeants have been trained, that Goal will cease to be relevant. However, a Goal aimed at reducing the number of burglaries could be conceived as having a continuous life, as it is unlikely the police will totally eradicate the crime, and therefore in reality such a Goal has an infinite range.

Some Goals may apply to a number of sections of the force. As an example, Goals directed towards the prevention of crime may involve uniformed patrol officers, but also include specialists such as the crime prevention and community relations officers, who may include crime prevention information in their presentations to public groups. Thus it is helpful in the Administrative Directions to establish relative to particular Goals, those parts of the force who are expected to contribute to the achievement of the Goal and, furthermore, how the co-ordination of effort between the various sections of the force will be achieved.

It has been noted earlier there is considerable danger in specifying within the Goal Statement and/or the Administrative Directions, suggestions as to how Goals should be achieved. Policy considerations may, however, oblige the group setting Goals to determine from the outset that certain methods will not be pursued. For example, the saturation policing of an area may be ruled out on grounds of policy as being inappropriate. However within the provisos set out above, it may be appropriate to establish a general range of strategies which can be used to pursue a particular Goal, providing sufficient freedom is allowed to members of the force to develop their own solutions.

The Administrative Directions will also include an assessment of why each Goal is being stipulated. To illustrate, a Goal may be generally relevant to the whole force, such as a Goal 'to reduce the rate of increase in suppressible crime', but in some parts of the force area, burglary may be the most important crime in terms of recent increases; whereas in another part of the force, robberies and thefts from the person may be a matter of greater concern. These differences of emphasis can be identified by, in this example, divisional commanders. Whilst it is essential that a Goal is seen as a directive to the force, a divisional commander or head of a department might wish to point out specific considerations to guide his officers in particular. In these circumstances it would be appropriate to accommodate such matters in the Administrative Directions. (See Example Figure 9.1).

When the Policy Statement is published, chief superintendents will review it in the context of their own areas of responsibility. Through the process described above, they will produce Provisional Goals which will be discussed at a meeting of all chief superintendents held prior to the Chief Constable's Policy Group meeting. This meeting will allow chief superintendents to exchange ideas and modify or amend their own ideas in the light of these discussions. It will assist their deliberations if some standardisation is introduced into the format of the presentation of Provisional Goals. A standard format which may be useful is shown on the Provisional Goals Worksheet (Figure 9.2). The narrative under each heading will allow greater understanding of the context of the proposed Goal, and will also provide material for inclusion in the Goal Statement or Administrative Directions.

Following the preliminary meeting of chief superintendents, the Provisional Goals will be submitted to the PBO Co-ordinator at headquarters for submission to the Chief Constable's Policy Group. The Policy Group will confirm the Goals, with any necessary amendments, and the PBO Co-ordinator will then prepare the Goal Statement and Administration Directions which will be published to the force.

Objectives

Introduction

Objectives are shown in Figure 8.6 as the third stage in the planning process. They provide the link between Goals and Action Plans. The Goals discussed in the preceding section will have been set by this time, and they should be seen as establishing the general policy directives and priorities for the force as a whole. Force Goals

Figure 9.1   Goal statement 1984

Crime control

The Policy Statement identified the control and reduction in crime as a primary responsibility of the force. The reviews that have been undertaken by divisional chief superintendents and the detective chief superintendent have identified some problems which concern the force as a whole, and some crime problems which fortunately only affect some areas within the county. The crime of burglary is one which affects the whole force and is one which causes great concern and distress for the victims. Therefore we will seek to reduce the rate of this crime in the county during the coming year. Although thefts of and from motor vehicles account for almost a quarter of our reported crime, these crimes are more likely to occur in large car parks, housing estates where cars are parked overnight and other specific locations. Therefore these crimes are ones which are of more concern to some sub-divisions than others, however, due to the large numbers of such offences it is believed to be sufficiently important to require action on the part of the force to control these crimes.

For 1984, Goals in the area of crime control will be as follows:

Goal 1   To reduce the number of burglaries.

Goal 2   To reduce the number of thefts of motor vehicles.

Goal 3   To increase the number of persons arrested for thefts from motor vehicles.

Figure 9.2 Provisional goals worksheet

1 **General area of concern**
   (Policy statement para. no.)

2 **Brief statement of problem**

3 **Description of the nature of the problem**
   (stating sources of information and measures/indicators)

4 **Additional information requirement**

5 **Sub-divisions or department effected**

6 **Resources available**

7 **Possible strategies**

8 **Results measurement**

9 **Provisional goal:-**

will have a relevance to every sub-division, but there will be differences in the degree to which a specific problem applies to individual sub-divisions. For example, the pattern and frequency of road accidents may vary throughout the force. It is equally likely that the capacity for police to influence and thereby reduce the number of road accidents will also vary throughout the force. It must be remembered there is nothing in the PBO model which requires police officers to achieve miracles, or indeed achieve the impossible. Policing by Objectives requires police managers to analyse their problems and direct resources at solving those problems, based on a realistic assessment of the likely results to be achieved.

Therefore, the role of Objectives is to allow sub-divisional superintendents to analyse their own particular problems within the context of force-wide Goals, and having made the analysis, to adopt Objectives in an order of priority which reflects their own specific requirements and capacity to respond to those problems. Objectives thus are the link between Goals and Action plans. Their purpose is to describe *what* is going to be achieved and *when* , and the time scale in which those results are going to be measured.

Definition

An Objective can be defined as:-

A single sentence statement of a specific, measurable result to be achieved within a given time period.

When an Objective is written it must identify a *specific measurable result* . If an Objective is not capable of being measured, then it is not possible to determine whether the problem being addressed has become more or less serious during the period under review. An Objective must also specify the *time period* during which it is to run. Once again, this is essential for the evaluation process.

When an Objective is written, the question should be asked, "If I achieve this Objective, what will it contribute to achieving a Goal". It is possible to write an Objective which addresses a specific problem on the sub-division and subsequently results in a solution, without contributing to the achievement of a Goal. If that is the prospect and there are limited resources on the sub-division, then it may not be appropriate to pursue such an Objective.

The definition of an Objective given above refers specifically to Performance Objectives. However, in the same manner as there are Maintenance and Development Goals it is possible to define Maintenance and Development Objectives. For example, a sub-divisional commander may be concerned that the quality of police response to emergency calls could become reduced through diverting resources into other activities. He may therefore write a Maintenance Objective with a view to preserving existing standards.

During the Action Planning consultations which lead to the formulation of Objectives, it may be apparent there are insufficient sources of data on the sub-division to identify a specific problem. In these circumstances, it may be necessary to define a Development Objective which directs all or some of the officers on the sub-division to produce better information, towards identifying that specific problem. Performance Objectives could then be defined when the information becomes available.

The Measurable Result

An Objective must specify in measurable terms, a result which is to be achieved. In some cases measurement can be relatively straightforward, for example, if the number of burglaries in dwellings is known, then any change in the number gives a direct measure of a result. In reality, such direct measures are not easy to identify as there may be a number of factors affecting the rate at which burglaries are reported. However, such factors do not prevent these direct measures being employed, providing they are used in the circumstances described below.

The direct measures are called Quantifiable Objectives in PBO, but of equal importance are Qualitative Objectives. A Qualitative Objective is used where the force is endeavouring to improve the quality of the service it provides to the community. Such a Qualitative Objective might be to 'improve police/ community relations during 1984'. It is apparent the measurement of such an Objective is not easy, but it is not impossible.

The necessity to measure Qualitative Objectives can be illustrated by reference to any report which has been written in the past five years concerning community policing. In several of these reports, the reader can find various objectives which are written to describe the purpose of introducing a specific community policing project. However, when the reader turns to the section concerned with evaluation, if indeed such a section exists, it is difficult and in most cases even impossible, to determine the real measurable results which have been achieved in terms of improving police/community relations. In some instances substantial claims are made for the success of such schemes, based upon virtually no evidence apart from subjective and anecdotal references.

Objectives should only be written if they are in response to some specific problem which has been identified on the sub-division. If this problem has been identified and exists in reality, rather than in the imagination of a well-meaning police manager, the evidence that disclosed the problem can be used as an *indicator* to develop a measure of improvements. For example, public dissatisfaction with the police may be indicated by the results of a social survey conducted in the force area, which shows that the public are unhappy about the attitude taken by officers when responding to calls for help from the public. The public might also be dissatisfied with the failure of police officers to communicate the result of enquiries or cases to witnesses and complainants. Letters may be received which criticise officers for being discourteous when reporting motorists for traffic offences. Complaints may be received from the public who state when they telephone their local police station, the "telephone rings for several minutes before it is answered".

The range of issues can run from the relatively serious to the minor or trivial. However, if a force examines its relations with the community, there are a number of indicators which may suggest there are problems to be addressed in terms of enhancing public satisfaction with the service they receive. When a qualitative Objective is written, it can specify the particular areas requiring attention in Action Plans, and it will be those indicators capable of measurement which can then be used to establish an improvement in police/community relations. No one indicator should be used on its own, and it is recommended at least three indicators are employed as measures to determine performance in respect of a qualitative Objective.

Who Sets Objectives?

The superintendent of the sub-division will have the specific responsibility for setting Objectives, and these will be confirmed by the chief superintendent. The process of setting Objectives however, relies upon the top down, bottom up planning process of PBO. With this procedure superintendents will consult throughout the sub-division, and each level within the sub-division will have a responsibility for communicating ideas up through the rank structure to the superintendent. It is possible that a sub-divisional group could be established in which all ranks and departments are involved; it could be this forum which consults throughout the sub-division, before sitting together to finally define those Objectives which will be accepted by the sub-divisional commander. There is no right or wrong way by which this consultation should take place, providing it does take place. For the purpose of the exercises given below, the consultation group will be called the Sub-Divisional Planning Group.

How Will The Objectives Be Set?

In the Goal-setting process described in the preceding section, it was suggested those involved should ask themselves a series of questions in a specific sequence. Having answered a question, they can then move on to the next stage. It is recommended in the consultation process which takes place to set Objectives, a similar question and answer format should be adopted.

Having received the Goal Statement and Administrative Directions from the Chief Constable's Policy Group, each Goal should be examined in turn to establish exactly how it relates to the sub-division and the problems being experienced by the police.

Before taking specific examples of Goals and translating them into Objectives, the process can be described in the abstract by going through the series of questions and answers. This process would be undertaken for each of the Goals.

Question 1

In terms of the Goal, what specific problems are we experiencing on this sub-division?

If for example, the Goal in question relates to a reduction in the number of burglaries, then it must be asked if this is a problem relevant to the sub-division. If so, to what parts of the sub-division is it a problem and, more specifically, what exactly is the nature of the problem? In order to answer these questions, it will be necessary to make a careful analysis of current management information. It is possible of course this process will highlight deficiencies in the management information system. Should this happen it may preclude a detailed analysis of the problem at this stage, and steps will have to be taken to remedy the deficiency before an Objective can be proposed.

If the Sub-Divisional Planning Group is satisfied it has sufficient information to answer this question, then it can proceed to Question 2.

Question 2

Given the scope and nature of the problem, what can we do on this sub-division to solve the problem?

An essential component of any Objective is to determine what is going to be achieved in a given time period. For example, are we going to reduce burglaries by 5 per cent, 10 per cent or by an even more ambitious proportion? Setting the target for an Objective can never be an exact science. However, the distance which the leap of faith must make in determining the target can be significantly reduced by the quality of the analysis undertaken in response to Question 1, and second, by a careful consideration of the possible methods which could be applied to solve the problem.

Therefore, although Action Plans will be discussed in more detail in the next chapter, at this stage it is necessary to consider Provisional Action Plans, and here as many ideas as possible should be obtained on the sub-division and considered, analysed and assessed. It would not be appropriate at this stage to undertake detailed Action Planning, but the Sub-Divisional Planning Group should ensure they have the resources to carry out a proposed Action Plan. They should consider the cost/benefits of prospective Action Plans, the degree of support required from other sections of the force, for example the traffic department, any special skills or training which may be required, and any additional equipment which will be necessary to carry through the Action Plan.

Having considered the nature of the problem and discussed what could possibly be done to solve it, the subsequent evaluation has to be considered.

Question 3

How will we know we have achieved our Objective; in other words, what measures will we use?

Once again, we turn to the critical and difficult issue of measurement. Measures of police effectiveness have been elusive in the past but, under the PBO process, the method of analysis and planning which is fundamental to the model actually helps to identify things that can be measured. To answer Question 1, the analysis undertaken to identify the exact nature of the problem will have involved some matters which can form the basis of measurements of effectiveness. For example, in the case of burglary, the number of crimes reported in a given period will form part of the measurement process.

It is essential at this stage of the planning process to consider the measurement of Objectives. If not, the whole system could become discredited should considerable effort be mounted to address an Objective, only to find it is impossible to determine whether the effort made any difference to the size of the problem.

The setting of Objectives will usually be the responsibility of the sub-divisional superintendent. The process will inevitably involve consultation throughout the sub-division but, in the implementation stage, some delegation will be essential to specific members of the sub-division in order to pursue Action Plans. Thus, at this stage, it is important to ask the following question:-

Question 4

Who will be responsible for writing Action Plans to achieve this Objective?

It is necessary at this stage of the planning process to establish individual responsibilities on the sub-division. Whilst all members of the sub-division will have some level of responsibility for Action Plans, the planning, implementation, co-ordination and evaluation of specific Action Plans can be a major task. Therefore, it is essential to avoid defining a range of Objectives which will place an undue burden in subsequent Action Planning on one or two members of the sub-division. If this appears likely, then a number of alternatives should be considered. As an example, the load could be spread between other officers who do not have the primary skills but, nevertheless, would be capable of carrying the Action Plan through, or other work could be delegated further down the structure to leave the individual with more time to perform the additional duties. Alternatively, it may be necessary for Objectives in that particular area to be reduced on the grounds there is insufficient time for officers to co-ordinate and evaluate the Action Plans.

These considerations bring us to the next question:-

Question 5

What resources are available?

The major, yet often neglected, primary resource on the sub-division is the man hours available to perform all the duties, responsibilities and functions required of the sub-division. The measurement of time and, more specifically, the amount of discretionary time which is available on the sub-division, is a crucial prerequisite of PBO. As far as first line personnel are concerned, uniformed patrol officers and detective constables, it is essential to establish they have discretionary time available before being given additional work to perform in connection with Action Plans. Similar considerations are necessary for other ranks within the sub-division who are being given additional functions such as the planning, implementation, co-ordination and evaluation of Action Plans.

This aspect was discussed under the previous question but it cannot be over-emphasised. If say a detective inspector is being made responsible for the implementation of a specific Action Plan directed towards crime control, then it is essential to clearly establish he has sufficient discretionary time in which to plan, co-ordinate and evaluate the Action Plan. If such time is not available, then this matter has to be confronted and solved before any further demands can be made on the officer's time.

When an assessment has been made of the resources available, the final question in the planning process can be asked:-

Question 6

What are the priorities of this sub-division?

The question is most appropriately asked after all the Goals have been considered and the process described above has been undertaken in turn for each Goal. A sub-division would be very fortunate if it had sufficient manpower resources to undertake a number of Action Plans directed towards every Goal. Therefore, it is suggested that all possible Objectives are arranged in an order of priority, and defined and submitted to the divisional commander on the basis of resources available to pursue them.

Setting Objectives – A Case Study

For the purpose of this exercise, we will assume two Goals have been formulated by the Chief Constable's Policy Group. These two Goals have been written thus:-

To reduce the amount of suppressible crime; To enhance public tranquillity.

We will now deal with the Objective-setting process in respect of each Goal. The procedure described below should not be interpreted as the only means by which this process can be undertaken, but rather as a brief description of one method which may be appropriate to the particular circumstances. It should also be understood this is a brief guide, and does not attempt to cover all the issues that may arise in the process of defining sub-divisional Objectives.

Goal No. 1 – To Reduce the Amount of Suppressible Crime

On receiving the Goal Statement from headquarters, the sub-divisional commander requests an analysis of the current crime situation on the sub-division from the detective inspector and the collator. He asks for papers to be prepared for discussion by the Sub-Divisional Planning Group at its first meeting to consider the sub-division's Objectives.

At the initial meeting of the Sub-Divisional Planning Group, it is established from the analysis undertaken within the Sub-Division, that the most significant change in crime patterns during the last three years is a substantial increase in the number of reported burglaries. There appears to have been no additional population influx which could have accounted for this increase, and it is agreed by the Planning Group that a reduction in the increase of burglaries in dwellinghouses should be examined as a possible Objective for the coming year.

At this stage, ideas are floated as to possible explanations for the increase in burglary. The detective inspector and collator are given the task of preparing a more detailed analysis of the burglary pattern on the sub-division, the type of property being stolen, the type of houses which are being attacked, the time of day of offences, any information on the disposal of stolen property, and intelligence concerning the persons who have been arrested and admitted offences of burglary.

At the following meeting of the Sub-Divisional Planning Group, it is established that two distinct burglary patterns exist on the sub-division. The first pattern relates almost exclusively to a municipal housing estate and houses adjoining. Here properties are being attacked during the daytime between 10.00 am and 4.00 pm when cash and small carry away items such as portable radios, jewellery and so forth are being stolen. It has been found from detected offences that juveniles appear to be responsible for the majority of these crimes, and the property is either being sold or exchanged at schools or being disposed of in local second-hand shops.

The second burglary pattern is more difficult to determine but appears to be the work of more professional burglars, who are attacking carefully selected houses and stealing relatively high value property such as televisions, videos, stereos and the like. The sources of disposal of this property are not readily identifiable. The Sub-Divisional Planning Group agrees the first pattern of burglary, which apparently is the work of juveniles, is a matter which can be addressed on the basis of the present information. However, the members also agree the second pattern of burglary requires more detailed analysis, information and intelligence before Action Plans can be proposed.

Members of the Sub-Divisional Planning Group are then asked to consult officers throughout the sub-division, with a view to their proposing possible Action Plans which could be devised to combat the problem of juvenile burglaries. We have now reached the stage where the question concerning problem identification has been asked and answered. We are now posing the question "What can we on the sub-division do, to find a solution to the problem?" (Question 2)

At a subsequent meeting of the Sub-Divisional Planning Group, a number of Provisional Action Plans are suggested by the members. These can be listed as follows:-

1   Following the analysis of the burglaries believed to have been the responsibility of juveniles, a reduction of truancy from local secondary schools is proposed as a means of reducing them. By reducing the number of potential burglars in the neighbourhood, at times when houses are most likely to be unoccupied, the number of burglaries is likely to be reduced. The strategy would involve police officers paying particular attention to young people of school age seen out of school during school hours.

    This plan, it is suggested, would have a deterrent effect on juveniles who are truanting from school. Second, it would provide a basis of intelligence which may establish a pattern of truanting amongst the most severe offenders. Third, it might establish patterns of associates which could be used if a juvenile was arrested for burglary and his associates were known and suspected of being involved.

2   Local publicity to ask members of the public to report young

people who are seen hanging around the street during school hours in suspicious circumstances.

This too, would have a deterrent effect on the juveniles. Second, it would highlight the problem of burglary to the community, thus encouraging citizens to take more care of their property and, third, it should greatly enhance the volume of information coming to the police, and therefore increase the likelihood of a crime in progress being detected.

3   Liaison with local schools, which should ensure they are aware of the police concern with juvenile crime in the area. It might also make them more aware of the truancy problem and encourage them to take steps to assist the police in reducing truancy. Finally, it might also generate a deterrent effect by publicising the police stategy in schools. School teachers could also be encouraged to assist the police, by reporting instances where property is brought into the school for the apparent purpose of being traded between pupils.

4   More frequent visits to second-hand dealers' premises. This strategy might discourage unscrupulous dealers from trading with juveniles, or alert and encourage them to report instances where young people attempt to sell the type of property being stolen from houses.

The Sub-Divisional Planning Group accepts all the Provisional Action Plans as possible methods which could be implemented. The Group's next concern is to establish what measures will be used to determine whether these Action Plans are achieving tangible results if implemented. The overall measure to be used, termed the *primary measure*, will be the number of reported burglaries in dwellinghouses over a specified period. This decision is made as it has been established through the victim survey section of a social survey conducted in the community, that more than 90 per cent of all burglaries in dwellinghouses are reported to the police.

Whilst these figures will form a basis of determining whether the Objective has been achieved or not, there are other measures which may be helpful in identifying the effectiveness of specific Action Plans. Therefore, *secondary measures* must be adopted.

The detailed analysis undertaken on the sub-division has

already suggested measures of effectiveness. It is possible to keep a record, and therefore count, the number of juveniles who are seen out of school between 10.00 a.m. and 4.00 p.m. It may be possible to obtain, with the co-operation of schools, a count of the number of unexplained absences from school both before the Action Plan is implemented and during its implementation. The impact of the publicity campaign encouraging members of the public to report suspicious incidents to the police, can be evaluated by the number of calls received from the public. Furthermore, the number of arrests made for crime directly following calls from the public, can also be measured before and during the Action Planning period. Similarly, it is possible to count the number and frequency of visits to second-hand dealers, the number of occasions on which dealers report suspicious transactions to the police, and the number of persons who are arrested as a result of these calls.

Although a reduction in the number of reported burglaries will indicate a successful achievement of the Objective, it is equally important to ascertain which, if any, of the Action Plans contributed to achieving the Objective. For example, if virtually no property is sold by juvenile housebreakers to second-hand dealers, then the Action Plan of regularly visiting second-hand dealers may be an activity which should be discontinued.

It should also be recognised that this process of evaluation is enhancing the overall fund of knowledge the sub-division has about the way it performs its function. Over the years, it may develop and store a range of Action Plans to counter specific problems which, having been solved, arise again at some later time. At this stage of setting Provisional Action Plans however, the Sub-Divisional Planning Group is only required to ensure there are measures available to be used should these Action Plans be adopted.

During the process described, some duties and responsibilities have already been assigned. For example, the superintendent has been exercising his role as the person responsible for ultimately defining the Objectives. Similarly, the detective inspector and collator have been involved in problem analysis. At this point, however, it is helpful to use the Provisional Action Plans proposed previously, as a means of identifying those officers who will have direct responsibility for implementation, co-ordination and evaluation.

It is unnecessary to describe all the roles that have been outlined in the Provisional Action Plans, but it can be seen that the uniformed patrol officers will have a major responsibility for the observation of juveniles of school age seen on the streets during school hours. It will be a matter for the superintendent's judgement as to who should undertake the school liaison role and, finally, it is likely the detective inspector or the collator will have a role in evaluating the consequences and impact of these Action Plans.

It has been emphasised there is a critical requirement within PBO to establish the amount of time available for devoting to Action Plans. In some cases existing data may not provide Action Planners with an accurate assessment of the amount of time available. However it should be possible to make some reasonable estimates of this time, but it is equally possible that some Action Plans will require little, if any, dedicated time, that is substantial portions of specifically allocated time. For example, the observation and contact with persons on the street is an every day activity of uniformed patrol officers and therefore the proposed Action Plan is not in the least innovative. What is important in respect of the Action Plan, is that the activities will be directed towards specific target areas and, furthermore, the results of those activities will be evaluated. Thus, as well as establishing the amount of time available for Action Plans, it is equally important, at the stage of Provisional Action Planning, to make some realistic estimates of the number of man hours that will be consumed in those Action Plans by the various officers who are involved.

The next stage in the exercise assumes a reduction in the number of burglaries on the sub-division is seen as a priority to be pursued. When all possible Objectives have been explored by the Sub-Divisional Planning Group, the agreed Objectives should be arranged in a list of priorities, and those first in the priority list should be given the first allocation of limited resources.

As a result of the analysis carried out on the sub-division, it is established that twenty five per cent of all burglaries reported during the previous year were committed between 10.00 a.m. and 4.00 p.m. From the detection figures, and an analysis of the M.O., it is estimated the majority of these burglaries were committed by juveniles. It is anticipated the proposed Action Plans could reduce these crimes by half. Accordingly, it is decided to set an Objective viz:-

'*To reduce the rate of burglary in dwellinghouses on the Sub-Division by 10% in 1984*'.

This Objective would then be submitted, together with the other Objectives, to the divisional chief superintendent for ratification.

Goal No. 2 – To Enhance Public Tranquillity

Goal No. 1, which addressed the reduction of suppressible crimes, was very obviously a Performance Goal which led to the development of a *Quantifiable Performance Objective*. The second Goal emphasises the qualitative aspects of the police service and thus we will be looking towards defining a *Qualitative Performance Objective*. However, the strategy adopted will be identical to that undertaken in defining the Quantifiable Performance Objective.

The first step taken by the sub-divisional superintendent on receiving Goal No. 1, was to call upon the services of the detective inspector and collator to analyse the current position using historical data. With Goal No. 2, the sub-divisional superintendent may be in the best position to assess the nature and scope of the problem in relation to public tranquillity. He is the officer who may be a regular visitor at public meetings and the meetings of various residents' and community associations. He may also be responsible for answering letters of complaint from members of the public who are concerned about noise in their area, incidents of drunkenness and so forth. Therefore, the sub-divisional commander may be a person with key information in respect of this Goal. However, even if this is the case, it is likely other members of the sub-division, for example area constables, will have some knowledge of matters affect feelings of public tranquillity. For the purposes of this exercise, we will confine the examination to problems that have been identified on a large municipal housing estate.

When the Sub-Divisional Planning Group meets, it is established that during the previous year on this housing estate, complaints have been received from members of the public and the residents' association concerning the following matters:-

Incidents of drunkenness and rowdiness outside the two public houses on the estate, mainly at closing time.

Vandalism to publicly owned property, in particular telephone kiosks and bus shelters.

Defacing of walls and other amenities on the estate, by the use of spray paint.

Noise and speeding by youths on motor cycles.

The local youth club has been the focus of a number of complaints concerning noise, litter and vandalism in the adjoining area.

As a result of its discussions, the Sub-Divisional Planning Group members are not only aware of the scope and nature of the problem, but they are also able to locate the problem to specific sites within the housing estate, for example, the public houses, youth club and public amenities such as telephone kiosks, bus shelters and so on. There is ample evidence of a problem, and the next issue concerns Action Plans to solve some, if not all, of the various aspects to the problem.

At a subsequent meeting of the Sub-Divisional Planning Group, a number of Action Plans are proposed:-

1. Use directed patrol by uniformed officers who will position themselves at known trouble spots at relevant times in an attempt to deter or, if necessary, enforce laws in relation to drunkenness and public order. This plan would involve officers attending the public houses at closing time, or parking the police car in a prominent position outside the youth club at relevant times, and so forth.

2. Observations on specific known targets of vandalism. Here, surveillance could be carried out either entirely by police officers or with the help of technical equipment such as television cameras or night vision equipment.

3. Specific enforcement of traffic laws in relation to motor-cyclists, having particular regard to licensing and insurance

legislation, and the Construction and Use Regulations relating to exhaust systems.

4. Liaison with the youth club. This could take a variety of forms, such as attending the youth club to give advice to the members and management concerning the nuisance apparently being caused in the locality. It might be thought appropriate for a police officer to become a member of the management committee but, more importantly, it may be useful for the police to encourage local residents to become members of the committee, in order that their viewpoint could be communicated directly to the young people.

5. Liaison could be established with the local bus company, British Telecom, shopkeepers, the Parks and Gardens Department and local publicans in order to introduce improved means of identifying trouble-spots when they arose.

When pursuing a qualitative Objective, it is all too easy to assume activities will necessarily produce results. For example, there has been a trend in recent years to presume that police involvement with youth clubs will automatically produce tangible, beneficial results. This may or may not be so, but such benefits cannot be assumed and, before the police become involved in the committees of youth clubs, they should be sure of the results they are trying to achieve. Similarly, it is important not to confuse some quantifiable results as necessarily bringing an improvement in qualitative results.

To exemplify, it would be preferable to have no complaints of noise or disorderly conduct outside public houses, rather than an impressive record of arrests for public order and drunkenness offences. However, such data should not be disregarded. Although arrests may be made outside public houses it may not result in less complaints from citizens. Therefore, other strategies may need to be adopted. For example, a more positive supervision of the public houses themselves to reduce under age drinking or other problems which may, in fact, be more effective in reducing complaints than arrests made outside on the car park.

In the final analysis, the indicators that will tell us whether or not we have made some impact on this Goal, will be public opinion and their perception of any improvements in public tranquillity in the neighbourhood. Therefore, when we come to establish the measures of determining the achievement of an Objective, it will be necessary to identify at least three measures to provide an answer to the question.

Once again, our examination and analysis of the specific problem produced a number of potential measures. To illustrate, the volume of letters of complaint received from residents' associations and community groups, the number of complaints from individual citizens concerning noisy motor cycles, and the number of complaints from the bus company or British Telecom concerning damage to their property, are all measures of the results of police activities.

By this stage in the process, the Sub-Divisional Planning Group has identified a specific problem, has considered the means by which the problem might be solved, and has established performance measures which can be used to establish the degree to which the Objective has been achieved. By going through this process, the Group has suggested possible strategies in terms of Provisional Action Plans. It is now appropriate to discuss who will be responsible for writing Action Plans when the Objective becomes operational.

In the discussions concerning Goal No. 1, which related to the Goal addressing suppressible crime, the specimen Objective concerned the whole sub-division and involved a number of officers in Action Planning, both in uniform and C.I.D., and at a number of different ranks. In the case of Goal 2, the Objective is related to specific problems concerning an individual housing estate. This housing estate will be on a beat patrolled by an area constable. If this officer's full potential is to be exploited, he could be conceived as a 'beat manager' and thereby made responsible for co-ordinating all police activities on the beat. If this position was accepted then it would be appropriate for the area constable to be responsible for the preparation of Action Plans. Should the proposal be agreed, it would add status and credibility to the role within the force. Additionally, and equally as important from a management viewpoint, it would place responsibilities upon an officer who has an intimate knowledge of the problems of the area and, furthermore, likely to have a professional commitment towards finding the solution to those problems.

Before leaving the planning process, the availability of resources must once again be discussed. Some of the Action Plans that have been proposed can be carried out in the normal course of patrol, but observations of specific targets to detect vandalism will require the specific allocation of time. Also, the directed patrol to potential trouble spots will require the same status as attending a call from the public. After all it would be self-defeating if an officer, in carrying through an Action Plan, stationed his vehicle in a prominent position overlooking a public house car park or the youth club, and after five minutes was directed elsewhere to attend a call from a member of the public. If directed patrol is adopted as an Action Plan strategy, then the strategy must include safeguards to ensure officers do in fact implement the Action Plan, and not merely go through the motions.

Following the discussions within the Sub-Divisional Planning Group and the review of Provisional Action Plans, an Objective can be written to cover the issue of public tranquillity on this housing estate. The Objective is written as follows:-

To improve the public's perception of public tranquillity on housing estate X during the next year

As this is a Qualitative Performance Objective, it will also contain performance measure as specified below:-

1. There will be a reduction in the number of letters of complaint received from residents' associations and community groups in the next year.

2. The number of incidents of damage to public property and amenities will be reduced during the next year.

3. There will be a reduction in the number of complaints from members of the public concerning drunkenness and rowdiness outside public houses on the estate during the next year.

Summary

The sub-divisional superintendent will have to review all the proposed Objectives before submitting them to the divisional chief

Figure 9.3   Provisional objectives worksheet

1 Goal

2 Description of the problem
(stating sources of information and indicators/measures)

3 Additional information requirements

4 Possible strategies
(Provisional action plans)

5 Results measurement
(performance measures)

6 Officers involved and responsibilities

7 Resources available

8 Provisional objective

9 Priority rating

superintendent for confirmation. It was suggested in the section which described Goals that a standard format should be adopted for the preparation of Provisional Goals. The same suggestion applies in the case of Objectives. A proposed format is shown in the Provisional Objectives Worksheet in Figure 9.3, and the headings follow the questioning sequence which has been described on the preceding pages. The use of this format will produce a standard approach to the setting of Objectives, and provide the necessary background information to accompany the Provisional Objectives for review by the chief superintendent.

Confirmation Of Objectives

When the sub-divisional superintendent is satisfied he has prepared Objectives which are both challenging and reasonable targets, and he believes he has the resources to pursue them, they will be submitted to his divisional chief superintendent.

Objectives should not be submitted on their own, but be accompanied by a narrative description of the basis on which each Objective has been prepared and the Goal to which it is related. The narrative will enable the chief superintendent to understand the reasoning behind the Objective, as he is required to review each Objective and either confirm it, or return it for further information and modification. To review Objectives, the chief superintendent will ask himself the following questions in respect of each:-

(a) How is the Objective linked to the Goal?

(b) Will achieving the Objective contribute to achieving the Goal?

(c) What is the nature of the problem on the sub-division?

(d) Are the conclusions which have been drawn from the analysis reasonable?

(e) Have steps been taken to assess the resource requirements?

(f) Are there resources available?

reasonable?

(e) Have steps been taken to assess the resource requirements?

(f) Are there resources available?

(g) What measures are to be used to establish the results?

(h) Is the Objective realistic, in so far as it will be challenging to the participants but not impossible to attain?

When this review of each Objective has been completed, the chief superintendent should look at all the Objectives on a sub-division as a package. The Objectives should reflect the priorities of the sub-division, but inevitably there will be differences of emphasis in the Objectives between sub-divisions. If resources are limited, then it will be necessary to identify those Objectives which merit the first priority allocation of resources. This point can be made by looking at all the Objectives and assessing one against the other.

The outcome of this process will be confirmation of Objectives by the chief superintendent, who will return them to the sub-divisions for the preparation of Action Plans.

10   Action Planning

At this stage in the Policing by Objectives model, we have to assume the Objectives which were defined by the Sub-Divisional Planning Group following the process described in the previous chapter, have been returned from the divisional commander to the sub-division with authority to proceed to implement Action Plans to achieve those Objectives. We have now arrived at the fourth step in the PBO planning process.

By adopting this process the chief constable has shown his intention to give the widest possible discretion at this stage. The purpose of adopting the PBO model is to allow a greater degree of decentralised decision making within the force, whilst maintaining an appropriate command structure. There has been an absolute requirement for the force to go through the procedure of producing a Policy Statement, followed by Goals and Objectives. It will be recollected that, during the process of setting Objectives, Provisional Action Plans have been suggested as this is the only practical manner in which the system can be carried out. However, whilst a wider degree of discretion will be allowed in the Action Planning process, if there is one single key to the successful implementation of PBO in the force, it will be the skill with which sub-divisions can undertake the preparation, co-ordination and measurement of Action Plans.

It is possible, at this stage of the PBO model, to lose sight of its central purpose. That purpose is to *improve police management* and *not to be overwhelmed* in a paperchase where every single activity undertaken on the sub-division must be preceded by a written Action Plan. Such an outcome is not an inevitable and automatic consequence of adopting PBO, and in fact it is worth recalling the central component of the model, which is to perform only those police activities which can be demonstrated to produce some tangible and beneficial result. If an avalanche of paper does accompany the adoption of Policing by Objectives within the force, then it should be understood this is not the fault of the PBO model, but a lack of understanding and commitment to the underlying concepts. The danger will be discussed later in this chapter.

The learning objectives of this chapter are as follows:-

1   To understand the value of Action Plans as a means of providing direction and structure to the day to day policing activities of officers.

2   To understand the place of Action Plans in the PBO cycle.

3   To understand the criteria which must be applied to Action Plans when a choice is being made between them.

4   To understand the need to establish the roles and responsibilities of officers in relation to Action Plans.

5   To be able to apply the criteria to Action Plans to choose the most appropriate policing method.

6   To understand the distinction between primary and secondary measures and their use.

Action Planning brings the process right down to the constable on the beat and therefore it is worth pausing to ask some questions about the benefits the management process can bring to operational officers. To adopt a process such as PBO requires the active commitment of all officers and they are entitled to ask why they should be committed and what benefits they will receive. In fact when constables are introduced to this system of management they may simply ask "What is so different about Policing By Objectives?"

The question raises a number of key issues in relation to Policing by Objectives, and it is worth asking further supplementary questions and inviting the reader to reflect upon the answers based upon his or her own experience of police work. The first question is simply, "In the past have you been aware of the force policy concerning the prevention and detection of crime, enforcement of road traffic law, enhancement of public tranquillity and so forth?" It is all too easy to make assumptions about these critical issues based upon some vague definition handed down by Rowan and Mayne. But can these vague concepts really help in determining in the minds of individual officers, the priorities he or she should be pursuing to serve the needs of the community?

This brings us to the second question which is equally important, "Do I always know why I am performing a particular aspect of police work?" In connection with answering calls for service, dealing with demonstrations and other straightforward matters, this question is not too difficult to answer. But in relation to the more mundane and everyday activities, such as the enforcement of road traffic laws, preventive patrolling, visits to schools and so on, is it always clear exactly what this work contributes to the overall policies of the force?

Even if an officer does know why he is performing a range of police activities, he may not be able to answer the question, "Do I know what I have achieved as a result of these activities?" It has been shown that a significant contribution to job satisfaction is giving an employee information reflecting the results he achieves from his work.

Finally, even if an individual is aware of what he is achieving, there is the further question of, "Do my supervisors know what I am achieving?" Criticisms have been levelled at staff appraisal systems but it is not the concept of staff appraisal which is usually at fault, it is more likely that the person making the appraisal has extreme difficulty in giving an objective assessment and evaluation of an officer's performance. This fact is not a criticism of individual police supervisors, but more a consequence of a management system which has not, in the past, been very good at clearly determining the results of individual effort.

By adopting PBO as a management model, the chief officer has prepared a Policy Statement which is available to every member of the force, who should therefore be fully aware of the overall direction and policies of the force. This general policy directive has been followed by a set of Goals which establish priority areas for police action, and should ensure a more co-ordinated and forthright attitude towards pursuing the policy determined by the chief officer. These broad policy directives prompt, at sub-divisional level, an analysis of the problems facing the sub-division, and possible solutions to those problems. This sub-divisional analysis will involve as many officers as possible, and thus they will not only be contributing to the design of the solutions to problems, but they will also be consulted on why these problems need to be the subject of police efforts. Therefore, officers throughout the force should have a clear knowledge of the overall policy and strategic Goals of the force and, furthermore, have a good working knowledge of the problems facing their sub-division.

When Action Plans are prepared and implemented, individual officers should have a precise awareness of reasons why they are carrying out particular activities and the results they are expecting to achieve, together with a clear understanding of their individual responsibilities and how those individual responsibilities fit in to the overall strategy.

The aspect of PBO which makes it radically different to previous management innovations in the police, is the absolute commitment to measuring and evaluating results. By undertaking this measurement and evaluation strategy, not only will the force be in a position to determine the results it has achieved, but individual officers will also be able to establish their achievements and be held accountable and rewarded for those achievements. Therefore, to return to the question, "What is so different about PBO?", the answer lies not in the individual component parts of the model, but in the way in which all elements are brought together in a coherent and co-ordinated process which leads from broad policy to action on the streets and subsequent evaluation.

Action Planning Procedure

The Action Plan is the final step in the planning stage. It serves as a direct instruction to operational officers to perform certain tasks related to a given Objective, which will be evaluated by specific pre-determined measures. Any Action Plan must satisfy two basic tests. First, the Action Plan must be reasonably likely to achieve the desired result. Second, it can be pursued by the officers, or group of officers, who are proposing to use it. If an Action Plan fails on these two criteria, it should be rejected and alternatives proposed. If the process described so far has been followed to this stage, it is very unlikely that a proposed Action Plan will fail the standard tests, as in the Objective setting stage, Provisional Action Plans have already been proposed and tentatively agreed by the sub-divisional superintendent.

The Action Planning procedure at this stage of PBO is mainly concerned with making choices between alternatives, assigning specific responsibilities for the various parts of the Action Plan, and establishing time periods at which evaluations will occur.

Choosing Options

In the section which discussed the formulation of Objectives, a number of Provisional Action Plans were proposed for illustration. When this stage of the process is reached in practice, it is likely there will be many more Provisional Action Plans than the number set out in the examples. Therefore, the difficulty of choosing between Action Plans will be related to the number which are available. Whatever choice is made, providing the choice has been made upon sound grounds, it cannot be open to criticism, as it is the sub-division's responsibility to manage their resources at this stage of the PBO process.

To assist in making these choices, it may be useful to assess each Provisional Action Plan against a check-list of criteria:-

(a) *Cost-Benefits:* If there is one central philosophy for changing management strategy, it surely must be the desire for the force to be more efficient and effective in the future. Therefore, all Action Plans must be carefully examined to establish if they are an effective use of resources, and of equal importance, whether the use of resources will be efficient. By efficient, we mean there may be a number of ways of achieving a given Objective, but our responsibility as managers of scarce resources is to ensure we achieve the Objective with the least cost. To take a very simple example, a particular Action Plan may require 16 man hours a day to carry out. This time could be found from within existing duty time, or it may be necessary to employ officers on overtime. If it is only possible to find the resources by using overtime, then so be it, but if a more careful use of resources enables the same task to be performed in duty time without incurring additional costs, this latter strategy must be more efficient.

This first criteria will require a careful consideration of all the cost implications of the Action Plan. In cases where special equipment is needed, the costing is relatively straightforward to calculate. But in cases where man hours are the significant cost, it should be remembered this involves not merely the man hours which will be used to carry through the Action Plan, but also those man hours required in planning the strategy, the co-ordination and monitoring, and possibly other factors such as additional training for officers.

Unfortunately, costings of police services, particularly where precise cost data are not available, is a difficult task, but it is something to be borne in mind throughout this process. In many instances it may be possible to give only broad estimates of costs, but even this is better than no consideration at all being given to this very important management matter.

(b) *Range of Activity:* The sub-division, or the unit within the sub-division proposing the Action Plan, must be capable of carrying it through on its own. The Action Plans which were proposed in the previous section were all assumed to be, and indeed were, capable of being performed by sub-divisional resources.

However, an Action Plan related to improving road safety could involve a wide-spread publicity campaign concerning the dangers of drinking, and warning motorists that particular attention would be paid to this offence in the coming months by the officers on a specific sub-division. Whilst this strategy may well produce the desired results, a sub-divisional commander would need to ask himself if it is appropriate for him, as an individual, to undertake an Action Plan which has obvious ramifications beyond the boundaries of his sub-division. This does not mean such an Action Plan should automatically be dismissed as an option, but it is something which might be considered at force level as more appropriate as a common Action Plan across the force area, and additional to sub-divisional Action Plans.

(c) *Additional Support:* When considering the range of activities above, managers were cautioned against actions going beyond their sub-divisional boundaries. Here we are concerned with requests for additional support from specialist departments to assist operations within the sub-division. It is important to consider the possibility of obtaining additional support from specialist officers at the earliest possible stage in the Action Planning process. If this is not done, then it is possible it may not be available. If the support is not available, then the Action Plan may have to be radically altered at this early juncture or abandoned altogether. In the bottom-up consultation process which takes place in the planning stage, the requirements for specialist support can be communicated through the linking pin process to the Policy Group when they are considering Goals.

(d) *Preparation and Development:* In some cases, Action Plans can commence immediately they are formulated, but in other instances there will be a need to undertake a period of preparation and development before the plan can be implemented. The requirements for preparation and development must be carefully considered, as it is very damaging to arrange for manpower to be available on a particular date in order to proceed with an Action Plan, only to find the necessary preparation has not been done in advance and the plan has to be postponed.

(e) *The Effects on Other Police Efforts:* One of the more difficult tasks of the police manager is to attempt to predict the likely outcome of a course of action on other areas of police activity. These implications can be seen under two headings; first, the question of implications for the police organisation – that is internal implications, and second, implications for the community – external implications.

A simple example of internal implications is where an Action Plan requires a number of officers to perform certain activities at a particular time, which means as a consequence these officers are not available to do duty elsewhere. Thus, if area constables are encouraged to be involved in youth activities, then the same officers, during the hours they are in youth clubs and schools, would not be providing a visible presence on the street. Therefore, when it comes to assess the impact of patrolling officers on the perceptions of police visibility by the public, the fact officers spent many hours inside youth clubs and schools must be a consideration when the results are being assessed.

To take another example of police involvement with youth, a policy of greater contact between young people and area constables may provide benefits and gains to the police image, but these could be eliminated entirely by an Action Plan which required strict enforcement of road traffic regulations in respect of young people riding motor cycles.

In most cases, Action Plans will have implications either internally or externally or both, and it is not being suggested here that such Action Plans should automatically be discarded. Far from it, as it is likely that a carefully managed Action Plan which appears to have conflicting implications, can simultaneously produce successful outcomes. However, this is only likely to occur if the wider implications of such Action Plans have been considered from the outset, and steps have been taken to minimise the possible conflict between them.

(f) *Special or Additional Skills:* Where Action Plans will require special or additional skills, then these must be identified at an early stage and either be provided within a sub-division by 'on-the-job' training, or a request made to the training department for assistance and co-operation. A simple example would be where an Action Plan involves uniformed patrol officers undertaking crime prevention surveys in houses in an effort to reduce the opportunities for burglary. It is likely the officers undertaking these surveys, if they are to be conducted in a professional manner, will require some form of crime prevention survey training. Thus it is a prerequisite of the Action Plan that this training be provided before it can proceed.

(g) *Equipment Requirements:* In many cases, equipment will either be or can be made available on the sub-division. However, this aspect must not be overlooked. For example, if night vision equipment is not available to pursue an Action Plan involving evening observations of areas being subjected to vandalism, then the Action Plan could not be undertaken.

(h) *Manpower Resources:* The critical issue of manpower availability has been stressed at length, if manpower is not available for Action Plans then they simply cannot be executed. There are two general ways in which manpower can be made available. First, having established the amount of discretionary time available to uniformed patrol officers, a number of officers can be detached from uniformed patrol duties to perform specific tasks in a small squad. However, it must be remembered sufficient manpower resources must remain within the unit, to carry out those tasks which are designated as essential activities. Thus under this strategy, if the discretionary time of a unit of officers is 50 per cent it may be possible to reduce the discretionary time of some officers to 20 per cent and thereby release officers for alternative work, however this will mean the remaining officers will have to work harder.

The second strategy is to start to fill those periods of discretionary time with specific activity. This is what typically occurs at present, where officers who are not responding to calls or otherwise engaged, will patrol potential trouble spots on foot or check cars for crime or road traffic offences, and generally perform those tasks which are called self-initiated. The Action Planning strategy would not radically change this mode of operation. However, it would attempt to ensure all these self-initiated activities undertaken by officers from time to time are directed towards specific Objectives, and therefore every activity would be channelled towards some measureable and achievable results. This is known as *directed patrol*. [1]

The proposed Action Plans in respect of burglary discussed in the preceding section involve both these strategies. For example, during discretionary time, officers could direct their attention towards young people on the street who appeared to be absent from school. The plan to visit second-hand dealers, however, could involve detaching two men from uniformed patrol duties and having them working in plain clothes. Whichever strategy is chosen, it must be remembered that PBO is not a process for getting 'blood out of a stone'. If there simply is not the time available to perform Action Plans, then they should not be implemented.

In previous sections a question and answer approach was suggested as a very useful way of dealing with the issues raised by particular aspects of PBO, and the strategy of choosing options is no exception. Thus, we can summarise all the preceding points by these questions:-

(a) Will the Action Plan be effective and is it the most cost effective means of achieving the desired result?

(b) Does the range of activity proposed by the Action Plan extend beyond sub-divisional boundaries, or is it outside the scope of activities normally associated with the duties of the officers involved?

(c) Does this Action Plan require support from specialist departments at headquarters?

(d) Does the plan require a period of preparation or development before it can be implemented?

(e) Will the proposed Action Plan have an impact on other police activities and, if so, what are the consequences of this impact? Are they tolerable or do they make the Action Plan inappropriate?

(f) Does the Action Plan require special or additional skills and, therefore, training for the officers of this sub-division?

(g) Does the proposed Action Plan involve any additional equipment, and if so, will it be, or can it be made available?

(h) Is there sufficient manpower resources to carry through this Action Plan?

Establishing Roles And Responsibilities

At this point, we are concerned with who will do what and when. During the period of analysis which accompanied the setting of Provisional Action Plans, responsibilities have already been assigned. For example, in matters relating to crime, the detective inspector and/or the collator may have been involved. Having established the area of action, the person to have responsibility for overseeing implementation must be decided. Here it is possible the responsibility might change from CID to the Uniformed Branch if the Action Plan involves uniformed personnel. Thus implementation may be under the general direction of a uniform inspector.

During implementation it will be necessary to monitor each Action Plan and subsequently to provide an evaluation. This might be done by the person responsible for implementation, or it may be appropriate to return the evaluation process to the officer who made the original analysis, as he has a more detailed knowledge of the broad aspects of the particular problem. There exists a considerable degree of flexibility as to who should perform these tasks, but it is essential the specific roles are all assigned. Accordingly every Action Plan will have an officer responsible for the analysis and definition of the problem, preparation of the detailed Action Plan, overseeing the implementation, providing the day-to-day monitoring, and producing the final evaluation report. In some cases, it may be one individual officer who will have all these responsibilities. In most cases it is likely several officers will be involved at various stages.

Throughout this process, the sub-divisional commander will be involved in ensuring the component steps are undertaken, and the officers are competent to perform them. The sub-divisional superintendent will be responsible for the final review of these Action Plans and the preparation of the sub-divisional evaluation report.

Action Planning – A Case Study

After the Sub-Divisional Planning Group had made a detailed review of the crime problem on the sub-division in response to the force Goal 'to reduce the amount of suppressible crime, the following Objective was defined:–

To reduce the rate of burglary in dwellinghouses on the sub-division by 10% in 1984.

In the process of developing this Objective, four Provisional Action Plans were proposed and can be briefly described as follows:–

1   Special attention by uniformed officers on juveniles of school age who are seen out of school in school hours. This will be known as the Truancy Project.

Figure 10.1   Action plan comparison worksheet

Action plan descriptions	Truancy project	Publicity	Schools liaison	Dealer checks
Cost/benefits 1 = V. unlikely 4 = V. likely	4	3	3	2
Activity range Yes = confined to sub-division No = extends beyond sub-division	Yes	Depends on the medium chosen	Yes	Yes
Specialist support	4	4	4	4
Preparation/ development	2	4	4	2
Adverse effects on other APs	2	4	4	4
Special/ additional skills	4	4	4	2
Equipment required	3	4	4	3
Time NP = During patrol SM = Separate man-power	NP	None	NP	SM

SCALE

1   =   A great deal of this required for the Action Plan
2   =   Some of this required for the Action Plan
3   =   Very little of this required for the Action Blan
4   =   None of this required for the Action Plan

2   Publicity asking members of the public to report young people loitering in the streets in suspicious circumstances. This Action Plan will be known as Publicity.

3   School liaison to explain the problem of juvenile crime in the area with particular reference to burglaries, accompanied by a request to enlist the aid of schools to reduce truancy and report instances where suspected stolen property is being traded between pupils. This will be known as Schools Liaison.

4   Regular checks on second hand dealers to trace and recover stolen property. This will be known as Dealer Checks.

The process of choosing options is one of comparisons. All the above Action Plans seem likely to produce some positive results but it is worth comparing the cost, the benefits and all the additional questions in relation to these plans before settling for one or more Action Plans.

Such comparisons in police work can never be an exact science. A simple matrix grid may assist to clarify thoughts and make the choice a more objective process. The matrix grid has been prepared and appears at Figure 10.1. Across the top of the page, the brief descriptions of the four Action Plans have been arranged and are shown as Truancy Project, Publicity, School Liaison and Dealer Checks. Down the left-hand side of the grid are shown the eight specific questions which it was suggested should be asked in comparing Action Plans. The first row relates to cost and benefits, and under this item, we are most concerned with the likelihood of the plan producing the desired result. To illustrate this and to assist with comparisons, a scale of 1 to 4 is proposed where a score of '1' = very *unlikely* to achieve result' and a score of '4' = 'very *likely* to achieve the result'.

The second row, the Activity Range, can usually be answered 'Yes' or 'No'. An answer 'Yes' would indicate the activity is one which can realistically be confined to the sub-division and be implemented without interference with other sub-divisions. If the answer is 'No', it would indicate the plan will certainly spill over on to adjoining sub-divisions or, perhaps, the force area as a whole.

The next five rows, which are headed Specialist Support,

Preparation or Development, Adverse Effects on Other Action Plans, Special/Additional Skills and Equipment, can all be answered on the same scale. It is proposed a scale of 1 to 4 is used again but, in this case, a score of '1' would equal 'a *great deal* of this in the Action Plan' whilst '4', would indicate ' *none* ' of this in the Action Plan'. Thus, when considering specialist support for the Truancy Project, it is clear this is not required, and therefore a score of '4', ie 'there is no need for specialist support in this Action Plan', can be assigned to this aspect of the plan.

The final row concerns the man hour resources required. It is not the purpose at this stage to assign specific man hours to these Action Plans, although it may be desirable at some time. However at this point a decision can be made as to whether the Action Plan will be performed in the discretionary part of normal patrol time, or be carried out using separate manpower either drawn from units on the sub-division, or by reducing the discretionary time of uniformed patrol officers by taking away some of their number to perform separate duties.

For this case study, we will briefly examine each of the Action Plans proposed during the Objective setting process, to show how these comparisons can be made.

Truancy Project: The strong evidence of the involvement of juveniles in housebreaking, particularly during day-time hours, encouraged the Sub-Divisional Planning Group to believe activity by uniformed patrol officers would both deter juveniles from committing burglaries, and also raise the possibility of increasing detection through the checking of youths who had been involved in such crimes. In these circumstances, it is believed the Action Plan is very likely to achieve the result, and therefore it is given the score of '4'.

It is believed this is an activity which can be performed on the sub-division without encroaching on other areas of the force. Therefore its activity range is appropriate, and it is marked 'Yes' in that row. Specialist support is not required for implementation, and therefore it scores '4', but there will be some limited preparation or development, as the collator will be required to establish an index of juveniles who are found truanting from school. He will need to keep particular records of juveniles who are found to be involved in committing offences of burglary, and he will be required to prepare material to brief uniformed officers on crime patterns and so forth. Therefore, to indicate some preparation for the Action Plan, it is scored '2' in that row.

It is possible the Action Plan could have some adverse affects on police relations with young people, therefore under this item a score of '2' is once again assigned. As far as additional or special skills are concerned, these are not thought to be required in this case and a score of '4' is allocated under the heading. A very limited amount of equipment is going to be needed by the collator and this it is believed can be made available so a score of '3' is given. Finally, the manpower resources are to be drawn from normal patrol time and this is indicated by marking 'NP' in that row.

On the comparison criteria used, it can be seen the Action Plan is believed to have a very good chance of reducing the amount of burglary on the sub-division, it is specific and can be contained within the sub-division. It also appears to be very cost efficient, as it can be carried out during normal patrol activity.

Publicity: If a deterrent effect can be demonstrated by the use of publicity which encourages law-abiding citizens to report suspicious incidents to the police and, simultaneously, encourages potential juvenile criminals to believe they may be reported to the police by concerned citizens if they are seen acting suspiciously near houses, then this Action Plan has some likelihood of achieving the result. Therefore a score of '3' has been assigned under this heading.

The activity range of this Action Plan will depend to a certain extent on the type of media which is used for the publicity. If it is confined to local newspapers, then it is possible the activity could be limited to the sub-division, but if for example the local radio is involved, then this Action Plan will have an influence beyond the sub-divisional boundary. In these circumstances, an answer has not been given in this row but it has been noted 'it depends upon the media used'.

It has been assessed there will be no need for specialist support, no requirement for preparation or development, there will be no adverse effects on other Action Plans, and additional skills and additional equipment will not be required. The Action Plan will not necessitate any time allocation from operational officers, as the briefing can be done by the sub-divisional superintendent in the course of his normal media briefings.

To summarise, this Action Plan has little or no cost implications to the sub-division in terms of manpower. The likelihood of it achieving results is difficult to assess immediately, but if there is a good public response then the possibility of being reported by concerned citizens might well deter potential juvenile burglars from committing these crimes.

Schools Liaison: Once again, the amount of support received from the schools, and the deterrent effect which might be accrued from this support, is difficult to estimate at the outset.

However it is known from previous dealings with schools in the area that they are more than likely to co-operate, at least in a limited way, and therefore it can be reasonably believed this Action Plan is likely to achieve the desired results. For these reasons it is given a score of '3'. This is a matter that can be dealt with exclusively on the sub-division, therefore the answer to the question concerning activity range is therefore 'Yes'. The Action Plan will not require specialist support, preparation or development; it should not have any adverse effects on other Action Plans, it will not require additional skills or training, and no additional equipment will be required. It can also be performed during normal patrol time by area constables who, in their course of duty, visit schools.

This Action Plan will not incur additional manpower costs on the sub-division and, although its exact effects are difficult to predict at this stage, it is very strongly linked to the Truancy Project Action Plan. Some additional benefits may be accrued from this School Liaison Action Plan as a direct spin-off from the Truancy Project Action Plan. Indeed, it could be seen they complemented each other.

Dealers Checks: Regular checks with dealers may lead to the recovery of stolen property and the identification of those persons responsible for its theft, which in turn may stop those people committing further offences. An additional effect of this Action Plan could be to deter burglars from taking their property to the second-hand dealers for disposal, or at least to make such transactions difficult. What cannot be assessed of course is the extent to which these crimes will still occur and other means used to dispose of property. It cannot be said categorically therefore this Action Plan will be very likely to achieve results, but it is equally unlikely it will not achieve some results. A score of '2' under this heading would seem appropriate.

This is an activity which can be confined to the sub-division, although there is the possibility the Action Plan may displace the disposal of stolen property to second-hand dealers to other areas of the force. The Action Plan will not require any specialist support. The officers who are making the dealer checks will need to be aware of the description of property recently stolen, and this information will have to be extracted from crime reports and collated locally. This will require some preparation and background work to check up on recent crimes before the plan can be set in motion. In recognition of this development need, a score of '2' has been assigned under this heading. It is believed this Action Plan will not have an adverse effect on other Action Plans, and it is therefore given a score of '4'.

The officers who undertake responsibility for executing this Action Plan will require some training to prepare them for the task, for example as to the means of identifying property through serial numbers and the like, the records dealers maintain and the force policy and statutory authorities related to the seizure of property believed to be the subject of crime. To indicate this training need, a score of '2' has been assigned. There will be a limited requirement for additional equipment for the maintenance of certain indices and other records, and a score of '3' has been assigned under this heading.

Having considered the necessity for a detailed knowledge of property recently stolen, the need for officers to get to know second-hand dealers, and the requirement of a consistent policy concerning the procedure for recovering stolen property, it is thought appropriate to give the execution of this Action Plan to two officers on a full-time basis. Thus, there is a need for separate manpower to be allocated, and this has been indicated by marking 'SM' in the last row.

To summarise, it is believed this Action Plan will lead to the

Figure 10.2   Action plan

Objective

To reduce the rate of burglary in dwellinghouses by 10% in 1984.

Action plan title and description

Truancy project:-

To observe and where appropriate check juveniles of school age during school hours with a view to determining whether they are authorised to be absent from school and have been involved in committing crime.

Units involved

Sub-Divisional	*Others* (i.e. HQ)
Uniformed Patrol Officer	None
Area Constable	
Collator	

Major tasks

Preparation

Brief Officers
Collator
Prepare index for collating the information obtained by officers
Inform schools

Execution

Carrying out observations and checks on juveniles during school hours

Results management

Primary measure

Number of relevant offences of burglary reported

Secondary measures

Number of target juveniles observed and checked
Number of juveniles truanting from school
Number of burglaries detected

Co-ordinator

Sub-Divisional Chief Inspector

Review Periods

4 weekly

recovery of stolen property, which may produce detections of the persons responsible for its theft. However, it is likely this Action Plan will increase detection rather than produce a reduction in the absolute number of burglaries being committed. Further, it is likely property from other crimes, such as thefts from motor vehicles, will also be involved in the Action Plan. This particular plan is the most expensive one in terms of manpower as it requires a separate manpower allocation.

Making The Choice

The foregoing may at first sight appear to be a very laborious and unnecessary process, but it has only been used here in a relatively simple example to illustrate the concepts and procedures. In reality, there might be a number of Action Plans under consideration and it is only through this proper comparison that their relative strengths and weaknesses can be assessed. In making the final choice for Action Plans, the two most important criteria will be the likelihood of achieving a result and, second, the cost in terms of manpower to be used. On these two criteria, the Truancy Project is the most attractive. It has, on the analysis, the most likely chance of achieving the desired result and it is an activity which can be carried out at very low cost.

Publicity and School Liaison depend very much for their success on the co-operation of the public generally and schools in particular. The fourth Action Plan concerning dealers should be seriously considered, but this activity may be more appropriately combined with other crime Action Plans, providing they are conducive to the sub-division, for example plans relating to thefts from motor vehicles and the like. This fourth Action Plan is the most expensive in terms of manpower and also involves setting up yet another specialist squad, albeit of only two men, which once again removes an opportunity from the general uniformed patrol officer to become involved in the implementation of Action Plans.

It is decided after these considerations, the sub-division will implement the Truancy Project Action Plan. The process of preparing the Action Plan prior to implementation, assigning responsibility for the various parts of the Action Plan to individual officers and determining the evaluation measures is shown in the example at Figure 10.2.

The Figure 10.2 identifies the Objective to reduce the rate of burglary in dwellinghouses by 10 per cent in 1984. This is followed by a brief narrative comprising the Action Plan title and description. The Action Plan clearly shows units involved, namely uniformed patrol officers, area constables and the collator. The tasks which must be undertaken include a briefing of the officers involved. The collator will be responsible for preparing the index and collating information obtained by officers. Area constables will be responsible for informing the schools in their area that the police will be taking particular interest in young people who appear to be absent from school without reason. The final task shown is the major activity, which is the observation of juveniles on the street during school hours.

It is possible an Appendix to this Action Plan would need to be prepared to ensure all officers fully understand their roles and responsibilities and, in particular, officers are given instructions as to how to implement the Action Plans to ensure no adverse comments against police procedures. Area constables must be fully aware of the superintendent's policy before they can inform schools to ensure there are no misunderstandings and good relations between the schools and police are maintained. It will also be necessary to indicate to uniformed patrol officers the way in which any checks of young people are to be conducted and recorded. Care must be taken to ensure no damage is caused to relations between police and young people.

The example Action Plan also identifies, under the heading of Results Management, the measures to be used to evaluate the results of this police method. The *primary measure* will be the number of offences of burglary reported during the target hours. But it is equally important to provide information on a number of supplementary indicators, such as the number of target juveniles seen or checked, the number of juveniles actually truanting from school, (a figure which will have to be obtained in co-operation with the schools), and the number of burglaries detected as a result of the Action Plan. These are the *secondary measures*.

A distinction has been made between primary and secondary measures because they tend to serve different purposes. The primary measure will always be linked directly to the Objective, and is the primary evaluation criterion. Secondary measures are usually one step removed from the Objective as they measure things which on their own do not establish the achievement of the Objective, but measure contributions to the achievement. The primary measure is used to establish if progress has been made towards the Objective, the secondary measures should help to establish *why* or *how* the desired results have or have not been achieved.

From the outset, it must be clearly stated who will have responsibility for co-ordinating the Action Plan and in this case, responsibility has been assigned to the sub-divisional chief inspector. Finally, review periods will need to be established and as school terms are of a limited length, it is proposed that the Action Plan should be the subject of a four-weekly review to determine its results.

It was mentioned in the introduction to the Action Planning section there was a danger of becoming overwhelmed by the paper recording of Action Plans and associated matters. This is not an inevitable consequence of Policing by Objectives and is something to be avoided. However, the Action Plan is the key to the Policing by Objectives process and it is the one thing, above everything else, that will provide the base to the successful evaluation of the efforts of the force to improve effectiveness and efficiency. Therefore, given the critical nature of Action Planning in relation to the overall policy of the force, time spent on the administration of Action Plans must be considered as a valuable contribution to improving the management of the force.

An Action Planning document such as the one shown in Figure 9.2 is recommended to be used, and a proper recording procedure should be introduced to enable Action Plans to be co-ordinated and monitored in a professional manner. It is a matter for individuals whether this recommendation is accepted but, in the final analysis, it will be the responsibility of the person making the decision to ensure he is in a position to provide a sufficiently detailed evaluation to support any claims of success in achieving results.

References

1 Howlett, J. R., Killman, S. H., and Hinson, J. B., "Managing Patrol Operations", *The Police Chief*, December 1981, pp 34 – 43.

11   Implementation and Evaluation

In the preceding sections, the Policing by Objectives process has moved from the Policy Statement (Step 1) to Goals (Step 2), followed by Objectives (Step 3) from which Action Plans were prepared (Step 4). These four steps are concerned with planning and organising resources, and the reader might be forgiven for wondering why this complex planning process has been undertaken if, as an end result, we are going to implement a plan which involves amongst other things paying special attention to juveniles found in the street during school hours. On a superficial examination, this may indeed seem to be a very long and laborious process to arrive at a point which has been visited on many occasions before by police officers attempting to control crime.

To emphasise the importance of the planning process it is worth making the following observations which, to some extent, were covered in the introduction to Action Planning. The PBO process does not require radical changes in the way police officers do their job on the street. However when the PBO process is adopted, constables should be able to stop to reflect on the principles underlying the activities they are performing, and they should be aware of the following matters:-

They should know how any particular police activity fits into the overall strategy of the force.

They should know exactly what their contribution will be to the policing strategy of the force.

They should know who is responsible for co-ordinating the activities and evaluating the results.

They should know the results they as individuals and the group of officers to which they belong, are achieving.

They should know that if there are no benefits being achieved from a particular activity then it will be changed or abandoned.

If they have this greater degree of knowledge then they should certainly feel part of a team, and therefore gain greater satisfaction from the work they do. Furthermore, the force should be infinitely more effective and efficient, as it will not contain a number of individuals all doing 'their own thing', but will gain strength from the co-ordinated efforts of officers who shared a common purpose.

The learning objectives of this chapter are:-

1   To understand the place of the implementation process in the management cycle.

2   To recognise the factors to be addressed in the day-to-day management of the implementation of Action Plans.

3   To understand the functions of the evaluation stage in the management cycle.

4   To recognise the difference between Tactical and Strategic evaluation.

5   To be able to recognise and apply various methods of evaluation.

6   To understand the considerations implicit in deciding the time scales of evaluations.

7   To be able to apply the checklist of criteria which must be used to evaluate Action Plans.

8   To understand the specific requirements of the evaluation of Development Goals.

9   To understand the requirements of the annual review process and the issues to be included in the evaluation reports.

If there is a radical difference in the implementation stage of the PBO cycle, then it relates to the ability of officers to understand why they are doing certain things. For example, a management directive which merely tells officers to 'get out and do a bit of process' or instructs area constables to 'get involved in the local community', is a far cry from the careful analysis of problems on the sub-division; the involvement of officers at all ranks in identifying strategies which may lead to solutions, and a subsequent careful and co-ordinated programme of implementation and evaluation. This may entail officers reporting motorists for traffic process or area constables being involved in youth activities in schools, and thus the 'actions on the street' may well be identical, but the management philosophy which is directing them is substantially different.

There are dangers in being deceived into believing that the implementation process under PBO is similar to the more traditional forms of police management. As far as individual officers are concerned, their key responsibility will be to ensure the effective and efficient management of their own time, and this is a matter which all officers, regardless of length of service or rank, must make their guiding management principle. It is no longer sufficient for an officer to tell his supervisor he is 'busy', unless he can also inform the supervisor exactly what results he is achieving. It must be remembered that police activities have no value in and of themselves, they must be judged by the *results* they achieve.

Day To Day Management Of Implementation

The extremely diverse nature of police work creates on the one hand, an interesting and challenging management task, but on the other, makes it very difficult to provide instruction to managers which will cover every foreseeable eventuality. However, it is important to establish the structure and procedures to be used when implementing Action Plans. Random modifications to Action Plans must be avoided by establishing methods to make changes. Officers must be motivated and committed to the Plans. Systems for recording the essential elements of the Plan must be designed and adopted. In some cases Action plans will have implications for other aspects of police work. These must be co-ordinated by establishing appropriate procedures to prevent disruptions to the Plans or existing working arrangements. Finally, the force must understand the role of monitoring as a learning, rather than a punishment centred exercise.

(a) *Modifications to Action Plans*

Experience of executing an Action Plan may reveal sooner or later matters that have not been anticipated, thereby necessitating modification or amendment to parts of the Action Plan. Any such adjustments should not be done by individuals, but a system should be established whereby these problems can be dealt with by the officer responsible for co-ordinating the Action Plan. It will be his decision to make changes during the course of executing the Action Plan.

If the preparation for Action Planning has been done with sufficient care, then major alterations to the plan should not be necessary. There are dangers in making day-to-day modifications to a plan which is fundamentally sound, as the end result of these changes could affect the plan to such a degree that it becomes unworkable.

(b) *Motivation*

Any person who has been involved in changes at work is aware that initial enthusiasm and motivation can decline with performance returning to the level which may have existed before the change took place. This must not be allowed to occur. There is always the possibility of officers feeling that merely going through the motions is all that is required and, providing all the parts of the process appear to be carried out, this will be sufficient. In some cases, this may well be true but should this occur, it will be a criticism of the way in which Objectives and Action Plans have been formulated. If the Objectives can be achieved with little or no effort, then they have not been formulated in a sufficiently challenging way. This would not be a criticism of PBO, but a comment upon the way in which police managers have been more involved rather than *committed* to the process.

(c) *Recording*

In concluding the Action Planning section, a caution was given concerning the use of written Action Plans and the way in which making paper records can become an end in itself. It was pointed out this was not an inevitable consequence of PBO and should be avoided. Nonetheless it is essential for records to be maintained as this is the only means by which evaluation can be done.

During the implementation of Action Plans, it is equally important to maintain some key records, as it cannot be assumed that the directions or instructions given to officers can, or will, be followed. For example, when the Action Plan for the truancy project was being considered, accurate figures were not available for the number of truants who may have been on the streets during daytime hours. In choosing the Action Plan, it was also estimated that officers would have discretionary time available during which checks could be carried out. When the plan is implemented, records must be maintained to show when and where observations are made on juveniles to establish these checks are being conducted. If they are not, then it must be asked if this is because there are very few juveniles on the street, or because there is no time for officers to spend on this work.

An Action Plan in relation to public tranquillity, proposed officers should park their cars at conspicuous points in the vicinity of premises such as public houses and youth clubs, which gave rise to disorderly behaviour. If no reduction is recorded in the number of complaints received from citizens, then it must be established whether officers were able to carry through this Action Plan. If they were, then there is evidence the strategy is not a means by which these complaints can be reduced, and the activity can be stopped. However the lack of results may have been because the officers did not have sufficient time to spend at these locations, or they may well have visited, but within a few minutes were sent away to answer a call. The records must reflect these circumstances and this may lead to modifications of the Action Plan.

(d) *Establishing Procedures*

Where Action Plans involve officers using discretionary time to perform certain activities, the problems which were described at (c) above must be managed. Where officers are directed to patrol particular areas either in cars or on foot, or are required to make contact with individuals, or visit community groups, then policy must establish whether these activities will have the same priority as a non-urgent call for assistance. What rules will apply to these activities when a controller requires a vehicle or a foot patrol officer to service a call? Can he redirect officers engaged on these activities or will he only redirect officers when the call is a matter of life or death? These questions cannot be answered by this book but must be addressed on the sub-division in order that everyone is working to the same set of rules.

(e) *Monitoring*

It has already been emphasised that monitoring, and subsequent evaluation, are the radical differences between the PBO management process and other management techniques traditionally used by police forces. Nothing in the PBO process will change the fact that the police service is a disciplined organisation. However, there are dangers that any monitoring and evaluation will be used as a means of 'catching out' officers. As far as possible the monitoring process must not be seen as punishment-centred. Monitoring is a key part of the responsibilities of managers and it is their primary responsibility to ensure the more efficient and effective use of resources.

If officers are not working effectively, it should not be automatically presumed it is because they are either lazy, uncommitted or stupid. When problems do arise, the realistic manager should ask questions concerning the adequacy of the preparation, the briefing or the training of his officers, before assuming it is the individuals who are the source of the problem. It may be the shortcomings are within the plan, the organisation or its management. Monitoring and evaluation should be seen as a learning process for all concerned, and only as a last resort should they be associated with individual culpability and punishment.

There is little more that can be said about implementation but it should not be construed as indicating it is an unimportant part of the process. The force can develop the most sophisticated management planning capacity which has ever existed but, if the implementation of Action Plans is carried out in a haphazard, unco-ordinated and half-hearted way, the quality of planning will not redeem the situation. The reason for saying relatively little about implementation is simply, at street level, the activities undertaken by police officers will change minimally. The significant difference between yesterday and the future, is the philosophy underlying the reasons why these activities are taking place at all.

Evaluation

Evaluation is the final stage of the management cycle and is an important source of information for future planning. A manager must develop the skills of evaluation for the day-to-day monitoring of Action Plans and the longer term annual evaluation process. A distinction can be made between these two parts of the evaluation process, the day-to-day monitoring is the tactical evaluation, which may be the responsibility of several officers on the sub-division. The Action Planning Co-ordinator is the person who is given responsibility for the tactical evaluation of the plan. Strategic evaluation is the responsibility of the sub-divisional superintendent and those officers above him.

(a) Tactical Evaluation: The person co-ordinating the Action Plan will be the person responsible for informing the sub-divisional superintendent of the results being achieved. He must monitor the routine activities of the Action Plan, such as the recording of the observations of juveniles, the number of offences of burglary reported during the target hours and the number of offences detected. From this information and his overall knowledge of the police problems which led to implementation of the Action Plan, he is best placed to know when modification should be made to the plan and, in the longer run, whether the plan should be abandoned or continued.

Action Planners have been urged to ensure that the officers who are being asked to work on those plans, have sufficient time to perform all the related tasks. The same point can be made concerning officers with a responsibility for monitoring and evaluating Action Plans. If these officers do not have sufficient time to devote to these tasks, then it is unreasonable to give them the responsibility. Furthermore, this role of monitoring and evaluating should be given sufficient priority within the force to ensure it is not left as a task to be done when everything else has been completed. If the person responsible for evaluating is not able to perform these tasks correctly, for whatever reason, then the whole concept of planning, executing and assessing will fall into disrepute. In brief, tactical evaluation is concerned with asking the questions, "Which

231

police activities produce a desired result?" and "Which police activities do not?"

(b) Strategic Evaluation: The results of strategic evaluation are something which in the first instance affect the sub-division, but they should also be seen as being of value to the force as a whole. In effect, strategic evaluation should be the process by which the force increases its fund of professional knowledge.

As individuals, police officers are able to learn by their own experience, however, as an organisation, the evidence would suggest that police forces do not learn very well by past experiences. There are examples where police forces have introduced some policing method which in the past had been introduced elsewhere and abandoned as unsuccessful. Thus strategic evaluation provides the process and the structure to measure results and record the assessments for the information of others. Sharing management experiences and knowledge becomes an integral part of the management process.

Methods Of Evaluation

The specific methods to be used in the evaluation stage will have been suggested by the process of analysis and review which accompanied the designing of Action Plans. In fact where it is necessary to obtain data before the plan is implemented, the design of the evaluation will have to have been considered during the Action Planning stage. The method chosen will also depend upon the resources, information and skills available to the manager. The four methods which are described should not be seen as the only ones which are available for evaluating police methods. A manager must make his own decisions concerning his choice of evaluation method.

(a) *Before and After*

If we go back to the initial stages of establishing Objectives, you will recall the question, "What tells us we have a problem on the sub-division?" The analysis to answer this question will identify indicators which can be developed as measures to establish the extent to which the problem exists. Thereby, the very simplest form of evaluation can be comparisons of those measures used to define the problem, with the same measures some time after an Action Plan has been implemented. A word of caution – as with all the measures suggested in this section, no one measure in isolation should be used as evidence of a result. However a combination of measures can provide confirmation of a positive, or negative result.

To illustrate this point, the Action Plan example concerning the Truancy Project included one primary measure, the number of burglaries reported during the target hours. But the Results Management also included secondary measures, the number of juveniles seen, the number of juveniles found truanting from school and the number of burglaries detected. By using all four measures, a much clearer picture of what is happening as a result of the Action Plan will be produced. Whatever measures are used, they should be able to answer two management questions. First, what is being achieved by this Action Plan? Second, is it worth continuing the Action Plan?

(b) *Time Trends*

One of the problems with using traditional police statistics such as reported crime, detection and road accident rates, is that they can rise and fall during the time periods chosen, whether these are monthly, half-yearly or annual. However, if a long period is chosen, shall we say five years, then it would be possible to plot the specific measure using trend analysis to produce a straight line graph which illustrates the underlying trend over the period. This trend analysis can then be projected into the future to give a predicted rate. Programs are available for micro computers which will perform this type of analysis on data collected on the sub-division. Obviously there are a number of technical problems in producing these time trends, and furthermore, the accuracy of their prediction will always be subject to some variation. The accuracy of time trends can be improved if other factors are included. For example, it may be noticed over a five year period that there has been an average increase of 10 per cent each year in the number of burglaries reported to the police. Further investigation of this figure might also reveal the population of the sub-division has been increasing during the same period due to large scale housing developments. Therefore in this case, if the burglary rate is linked to the number of people living on the sub-division, the per capita burglary rate, then when it is plotted it would give a more accurate prediction of future trends.

Another factor known to affect the crime rate is the number of young persons in the population. A substantial proportion of crime is committed by people between the ages of 14 and 25 years. Demographic trends within the community will increase or decrease the proportion of the population on a particular sub-division within those age groups. For example, a housing estate which was built to take overspill populations from urban centres may initially be populated by young married couples with very small children, but within fifteen years, those children are in the age range most likely to be involved in crime. A few years after that peak has been reached, those young people will either have moved away or may have grown out of their desire to commit crime. This sort of information can be very valuable in examining time trends in crime patterns, and it may well be useful to visit the local authority and refer to the census data available there.

(c) *Comparison Between Groups*

Comparison between groups can also be called comparison between areas or locations. In principle the method takes a group or area where changes have been made to policing methods and compares the results with a similar group or area where no changes have been made. As an example, the number of uniformed foot patrol officers could be increased on a beat as a strategy to reduce vandalism. As this is a particularly prevalent offence and also one which occurs on impulse, it may be very difficult to assess the impact of additional police patrols in the short run. But if an area with similar social characteristics on the sub-division is chosen, and here no changes in police patrol strategy are introduced, the indicators which have been identified as outcome measures can be compared between the two areas.

Comparisons should only be made between two groups that are truly comparable. For example, there would be no point in identifying a housing estate with a high level of vandalism and social disorder, and making a comparison with another housing estate which has good amenities and a relatively low rate of vandalism and social disorder. If thefts from vehicles was the matter under consideration, then similarly there would be no point in comparing an area where substantial numbers of motor vehicles were left unattended in the open, with another area where vehicles were usually parked overnight in garages.

(d) *Controlled Experiments*

There are some similarities between a controlled experiment and group comparison. The major difference between the two relates to the level of sophistication of the measures. When making comparisons between groups, the approach requires two similar areas to be identified on the sub-division, and in one area the policing strategy is changed whilst in the other area it is held constant. Subsequently, the measures taken from both groups are compared to establish if any differences can be found.

In using controlled experiments, two separate areas are again identified, but here some relatively sophisticated measures are obtained before any changes occur in policing. These measures are applied to both areas and similar measures are taken at the end of a specified period. Thus the method entails both 'before' and 'after' measuring and comparison between groups. At its most sophisticated this strategy involves the type of public attitude survey described in Chapter 5 where 1,500 members of the public were questioned before and after a policing experiment.

This method is most useful when an Action Plan is concerned with changing the attitudes of members of the public. In the social survey described, the public were asked questions concerning their fear of crime and their satisfaction with the service they were receiving from the police. Although the survey is relatively sophisticated and time consuming to complete, some less elaborate forms of social survey could be used by sub-divisions to look at specific groups within the sub-division such as the examples given at the end of Chapter 5.

Crime prevention campaigns have been relatively frequent features of police/public relations. Although these campaigns appear to be superficially related to changing the public's attitude towards the security of their property, in the long term crime prevention campaigns can only hope to be successful if they are able to convince people to actually change their behaviour. There is little point in educating people that their cars are likely to be stolen or have property stolen from them, if simultaneously we cannot encourage people to lock their cars. Being worried about the possibility of having your car stolen in the absence of taking some positive steps to prevent it, will not discourage thieves.

Using the controlled experimentation method, it would be possible to check the proportion of insecure vehicles left in a particular car park. A crime prevention campaign could then be implemented and, during the campaign, a check could once again be made of the proportion of insecure motor vehicles. If there was found to be an increase in the proportion secured, then this would be a positive result. As crime prevention campaigns may have a limited period of influence on members of the public, it would also be useful to return some time after the campaign ceased to see if there had been a permanent change in the proportion of vehicles secured.

To summarise, there is no one best method to assess the results achieved by an Action Plan, as the evaluation method will always be determined by the type of problem being tackled, and the measures which identify the problem to the police manager in the first instance. The use of measures and the measurement strategy are matters which will exercise the imagination and innovation of members of the sub-division.

When To Evaluate

This is another question to which there is no right or wrong answer. As a generalisation, tactical evaluation may require to be done every week, but the long term strategic evaluation may be done at intervals of six months or more. There is a compromise to be achieved. First, if the evaluation is conducted too soon then there may have been no time for something to occur, and it will be impossible to discover whether the Action Plan will produce the results desired, or whether the time scale on which the results will be produced is longer than anticipated. Second, if an Action Plan is not producing the desired results and is costly in manpower, then the longer it continues without modification or being abandoned the greater will be the waste of valuable resources. In establishing the time scales for evaluation, the police manager must exercise professional judgement. However, it should be remembered, the responsibility of the Action Plan Co-ordinator is a continuous one, and not to be thought of as being restricted to monitoring Action Plans at the specified time periods. He should oversee these plans and monitor them on a day-to-day basis, and make formal evaluations at the specified periods.

Results Of The Evaluation

Obviously, the central question in the evaluation process is simply, "As a result of this Action Plan being implemented are we closer to achieving the Objective now than we were before we started?" By answering this question, we will also implicitly answer a supplementary question namely, "Was the original analysis of the problem correct?" It is important to consider this supplementary question as the Action Plan may have been sound in itself but applied to the wrong problem. For example, the Truancy Project was designed on the basis of an analysis which had indicated the involvement in burglaries of young people absent from school. In executing the Action Plan, no change may have been seen in the number of burglaries being recorded, but on the secondary measures it may be found that there were virtually no young people truanting from school. Therefore, questions should not be raised primarily concerning the Action Plan, but regarding the information and the basis upon which the initial assessment and subsequent Action Plan were founded.

To answer the two questions, it is necessary to go through a series of other questions in a sequence to establish exactly what has happened to the Action Plan and what results have been achieved. There may be other questions which could be posed during this sequence, and they should not be excluded if they appear to be relevant and appropriate to the particular circumstances. The following checklist can be used as a general guide to the sequence:-

(a) Were all the tasks completed in the preparation phase?

(b) Has the plan been executed?

(c) How many man hours have been used to date?

(d) Are the man hours that have been expended in accordance with those predicted in the plan?

(e) Are the man hours expended appropriate or should more or less manpower be assigned?

(f) What results have been achieved against the Primary Measure?

(g) What results have been achieved in terms of the Secondary Measures?

(h) Do these results confirm the original analysis of the problem?

(i) Have there been any adverse effects on other police actions?

(j) Do the results, to date, suggest the need for any changes to the original Action Plan?

(k) If changes are to be made, what are they and can they be achieved by sub-divisional resources?

(1) Should the Action Plan be continued or abandoned?

Probably the most difficult question to answer is the last one and this requires a decision to be made concerning the Action Plan. This would not usually be a decision that should rest with the Co-ordinator, but if he answers the sequence of questions which have preceded the final question, he should be able to prepare a case which will support his recommendation to continue or abandon the Action Plan. This final question does raise issues concerning the procedures to be adopted on the sub-division, and at what points and through what processes this decision should be made and by whom. It will be a matter for sub-divisional superintendents to decide how to review Action Plans, but it does seem an appropriate role for the Sub-Divisional Planning Group. If the Group was excluded from this decision making process, then the cycle of planning, implementation and evaluation would be effectively broken.

Evaluation Of Development Goals

Development Goals will usually not be pursued by defining Action Plans and therefore their achievement is not usually measured by aggregating small steps towards the whole. In most cases it will be self evident when a Development Goal has been achieved, in the example given in Chapter 9, when dictation equipment and word processors have been delivered to sub-divisions the Goal will have been achieved. This is a clear result, however good management practice demands a more detailed assessment of the consequences of the introduction of this technology. Although the equipment was delivered, was it taken into use? Did the equipment meet the criteria established by the users? Was sufficient preparation and training provided to all the users, typist and police officers? Was there any resistance by the users to the equipment? Was the equipment reliable? Did the productivity of the typists change and if so by how much? Can anything else be done to improve productivity? If these questions are not asked and answered then the implementation of the performance Goal "to reduce the amount of time spent by officers on typing" may fail before it starts merely because no training has been provided to enable officers and typists to use the equipment.

Annual Review

The first tier of the strategic evaluation will be completed on the sub-division by the Sub-Divisional Planning Group reviewing the results from all Action Plans, and assessing their achievements against the Objectives. This process in the first cycle will usually be completed after the first year, in accordance with the time schedule established at the beginning of the PBO cycle. It might be useful to conduct an interim review after six months to practice the technique and to monitor performance before the end of the year.

The sub-divisional superintendent will prepare an evaluation report based on the results from individual Action Plans, which will show the achievements that have been made under each Objective. Remember this is not a process which is judged by 'scoring points'. It is a professional management exercise where it is of equal value to have made *no* progress towards achieving an Objective, providing it is possible to give reasons, as it is to have recorded a decrease in reported crime. Of course the latter is the preferred result, but it is more important for a manager to know "why" or "how" something occurred than merely knowing that it happened.

The report will be prepared by taking each objective in turn and then looking at all the Action Plans which have been set to pursue that objective. The results achieved can be added together to give an overall assessment of the sub-division's achievements. Other data may also be available to add to the assessment. Consider the Objective which was set in Chapter 9 to reduce burglaries in dwelling houses by 10%. Action Plans would have been proposed and implemented with varying degrees of success measured on the reduction that occurred in the numbers of reported burglaries. The number of these crimes which occurred in the daytime may have been substantially reduced by the Truancy Project, however, there may have been an increase in evening burglaries. All these facts must be gathered to provide the overall assessment against the Objective and also to provide the evidence to plan policing strategy for the next year. The evidence which is produced in the evaluation process may show that the nature of the problem relating to burglaries has changed following successful police operations. These new facts must form the basis of the plans for next year. Each Objective will be reviewed in turn and assessed under four headings:-

1 The extent to which the Objective was achieved.

2 The contributions which were made by individual Action Plans to the achievement of the Objective.

3 The current nature of the policing problem identifying any changes which have occurred in the past year which may require specific police responses.

4 The quality of the management of Action Plans identifying any changes which should be considered during the next management cycle.

The evaluation report will be submitted to the chief superintendent for him to provide an assessment of the achievements of the division. These reports will also enable him to assess the relative management skills of his senior officers on the division and where necessary he will be able to plan management training to improve skills and strengthen weaknesses. A primary responsibility for the chief superintendents will be the identification of policy issues which will be considered in the development of the

Policy Statement for the next year.

The evaluation process to be followed by headquarters departments will be very similar to the sub-divisions. Where Objectives have been set then they will be reviewed under the headings which have been described above. Where Objectives were not set, as in the case of some Development Goals, some modifications may be necessary to these headings to make them relevant to the evaluation. Evaluation reports may be prepared by the officers in charge of squads and these will have to be assessed and co-ordinated by the chief superintendent in charge of the department.

When chief superintendents have reviewed the evaluation reports and prepared their overview of the achievements of the division or department they will pass the reports to the PBO Co-ordinator at headquarters. This officer will have the responsibility for producing the assessment of the achievements of the force. He will take the evaluations which have been made in the pursuit of Objectives and assess the force achievements in relation to the Goals. The evaluation report will include comments on:-

1   The extent to which the Goal was achieved.

2   The contributions that were made by the various policing methods which had been adopted.

3   The current nature of the policing problem making specific reference to any changes which have occurred which require changes in the police response or the priorities governing the allocation of resources.

4   Any management or organisational development issues which have been identified in the process.

5   Any policy issues which must be considered in the next management cycle when the Policy Statement is being prepared.

The value of this process will be seen in the ability of the force to answer questions which may be raised by Her Majesty's Inspectors of Constabulary, the Police Authority or local consultative committees. There will also be considerable value for the lessons that will be learnt by individuals, groups of officers and the force as a whole about their abilities to control crime, maintain public tranquillity and solve traffic problems. The management cycle (Figure 2.1) demanded a progressive approach to management through planning, organising, implementing and evaluation which would provide the basis of the planning for the next cycle. It is the learning potential of the process which should be exploited to the full. It is possible, in fact probable, there will be some parts of the force identified which contribute little or nothing to the efforts of the force. In these cases, management will need to grasp the nettle and disband them and transfer resources elsewhere. However, this should be seen and accepted by all concerned as a constructive and positive sign of a force determined to use its resources to the best effect. Learning will occur at all levels in the force. Constables will have a greater knowledge of the results they produce. Sub-divisional managers will be better appraised of the police activities and strategies which produce tangible benefits. Divisional and departmental chief superintendents will be more aware of resource and development needs. Executive management will have more opportunity to make their strategic decisions on information about the achievements and limitations of the force.

At the end of the first year, the force can assess its achievements against the issues identified in the Policy Statement which initiated the process. They can identify problems which have been solved, partially resolved or remained unchanged. On the basis of the evaluation the next annual cycle can proceed.

12   Resistance to Change

The evaluation procedures described in Chapter 11 will enable the force to determine how successful it was in achieving its targets. The force will also have a clearer understanding about the relative success of various operational policing methods. The evaluation process can and should be extended beyond the operational achievements to include an assessment of the management developments which have been achieved. The human dimensions of police forces were examined in Chapter 7 to illustrate the importance of understanding how people perceived their work and supervisors.

Chapter 7 included a check list of issues which managers were encouraged to use to identify the climate of their own organisation (Figure 7.1). The relative importance of each element should have been determined, and where it was seen to have an adverse effect on the achievements of the sub-division or department, remedial action was recommended. During the evaluation phase the same review should be done to determine if the original problems had been resolved and to see if new ones had arisen. When doing this review a distinction should be made between problems which can be traced back to the preparation phase before changes were made to the organisation and those which appear to have occurred during implementation.

This chapter is primarily concerned with the human side of the organisational change process. Targets may or may not have been achieved, but whatever the result it will have been caused through the endeavours or lack of endeavours of individuals. It would be dangerous to make assumptions about the quality of the management system of the force and therefore it should be subjected to an assessment to determine its contribution to the results achieved.

The learning objectives of this chapter are:-

1   To understand the need to assess the contribution that the management system made to the achievements of the force.

2   To understand that a management system cannot guarantee results, it can only facilitate the achievements.

3   To understand that the process of organisational change is based on the key issues of the understanding of the process and the results to be achieved, active commitment from the chief officer down to the lowest level in the force, the existence of trust, and the opportunities for personnel to have a 'better job' as a result of adopting the necessary changes.

4   To understand the impact of the resistance to change.

5   To recognise examples of the resistance to change and be able to suggest methods of resolving the management problems.

Evaluation Of The Management System

The system of management will only be as good as the people who direct and participate in the process. The force needs people to make it more effective and efficient, but those same people can also prevent those improvements being achieved. Policing By Objectives, like any other management system, can only *facilitate* improvements in the performance of the force – it cannot guarantee results. The evaluation of the management system must ask questions about the degree of understanding which exists within the force concerning the changes which have occurred. The commitment of all officers to the system must be assessed. The degree of trust between officers and their perceptions of their work will also form part of this evaluation.

Question 1

Do the members of the force have sufficient understanding of the process?

Members of the force should have realised why changes were being made to the management of the force and the consequences of these changes. If some officers or groups of officers believed they could stand aside and not become involved, then the total nature of the managerial process had not been understood. It would be very difficult for officers to make the maximum contribution to the force if they did not know or understand why procedures had been adopted. Officers must undertake their roles within the system and have a clear definition of their responsibilities and authority. If there were problems in relation to the understanding of the process, then the preparation strategy should be examined to determine if there was a need for additional training. The most likely cause of this problem is the quality of the communication systems and methods. If a year after implementation, there are still officers who do not understand the process, then the feedback mechanisms from officers to managers either do not exist or are suspect, because a sensitive manager should have recognised the problem sooner. Whatever the cause, a lack of understanding of the process will make a real commitment by officers to improving the effectiveness of the force virtually impossible.

Question 2

Does the process enjoy the support and commitment of the chief officer and his executive management?

Some might claim that the support and commitment of the chief officer is the single most important factor for the process of organisational change. On its own it would not guarantee success, but if it is absent then there is very little chance of success. Let us be clear what the process demands, it is making the force and individual officers responsible for determining priorities, establishing targets to be achieved and then evaluating results. In short, it is adopting a system which can identify failures of achievement and identify the groups of officers who are responsible. The fear of failure is a very powerful motivation to do nothing. Why should officers expose themselves to the chances of failure if they have doubts about the commitment of their leaders. If they do not achieve the success they hoped, then they should be able to rely on senior officers to understand the reasons for failure.

Support will be demonstrated in a variety of ways. The training which must accompany the preparation for change will raise issues of policy, resources and the delegated authority to make decisions. Many of these questions can only be answered by officers who are involved in the executive management of the force. If these officers do not contribute on a continuing basis to these training courses by being present, then these matters will remain unresolved and the entire training and preparation process may be significantly damaged. The pre-implementation training provides opportunities for officers to learn about the proposed changes and for executive management to become better informed of officers' anxieties, their lack of understanding and any gaps that may exist in planning and policy which must be addressed before implementation. One of the most tangible examples of top level support is when they obtain the resources which have been identified as a necessary prerequisite for success. If a force cannot provide key resources, it has built in the excuse for failure. Overt support must continue throughout the implementation phase, being careful not to allow enthusiasm and support to become interference with the operational autonomy which has been established by policy.

Question 3

Did the process receive commitment and active support throughout the force?

The commitment and support of the chief officer is essential to the success of the venture and it should act as an example of good management practice to the rest of the force. However, the chief officer must expect and receive the active support and commitment of all officers. Problems will occur if some parts of the force believe they are exempt from a drive to improve effectiveness and efficiency. Selection for promotion should reflect the new management needs of the force and seek the means of identifying those officers with real commitment who do not merely pay lip service to the system. If officers in senior management positions lack commitment, then the system of accountability and responsibility should be examined and modified accordingly. If they can continue to remain outside the corporate efforts of the rest of the force, the evaluation systems may need tightening to encourage these officers to co-operate or to be seen to be abdicating their responsibilities.

Question 4

Does trust exist between members of the force?

An important means of reducing the fear of failure in any new venture is to generate a climate of mutual trust. The chief officer may tell the force that he does not expect instant success on every Goal, but is realistic enough to recognise that success in some areas will be accompanied by failure in others. Despite this public statement, if his officers do not trust him then they will still fear the consequences of failure and may even subvert the process by 'fixing' the figures or not setting any challenging Objectives.

Trust is also a critical issue in the decision making process. The management process which has been described argues for decision making to occur as close to the problem and sources of information as possible. In most police forces this would require some devolution of decision making from a central point in the organisation to lower levels within the force. In fact the proposals made in this text would make the sub-division the basic operational unit and the policy would give more scope for decision making at that level. Inevitably errors in decision making will occur, but this can happen anywhere in the organisation, however, the urge to return to centralised decision making must be resisted. Trust and adequate training should be the foundations of the decision making system.

Question 5

Have there been any changes in the officers' perceptions of their work?

It will be misleading to over-emphasise the apparent differences and conflicts which exist between constables and their supervisors. However, the organisational climate, constables' morale and their job satisfaction can be damaged by this conflict. Where a manager is asking his staff to change their working practices or to take on additional work, he should try and identify the advantages that this will bring to them. If no advantages can be demonstrated then it should come as no surprise if the staff resist the changes. Managers have a responsibility to promote the positive aspects of the need to change working arrangements, therefore changes in the officers' perceptions of their work will give a good indication of the success or failure of the organisational changes. The following aspects of the work should have become more positive:-

(i) Officers should have a greater sense of involvement in the policy making of the force and the design of operational strategies.

(ii) Officers should be able to understand how their work contributes to the overall strategies and achievements of the force.

(iii) Officers should feel more confident about their own abilities and should gain a sense of achievement from their work.

(iv) Officers should have a greater sense of personal responsibility towards the use of resources, including their own time.

In Chapter 7, the predominantly hierarchical and authoritarian structures of police forces were seen to be at variance with the needs of police constables. The PBO process, if successfully implemented, will modify the management philosophy of the force to make it more suitable for the needs of its officers. Police work demands particular attitudes and behaviours from constables. Managers should seek to modify management philosophy to coincide with the needs of officers.

Resistance To Change

Throughout the force there may be a positive response by most officers to the changes required by the new management strategy, but some individuals may adopt attitudes or responses which have the potential to inhibit or prevent the achievement of all the possible improvements to the force. Some cases can be described to illustrate the more common problems which may arise when changes are made to the force. However, there are no text book answers to these issues. Each must be examined, understood and approached as a unique case. Thus, when suggestions are made about possible remedies they should be seen as *suggestions* and not prescriptive cures.

The Area Constable

A primary responsibility of the area constable is to develop a close affinity for the people on his beat. These officers can achieve a great deal of personal satisfaction by becoming recognised as the 'local constable' and the community receive benefits by knowing an officer has a special interest in their problems. Action Plans will need a flexible approach to using manpower and therefore there will be occasions when the area constable will have to work elsewhere than on his own beat. At other times other officers will come and work on his beat and there is a danger the area constable may feel he is losing his close identity with the beat. Sensitive management must be aware of these anxieties and ensure these officers recognise the need for flexibility in the use of manpower. Area constables should also be shown other benefits by making them responsible for planning the use of additional manpower on their own beat. The introduction of the concept of beat manager will help to reduce the problems which may occur.

The Sergeant Controller

To achieve a better use of constables' discretionary time, controllers will need to exercise more management control over manpower. Unless controllers are able to assess the response requirements of calls from the public, there will be disruption to directed patrol Action Plans, by taking officers from those tasks to respond to calls. The use of directed patrol strategies is potentially the most effective means of managing police patrol operations. If these problems arise they should be carefully examined. To issue a directive that officers will never be called away from directed patrol activities is a short road to disaster, because it ignores the realities of police work. If a problem arises the following questions should be asked:-

(i)   In the context of current workload, has the amount of discretionary time been over estimated?

(ii) Are there peak workload times when Action Plans should not be pursued?

(iii) Is the stacking of calls a viable option? Do controllers have sufficient information about incidents to make it safe to delay a response?

(iv) Is it necessary to increase the number of mobile officers to deal with peak workload demands?

(v) Should directed patrol activities be given to other officers, area constables for example?

When the problem has been examined, policy can be established with more confidence and a solution is more likely. The possibility of a deliberately disruptive sergeant should not be discounted but it should not be seen as the most likely cause.

The Patrol Sergeant

Action Planning will involve officers completing some additional forms. The reasons were explained in Chapter 10, but a point was also made concerning the danger of being overwhelmed in a paper chase. If forms are introduced, their use should be strictly controlled. Problems can arise with the introduction of PBO when sergeants insist their constables submit written Action Plans to cover everything they do in their discretionary time. If the paper chase appears to be occurring, it may suggest a lack of understanding of the process by sergeants. Whatever the cause it is not a matter which can be ignored. Sergeants should be asked why they believe the insistence on written Action Plans is useful. Where advantages can be demonstrated they should be continued, but where their strategy is clearly disruptive, action should be taken to solve the problem.

The 'Competitive' Unit Inspector

In Chapter 7, competition between groups was said to be a useful form of motivation. Competition between units of uniformed officers on sub-divisions encourages inspectors to motivate and lead their officers to achieve the best results. The PBO process encourages more co-operation and co-ordination of effort in the belief it is important for improvements to be achieved by all officers, not just small groups who are particularly well motivated. A unit inspector whose officers have consistently achieved better results than the other officers on the sub-division, may feel frustrated by a system which assesses the performance of the whole sub-division. The inspector may feel his efforts are only making the other officers on the sub-division look good and this may cause his motivation to decline. Two strategies would seem appropriate. First, a means must be found to enable individual effort to be recognised but it should be done in ways which do not subvert the co-operative approach to policing strategies. Second, ways should be found to increase the efforts made by the other inspectors to motivate and lead their officers.

The 'Retired' Unit Inspector

In certain circumstances it is possible for a manager to 'retire' but remain in his post and draw his salary. A unit inspector may take this course by delegating all tasks to his sergeant. At first glance the unit may seem to be performing from day to day without too many problems, but on a closer examination it can be seen there is no leadership, co-ordination, or drive. The delegation of most tasks to sergeants gives the inspector discretionary time which could be used to undertake some problem solving exercises. The sub-divisional superintendent could give specific problems to the inspector to analyse and ask him to propose policing strategies to resolve them. When he has made his proposals, the inspector could be made responsible for co-ordinating and monitoring the activities undertaken in pursuit of the strategy. This method of directing the involvement of the inspector would give him specific tasks and it would also give him a responsibility to other officers on the sub-division to help them improve their effectiveness. The added responsibility would provide an incentive to 'rejoin' the force and the process would be a learning experience whereby new skills were obtained and confidence gained. The remedy might not be so simple as it may appear, but for actions to achieve results, the sub-divisional superintendent would need a thorough understanding of the problem. It would be wrong to simply assume we are dealing with a lazy inspector, the reasons for his lack of motivation may be very complex and should be understood.

The Detective Inspector

In cases where the CID see themselves as something of an elite group there may be a reluctance on their part to join the co-operative efforts required by the new management strategy.

Consider the case of the detective inspector who believes PBO has nothing to offer the CID. He believes detective work is about investigating crime and he does not need any new management system. He may also be anxious that the evaluation aspects of PBO may remove some of the myth and mystique which has surrounded detective work. As a consequence he is not willing to commit his own time to the process and tries to prevent his sergeants and detective constables from becoming involved. Apart from being very disruptive for the other members of the sub-division, the attitude is extremely short-sighted. There are clearly important and skilled functions for the CID to perform. It is nonsense to cling to activities which produce marginal results when detectives can make positive contributions in the tasks of interviewing of suspects, and assisting and thereby training uniformed officers in crime related activities. The work of detectives could also be developed towards the new skills of crime analysis and the reviewing of intelligence to support the activities of other officers.

The whole process of management would be damaged if one group were unilaterally allowed to remain outside. Therefore the sub-divisional superintendent must develop strategies to resolve these problems. The most likely strategy is to demonstrate a role for the CID in the process and remove the anxieties that somehow the CID have become redundant. If they refuse to co-operate then they are almost certainly going to become less relevant to the work of the sub-division as the rest of the officers develop skills to replace those previously provided by the CID.

The 'Numbers Game' Superintendent

Nothing in PBO can prevent human nature from intervening in an attempt to subvert any part of the process and the evaluation aspects are no exception. Figures and statistics can be massaged to promote a favourable view of results. Academic studies by criminologists have identified circumstances where changes in police recording procedures have caused crime rates to rise or fall depending upon the circumstances. Another strategy can be to subsume the facts within a larger context. Consider for example the detection rate for burglaries. A sub-division claims it has achieved a 5 per cent increase in the proportion of burglaries which have been detected in the last year compared with the previous year. Although this figure is correct, further examination shows the *actual* number detected has reduced because the number reported has also declined. When the methods of detection are reviewed, it can be seen that the proportion of detected crime which has been the subject of a charge or summons against an alleged offender has reduced considerably. However the number which have been admitted by offenders serving a sentence of imprisonment has increased. These latter offences have then been 'written off' under the Home Office rules. Thus the performance of the sub-division in respect of burglary detection can be summarised as follows:-

Fewer burglaries have been detected in the last year and the proportion cleared by charge to an offender has significantly declined.

Whether these facts can be construed as a success or failure is not the point, the issue is to ensure the evaluation process is a realistic assessment of the sub-division's achievements and the process is sufficiently refined to reduce opportunities for the abuse of figures.

The tragedy with the 'numbers game' superintendent is that he is only fooling himself and he can hardly expect a professional response from his officers. Furthermore, if they have given him their commitment he has betrayed their professionalism by abusing the evaluation process. How can the officers claim any success even when they have worked hard, if the superintendent abuses the figures?

The 'Enthusiastic' Chief Superintendent

The management process involves establishing levels of accountability and responsibility. In some cases this will mean officers taking on new tasks, in other circumstances existing tasks will be transferred elsewhere. It is likely a major change will occur in the work of divisional chief superintendents, they will become more deeply involved in strategic policy and management, and less concerned with day to day operational matters. Relinquishing the day to day activities to which they may have grown accustomed over the years will not come easily to some, particularly as these tasks will be replaced with unfamiliar and challenging new work. In effect, chief superintendents are being asked to raise their horizons from day to day operations to take a much broader view of the needs of the community and their officers. Organisation analysis and review, strategic planning and evaluation will require a significant shift of emphasis in the chief superintendent's tasks. However, if they do not make the change, the management process will fail to produce improvements over the long term.

Another reason why chief superintendents should change their outlook is to allow sub-divisional superintendents to develop in their role and become managers in every sense of the word. If they are to be held accountable for the achievements of the sub-division then superintendents must have the freedom to act in accordance with policy. If chief superintendents are continually having to intervene or check on the actions on sub-divisions then they should look at their skills of defining policy and providing on the job management training to their superintendents.

Overcoming Resistance To Change

Resistance to change is a natural human response. The process of management which has been advocated will reduce the degree of resistance because the changes which occur in the force will have been the product of the efforts of all officers. The management review and the planning process demands consultation between officers. The Policy Statement is an unambiguous symbol of the chief constable's commitment to the process of improving effectiveness and efficiency. It also forms a contract between him and the force by identifying the support he will give to the efforts of his officers. Therefore the force is guided and motivated by overt leadership and a common purpose.

The style of management which has been described follows a learning approach. Managers must ensure that this style is not lost in the evaluation process to be replaced by a punitive and critical assessment of police performance. Where achievements have fallen short of the targets which were set, managers should look for reasons rather than seeking to blame individuals. The rational management approach is concerned with achieving operational improvements, however, improvements are likely to be facilitated by improved human relations. Therefore, improved policing methods should be accompanied by improvements in the interpersonal skills of all officers with managerial responsibilities.

Some resistance to change is inevitable and managers have the responsibility to be prepared to resolve problems as they occur. Therefore, before a manager can address problems associated with resistance to change he must have sufficient time and possess the necessary inter-personal skills. Any single issue might take many hours of counselling, policy review and on the job training to resolve. Managers must have the skills to listen to their officers. They must have an empathy with officers who are anxious about their new roles which should be balanced by the need to make progress towards the changes required to achieve improved effectiveness and efficiency. If the force is not prepared to make time available to managers in every rank for these tasks or provide the training for the development of skills, then the chances of the force improving its effectiveness and efficiency will be reduced. Management strategy is a package which only delivers results if all the parts are included.

13 Improving Effectiveness and Efficiency in a Changing World

Improving effectiveness and efficiency are demands which the police cannot ignore or resist. The key to achieving these two aims lies in the improvement of police management processes. The significant change for police managers will be the additional responsibilities of planning and evaluating. In the past the emphasis has been on conducting 'business as usual', with changes to policing methods occurring as almost spontaneous responses to individual problems. This approach will not be adequate in the future because the success of this method as a means of improving police performance is extremely suspect. Police managers will continue to conduct business as usual, but in addition they will have a vision of the future which will form the basis of the grand strategy of the force. Furthermore, they will cease to make assumptions that police activities have a value in themselves, the emphasis will be on the evaluation of the results produced.

In the initial stages of achieving improvements in cost effectiveness, the force will experience quite radical changes. These changes will be seen in the structures of the force, the roles and responsibilities of individual officers and civilians, the roles and relationships between parts of the force, and the introduction of new systems and technology. After the initial surge which accompanies these changes, the force will settle back to sustain the improvements which have been achieved, and make further progress through the pursuit of the management cycle. In fact the process of management which has been described will provide the mechanism for sustained improvements in cost effectiveness and the framework for the force to respond to the changing world. There is a danger that the force will believe that it is now committed to a permanent state of uncertainty and change. It will be true that the management philosophy of the force must accept the need to examine new methods of policing, however, this should be seen as a natural extension of the management process and not a matter which should be associated with uncertainty and anxiety. To reduce the anxieties which are associated with change, the force should have a period of consolidation after the initial changes have been implemented and evaluated. The process of consolidation will reassure the anxious that the force is not hurtling out of control.

Chapter 8 described two methods for the implementation of change to police forces to achieve improvements in cost effectiveness. The following chapters described methods of introducing a rational management process to implement methods to improve cost effectiveness. In the process which involves the review of procedures and functions, time can be made available to undertake the necessary preparations including providing information systems and training, before the force implements the rational management system. In the other model which was described in Chapter 8, the operational management review, a progressive step by step approach was recommended. It is almost inevitable that there will be wide variations in the abilities of the various sub-divisions and sections of the force to immediately implement the rational management system. However, at the end of Chapter 8 it was assumed, for the sake of maintaining a coherent description of the strategy, that all sections of the force had been able to undertake the management review with sufficient skill to answer all the questions which had been asked about measuring their existing performance and measuring improvements which they were suggesting. As a response to the wide variation in the quality of the answers which are likely to be given in the management review, it is necessary to have a process which recognised the limitations in the management skills of various members of the force.

The management review process was designed, in part, to be a learning experience for officers throughout the force, therefore the evaluation of the reports should be approached with the same philosophy. It would be misguided to allow officers to go ahead and implement changes without –

(a) knowing how effective they are now, and

(b) having reliable and valid measures to assess the results of the suggested change.

Therefore the reports which are collated at headquarters on behalf of the chief officer should be evaluated on the following criteria under each priority identified in the review agenda:–

Stage 1 – The report has identified activities which are undertaken at present in pursuit of the specific priority identified in the chief officer's agenda.

Stage 2 – The report has satisfied Stage 1, and has identified reliable and valid measures on which existing performance can be measured.

Stage 3 – The report has identified changes to improve performance.

Stage 4 – The report has satisfied Stage 3, and has identified reliable and valid measures of establishing the results achieved by the implementation of the change.

Stage 5 – The report has satisfied Stage 4 and has identified no constraint effecting the implementation of the proposed change.

Sub-Divisions which have achieved Stage 4 on at least one of the priorities in the chief officer's review agenda will be allowed to proceed to make changes to policing methods on the basis of the PBO system. The chief officer will prepare a Policy Statement and Goals will be established for the force in accordance with the processes which have been described. However, Objectives will only be set for those Goals and by those sub-divisions who have demonstrated an ability to reach Stage 4 on the matters related to the specific Goal. Therefore, the force will have to adopt a phased introduction of Policing by Objectives. The management development which was seen as an integral part of the process from the outset and was included in the management review model (Figure 8.1), will be concerned with bringing all sub-divisions to Stage 4 for them to achieve the necessary skills to enable the rational management process to be exploited to the full throughout the force. The content of the management development process will have to be tailored to meet the individual requirements of the force, but it will almost certainly contain changes to training, the introduction of improved information sources and improved data analysis techniques.

The Characteristics Of Successful Management Innovations

Improvements in the effectiveness and efficiency of police forces will not occur overnight by accident or chance. They will be achieved by professional and competent management which should be capable of learning from the experience of others. A study by the Rand Corporation examined the characteristics of successful innovations in the field of criminal justice which included police forces, and identified six key ingredients. [1]

1   All members of the force should share a sincere motivation to improve the effectiveness and efficiency of the organisation. Where the members of the force are responsible for analysing existing effectiveness and are able to propose methods for improvements, then commitment and motivation to change are more likely to occur. Where people do not see the need for change their commitment will always be suspect.

2   The study used to phrase 'key actor support' to identify the need to have the active leadership and commitment of the head of the organisation and also people who are located at various key points within the organisation. An important part of the preparation process is to identify the key personnel and to ensure their understanding and active commitment.

3   Closely related to the support of key personnel is the skill and competence of these participants in the process. Commitment alone will not bring success. Where people are being called upon to perform new and more demanding roles they must receive appropriate training. There can be few more threatening situations than to be asked to do something but not be given the skills to respond.

4   Where participants are being asked to change their working practices or undertake a more demanding role they will expect to see some advantages to them for responding. In short, they must be able to see some benefits if they are to be expected to accept the costs of the change. The study found that monetary rewards were not necessarily strong motivators. People were

more likely to respond to the more intangible benefits of having more challenging work, the satisfaction which could be gained by knowing they had achieved an objective and the feelings of being personally involved in the problem solving process.

5   Improvements in organisational effectiveness were more likely to occur where the participants had a clear definition of the goals they were seeking to achieve. It was not enough to simply state goals, they had to be defined unambiguously in terms which enabled staff to understand what was expected of them and how they would know when the goals had been achieved.

6   Finally, clear lines of authority were found to have a significant influence on the improvements which could be achieved through organisational change.

All the key ingredients found by the Rand Corporation study have been addressed. The method which the force adopts to initiate the process of change will be critical in generating the support, motivation and commitment of officers. If the chief officer and his executive management do not lead from the front and demonstrate their commitment to the process, then it is likely to be stillborn and fail to achieve any tangible improvements in the effectiveness and efficiency of the force. A force can write anything and call it a goal or an objective. However, if it has been produced on an inadequate understanding of its purpose in the management process, then do not be surprised if officers fail to understand what is expected of them and question the competence of their leaders. Finally, evaluation implies an understanding and knowledge of the existing performance of the force. Where information is not available to measure current performance there is no point in making changes because no one will be able to tell when or if the improvements were achieved.

Before embarking on the implementation of changes to improve police effectiveness and efficiency it may be worth considering the conversation Alice in Wonderland had with the Cheshire Cat.

Alice said to the cat, "Would you tell me please which way I ought to go from here?"

"That depends a good deal on where you want to go" said the cat.

"I don't much care where," said Alice.

"Then it doesn't much matter which way you go" said the cat.

A police manager may believe he knows which way he wants to go, but he must be certain he knows where he is starting from, otherwise the result will be the same, he will undertake a mystery tour. However, unlike Alice who travelled alone, the police manager may force several million pounds worth of expensive resources to accompany him into Wonderland.

References

1   Ellickson, P., Petersilia, J., Saggiano, M., and Polin, S., *Implementing New Ideas in Criminal Justice*, Santa Monica; California: Rand Corporation (1983).

Appendix 'A' Police Force Organisational Structure

In police forces other than the Metropolitan Police the organisation and rank structure are very similar. A typical organisation is shown in Figure A.1. To illustrate the principle components of a force the responsibilities of the senior officers will be described. A more detailed review of a sub-divisional structure appears in Figure 6.1 in Chapter 6. The various duties and ranks shown will vary from one police force to another although the general structure will always apply.

Chief Constable

The Chief Constable is constitutionally responsible for the conduct of his officers and the Force. The authorised establishments of British Police Forces range from around 1,000 officers to almost 7,000 officers in metropolitan forces outside London. In addition the Chief Constable is responsible for civilian staff, which in the large metropolitan forces may be as many as 1,500 additional people.

Deputy Chief Constable

This officer deputises for the Chief Constable and has specific responsibilities for the Complaints and Discipline Department, and the Public Liaison Department. The Complaints and Discipline Department deal with all complaints from members of the public and internal disciplinary enquiries which are initiated within the force. The Department is under the direct control of a chief superintendent. A superintendent is responsible for the day to day management of the Public Liaison Department, which is concerned with all aspects of community relations and liaison with the media.

Assistant Chief Constable (Administration)

The administrative support of the force is the direct responsibility of an Assistant Chief Constable who has three departments each headed by a chief superintendent. The Administration Department deals with all matters concerning finance, supplies and the maintenance of the force administrative systems. The Personnel & Training Department is concerned with recruitment, transfers, promotions and training. The Research & Organisation Development Department provides the research capability to the force. Its responsibilities concern the evaluation of systems and procedures, job evaluation and the reviews of establishments. The Department is also concerned with the development of policing methods and provides an evaluation service to other parts of the force.

Assistant Chief Constable (Crime)

This officer is concerned with all aspects of crime throughout the force but has specific functions for co-ordinating the activities of an Operations Department and a Support Services Department. Both departments are the responsibility of a chief superintendent. The CID Operations Department has squads with specific responsibilities for drug enforcement, stolen vehicles, fraud, and serious crime. The Support Services is concerned with providing a central information unit for criminal records and intelligence, scenes of crime and photographic sections.

Assistant Chief Constable (Operations)

This officer is responsible for uniformed operational personnel. The force is divided into five territorial Divisions, A – F Divisions, each of which is under the command of a chief superintendent who is supported by a Detective Superintendent and a Superintendent (Deputy). The Traffic Division is also under the command of a chief superintendent and comprises a sixth Division which is super-imposed on the other territorial Divisions. The Traffic Division is divided into three Sub-Divisions, Eastern, Central and Western, each of which is commanded by a superintendent. The territorial Divisions A – F are also divided into three Sub-Divisions each commanded by a superintendent.

Figure A.1

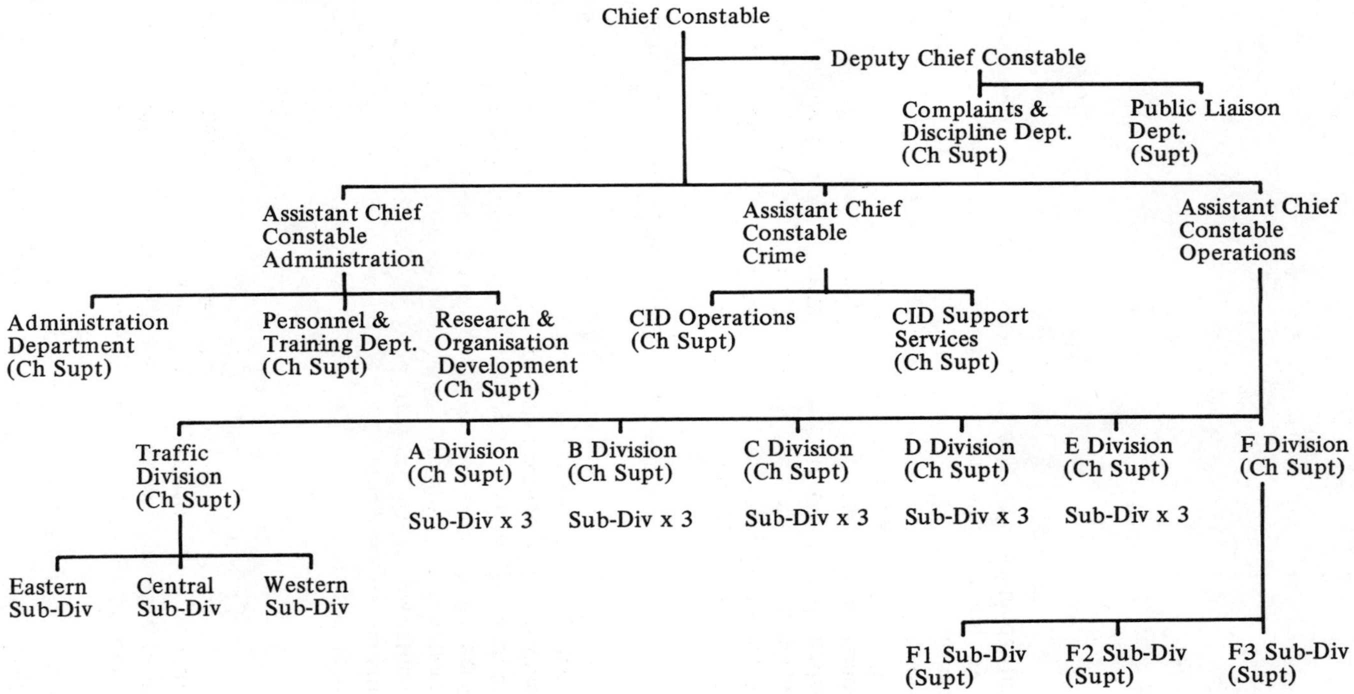

Chief Constable

Deputy Chief Constable

Complaints & Discipline Dept. (Ch Supt)

Public Liaison Dept. (Supt)

Assistant Chief Constable Administration
- Administration Department (Ch Supt)
- Personnel & Training Dept. (Ch Supt)
- Research & Organisation Development (Ch Supt)

Traffic Division (Ch Supt)
- Eastern Sub-Div
- Central Sub-Div
- Western Sub-Div

Assistant Chief Constable Crime
- CID Operations (Ch Supt)
- CID Support Services (Ch Supt)

Assistant Chief Constable Operations

A Division (Ch Supt) — Sub-Div x 3

B Division (Ch Supt) — Sub-Div x 3

C Division (Ch Supt) — Sub-Div x 3

D Division (Ch Supt) — Sub-Div x 3

E Division (Ch Supt) — Sub-Div x 3

F Division (Ch Supt)
- F1 Sub-Div (Supt)
- F2 Sub-Div (Supt)
- F3 Sub-Div (Supt)

Index